PEOPLE AND PLACES
OF THE ROMAN PAST

COLLECTION DEVELOPMENT, CULTURAL HERITAGE, AND DIGITAL HUMANITIES

This exciting series publishes both monographs and edited thematic collections in the broad areas of cultural heritage, digital humanities, collecting and collections, public history and allied areas of applied humanities. In the spirit of our mission to take a stand for the humanities, this series illustrates humanities research keeping pace with technological innovation, globalization, and democratization. We value a variety of established, new, and diverse voices and topics in humanities research and this series provides a platform for publishing the results of cutting-edge projects within these fields.

The aim is to illustrate the impact of humanities research and in particular reflect the exciting new networks developing between researchers and the cultural sector, including archives, libraries and museums, media and the arts, cultural memory and heritage institutions, festivals and tourism, and public history.

Acquisitions Editor
Danièle Cybulskie

Evaluation and Peer Review
The press has every proposal independently evaluated by expert reviews before any formal commitment is made by the press to the author. Further, all submitted manuscripts are subject to peer review by an expert chosen by the press.

PEOPLE AND PLACES OF THE ROMAN PAST

THE EDUCATED TRAVELLER'S GUIDE

Edited by
PETER HATLIE

British Library Cataloguing in Publication Data

A catalogue record for this book is available from the British Library.

ISBN Paperback: 9781942401551
ISBN Hardback: 9781942401544
e-ISBN: 9781942401568
e-pub: 9781641893244

https://arc-humanities.org

Printed and bound by CPI Group (UK) Ltd, Croydon, CR0 4YY

CONTENTS

LIST OF ILLUSTRATIONS

ROME

Città del Vaticano

Via Crescenzio

Piazza del Popolo

74

15

1

40

32

82

Piazza San Pietro

Via Della Conciliazione

10 Castel Sant' Angelo

Piazza Cavour

Via del Corso

Tevere

44

Palazzo Montecitorio

54

20

58

65

73

Piazza Navona

57

53

78

69

17

80

Corso Vittorio Emanuele II

49

Via Giulia

42

Campo de' Fiori

67

19

Largo Argentina

56

47 48

45

52

38

Ponte Sisto

Via Arenula

46

Janiculum

Isola Tiberina

Trastevere

61

Giardi deg Aran

85

Aventino

81

OVERVIEW MAP OF THE CITY OF ROME

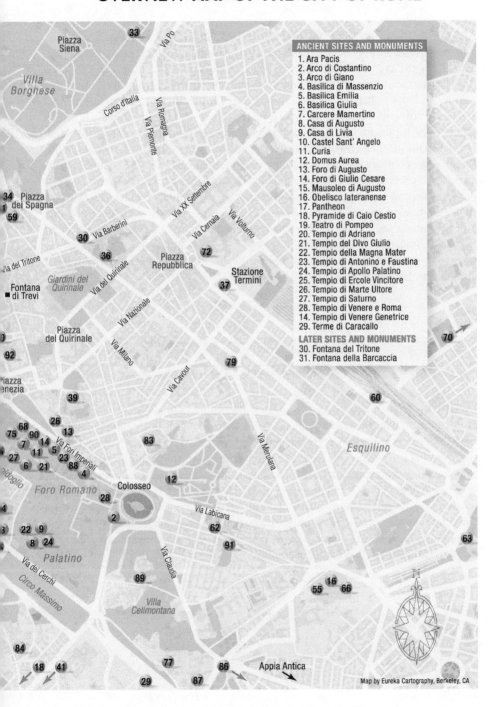

ANCIENT SITES AND MONUMENTS
1. Ara Pacis
2. Arco di Costantino
3. Arco di Giano
4. Basilica di Massenzio
5. Basilica Emilia
6. Basilica Giulia
7. Carcere Mamertino
8. Casa di Augusto
9. Casa di Livia
10. Castel Sant' Angelo
11. Curia
12. Domus Aurea
13. Foro di Augusto
14. Foro di Giulio Cesare
15. Mausoleo di Augusto
16. Obelisco lateranense
17. Pantheon
18. Pyramide di Caio Cestio
19. Teatro di Pompeo
20. Tempio di Adriano
21. Tempio del Divo Giulio
22. Tempio della Magna Mater
23. Tempio di Antonino e Faustina
24. Tempio di Apollo Palatino
25. Tempio di Ercole Vincitore
26. Tempio di Marte Ultore
27. Tempio di Saturno
28. Tempio di Venere e Roma
14. Tempio di Venere Genetrice
29. Terme di Caracallo

LATER SITES AND MONUMENTS
30. Fontana del Tritone
31. Fontana della Barcaccia

Map by Eureka Cartography, Berkeley, CA

ACKNOWLEDGEMENTS

ALL OF THE contributors to this volume are associated with The University of Dallas, a small, serious, and over-achieving liberal arts college in Dallas, Texas (USA) whose many strengths and virtues include a first-class study-abroad satellite campus in Rome (Italy). Many thanks to all of these colleagues and scholars for drawing upon their deep learning and love of Rome to make a meaningful contribution to this volume. Financial and moral support for this project came from the University itself, notably the Provost's Office led by Dr. Jonathan J. Sanford. Stace at Eureka Cartography deserves my deepest thanks for his diligence and patience in developing the maps. University of Dallas alumnus and photographer Michael Housewright is responsible for the beautiful image on the front cover; a handful of other individuals also generously contributed their pictures. Inspiration for the volume flies on the wings of hundreds of University of Dallas students who have studied at the University of Dallas Eugene Constantin Rome Program over the last decade and enrolled in a course called *People and Places of the European Past*. Their smiles of recognition and wonder, their penetrating questions, the willfully worn soles of their shoes, and their love of learning-to-learn are the reason why projects like this one come into being at all.

EDITORIAL NOTE

IN ORDER TO enhance value of this book for visitors to Rome, all place names are expressed in Italian; but see Appendix A for an Italian-English concordance. Italics are used sparingly in the volume, typically for books, specific works of art and on the first occurrence of certain foreign words, though not for Italian words nor for the names of churches, sites, museums and the like. Personal names are typically rendered in English, usually with dates of birth and death included. In the case of states(wo)men and popes, the duration of their reign or rule is rendered by the abbreviation "r." followed by the dates of the reign or rule. Finally, as for chronology, the symbols "BCE" for Before the Common Era and "CE" or Common Era are not used at every instance but rather only for the purpose of clarification in case of doubt.

LIST OF CONTRIBUTORS

Scott F. Crider is a Professor of English at the University of Dallas. A graduate of the University of California Riverside in English (Ph.D.), he is a specialist in early modern English literature and rhetorical studies with a particular interest in Shakespeare. Dr. Crider is the author of *The Office of Assertion: An Art of Rhetoric for the Academic Essay* (Wilmington, DE: ISI Books, 2005), *With What Persuasion: An Essay on Shakespeare and the Ethics of Rhetoric* (New York: Peter Lang Publishing Group, 2009), and *An Art of Persuasion: Aristotle's Rhetoric for Everybody* (Berkeley, CA: Sandala, forthcoming).

Sr. Catherine Joseph Droste, O. P. is a Tenured Lecturer and Vice-Dean of Theology at the Pontifical Institute of St. Thomas (Angelicum). A graduate of the Pontifical Institute of St. Thomas (Angelicum) in Sacred Theology (STD), she is a specialist in virtues and moral theology and the work of St. Catherine of Siena. Sr. Droste's many publications include the co-authored volume with editors T. Polakovic and M. Winstead, *Setting the World Ablaze: St. Catherine of Siena* (Denver: Endow, 2014) and *Servais Pinckaers: Renewing the Lamp of Moral Theology, Concili* OP 5 (Rome: Angelicum University Press, 2014).

David Dawson Vasquez is Instructor of Dogmatic Theology at the Pontifical Beda College and the Pontifical University of St. Thomas Aquinas (Angelicum). A graduate of The Catholic University of America (Ph.D.) in Theology, he has been teaching at various institutions in Rome since 2001. His research interests are in patristic theology, deification, and the intersection between the arts and theology and philosophy. Dr. Dawson Vasquez is author of the article, "St. Thomas Aquinas and Dionysius the Areopagite," in Harm Goris, Herwi Rikhof, Henk Schoot, eds., *Divine Transcendence and Immanence in the Work of Thomas Aquinas* (Leuven: Peeters, 2009).

Robert Scott Dupree is a Professor of English and former Chair of the Department of Modern Languages and Literatures at the University of Dallas. A graduate of Yale University in English (Ph.D.), he is a specialist in early modern and modern literature, he is a specialist in early modern and modern literature, with special interests in the city in literature and genre theories. Among his many publications is the monograph *Allen Tate and the Augustinian Imagination* (Baton Rouge: LSU Press, 1983). His current projects include problematics of a Menippean poetics and Lewis Carroll and the crisis of modern education.

Fr. Thomas Esposito, O. Cist. is an Assistant Professor of Theology at the University of Dallas and monk of the Cistercian Abbey of Our Lady of Dallas. A graduate of Rome's Pontifical Biblical Institute (SSD), he teaches courses in world religions, sacred scripture and biblical languages. His publications include *Jesus' Meals with Pharisees and Their Liturgical Roots*, Analecta Biblica 209 (Rome: Gregorian and Biblicum Press, 2015), *Letters of Fire* (New York: St. Paul's Press/Alba House, 2015), and *The Roots that Clutch: Letters on the Origins of Things* (Eugene, OR: Wipf & Stock, 2018).

Clare P. Frank currently teaches art at Great Hearts Academy in Irving, Texas, after having taught drawing and design at Auburn University. A graduate of University of Illinois at Carbondale (MFA) her prints have been widely exhibited, most notably at the Venice Biennale 54th International Arts in *States of the State: A Contemporary Survey of American Printmaking* and in *SLOW Invitational Exhibition* at Dodd School of Art, University of Georgia at Athens. Her work is included in the permanent collections of Purdue University Galleries, Kansas City Art Institute, Southern Graphics Council, and the Spencer Museum in Lawrence, KS.

William A. Frank is a Professor of Philosophy at the University of Dallas. A graduate of The Catholic University of America in Philosophy (Ph.D.), he is a specialist in medieval philosophy with particular interest in John Duns Scotus. He also works in the areas of the philosophy of personalism and the philosophy of education. Dr. Frank's many publications include a translation of H. S. Gerdil, *The Anti-Emile. Reflections on the Theory and Practice of Education against the Principles of Rousseau* (South Bend, IN: St. Augustine's Press, 2011) and, co-authored with Allan B. Wolter, *Duns Scotus, Metaphysician* (West Lafayette, IN: Purdue University Press, 1995).

Dustin Gish is an Instructional Assistant Professor at the Honors College of the University of Houston. A graduate of the University of Dallas in Politics (Ph.D.), he has expertise in American constitutionalism, American political thought, democratic theory, the history of political thought, classical and early modern political philosophy, and politics and literature. Dr. Gish is the author of many publications including, co-edited with D. Klinghard, *Resistance to Tyrants, Obedience to God: Reason, Religion, and Republicanism at the American Founding* (Lanham, MD: Lexington Books, 2013), co-edited with B. Dobski, *Shakespeare and the Body Politic* (Lanham, MD: Lexington, 2013), co-edited with B. Dobski, *Souls with Longing: Representations of Honor and Love in Shakespeare* (Lanham, MD: Lexington Books, 2011), and co-edited with W. Ambler, *The Political Thought of Xenophon*, in *Polis: The Journal for Ancient Greek Political Thought* 29/2 (2009). One of his forthcoming edited volumes is *Brill's Companion to the Reception of Xenophon* (Brill).

Peter Hatlie is a Professor of Classics, Dean, Director and Vice-President of the University of Dallas Rome Program. A graduate of Fordham University in History (Ph.D.), he is a specialist in late antique, medieval and Byzantine history, with particular interests in the fields of social, religious and culture history. Dr. Hatlie is the author numerous publications, including *The Monks and Monasteries of Constantinople, ca. 350–850* (Cambridge: Cambridge University Press, 2008). Among his forthcoming publications is, co-edited with D. W. Berry, *Bovillae: The History, Art, and Archaeology of A Lost City in the Roman Hinterland* (under review).

Fr. James Lehrberger, O. Cist. is an Associate Professor of Philosophy at the University of Dallas. A graduate of the University of Dallas's Institute of Philosophical Studies (Ph.D.), he is a specialist in the philosophy and theology of St. Thomas Aquinas. His many publications include the co-edited volume *Saints, Sovereigns, and Scholars: Studies in*

Honor of Frederick D. Wilhelmsen (New York: Peter Lang, 1993) and "The Anthropology of Aquinas' *De Ente et Essentia*," in *The Review of Metaphysics* LI.4 (June, 1998): 829–47.

Elizabeth Lisot-Nelson is Assistant Professor of Art History at the University of Texas at Tyler. A graduate of the University of Texas at Dallas in Humanities and Aesthetics (Ph.D.), she is a specialist in Italian Renaissance and baroque art history. Her research interests include artworks representing marginalized populations such as illegitimate children, servants, and slaves, Catholic art and doctrine, and Christian contemplative imagery. Her most recent publication is "Bleeding Bodies and Bondage: Signifiers of Illegitimacy in Ghirlandaio's *Adoration of the Magi* and Andrea della Robbia's *Tondi* at the Ospedale degli Innocenti, Florence," in Jana L Byars and Hans Broedel, eds., *Monsters and Borders in the Early Modern Imagination* (New York: Routledge, 2018).

John Norris is Associate Professor of Theology and Associate Provost of the University of Dallas. A graduate of Marquette University in Religious Studies and Historical Theology (Ph.D.), he is a specialist in Latin patristics with a particular interest in St. Augustine. Dr. Norris is the author of numerous articles including "Reason and Scripture in the *Confessions*: A Delicate Balance," in *Rationality from Saint Augustine to Saint Anselm*, eds. Coloman Viola and Joseph Kormos (Piliscsaba, Hungary: Ida Frölich, 2005): 95–104, and "Macrobius: A Classical Contrast to Christian Exegesis," *Augustinian Studies* 28 (1997): 81–101.

Andrew Osborn is an Associate Professor of English at the University of Dallas. A graduate of the Iowa Writers' Workshop in poetry (M.F.A.) and the University of Texas at Austin in English (Ph.D.), he specializes in modernist and contemporary lyric poetry. His many publications include the "Difficulty" entry in *The Princeton Encyclopedia of Poetry and Poetics*, 4th ed. (Princeton University Press, 2012), "'A Little Hard to See': Wittgenstein, Stevens, and the Uses of Unclarity," *Wallace Stevens Journal* 28.1 (2004): 59-80, and a collection of poems entitled *Plato's Aviary* (Aldrich, 2003).

Elizabeth C. Robinson is an Assistant Professor of Classics and Assistant Dean for Academics at the University of Dallas Rome Program. A graduate of the University of North Carolina at Chapel Hill in Classics (Ph.D.), she is a specialist in Roman archaeology focusing on the cultural and physical landscapes of Italy in the first millennium BCE and Italian urbanism in this period. She is the author of multiple articles and book chapters, the co-editor of a series of seven "Wall Maps for the Ancient World" (Routledge, 2010), and the editor of *Papers on Italian Urbanism in the First Millennium B.C.* (*Journal of Roman Archaeology Supplement* 97, 2014). Among her many current projects is a monograph entitled *Urban Transformation in Ancient Molise*, under contract with Oxford University Press.

Gregory Roper is Associate Professor and Chair of English at the University of Dallas. A graduate of the University of Virginia in Literature (Ph.D.), he specializes in medieval literature with a particular interest in Chaucer. His numerous publications include *The Writer's Workshop: Imitating Your Way to Better Writing* (Wilmington, DE: ISI Books, 2007) and "Dropping the Personae and Reforming the Self: The Parson's Tale and the

End of *The Canterbury Tales*," in *Closure in The Canterbury Tales: The Role of The Parson's Tale*, eds. David Raybin and Linda Tarte Holley (Kalamazoo, MI: Medieval Institute Publications, 2000): 151–75.

David Sweet is Associate Professor and Chair of Classics at the University of Dallas. A graduate of the University of California at Berkeley in Greek and Latin languages (Ph.D.), he is a specialist in Latin literature with special interests in Cicero, Catullus, and Juvenal. Dr. Sweet's recent publications include, "Some Principles at Work in Hesiod's *Theogony*," *Expositions: Interdisciplinary Studies in the Humanities* 6.1 (2012): 90–97 and "Catullus 65: Grief and Poetry," *Studies in Latin Literature and Roman History* 13 (Brussels: Editions Latomus, 2006): 87–96.

Tyler Travillian is an Assistant Professor of Languages and Literatures at Pacific Lutheran University. A graduate of Boston University in Classical Studies (Ph.D.), his scholarly interests include Latin poetry of the late republic, Augustan era and early Empire, textual criticism, paleography and ancient sexuality. His recent publications include *Pliny the Elder: Natural History VII (with Book VIII 1–34)* (London and New York: Bloomsbury Academic, May 2015) and "Horace *Odes* 3.1–3.2: *Carmen* or *Carmina*?" *Latomus* 72 (2013): 984–96.

Bernadette Waterman Ward is an Associate Professor of English at the University of Dallas. A graduate of Stanford University in English and Humanities (Ph.D.), her research interests include nineteenth-century English literature, Christian theology in literature, drama, John Henry Newman, and Gerard Manley Hopkins. Her many publications include *World as Word: Philosophical Theology in the Poetry of Gerard Manley Hopkins* (Washington, D.C.: Catholic University of America Press, 2002) and "Evangélisation et assentiment vivant chez John Henry Newman," *Etudes Newmaniennes* 31 (2015): 179–93.

Roman Warden is an independent scholar.

Chapter One

THE EDUCATED TRAVELLER'S GUIDE

PETER HATLIE

THE CITY OF Rome has an infinite number of stories to tell—ancient, modern, and everything in between. Some of these are an invitation to the city's beauty and pleasures. Others are lessons or teaching-moments emerging, like searching spirits, from Rome's eventful and densely-layered past. Still others bring us face to face, sometimes intimately and often poignantly, with the peaks and valleys of Rome's three thousand years of lived existence, its epic tragedies and triumphs, along with its deeply-felt wounds and its liberating heights of joy.

As one of the world's oldest and most beautiful cities, Rome is admired by travellers the world around. And on certain days—and in particular on certain moments of certain days—Rome is perhaps even more beautiful than descriptions will allow. It can be a feast for the eyes and a banquet for all the other senses, too. As travellers for centuries have found, there are ever so many particular attractions to recommend Rome. Take, for example, one of the city's many world-class museums. Or maybe it's a lonely alleyway or neighbourhood that will seduce you with its charm and local history. Maybe again it is the sight of Rome's seemingly eternal and all-seeing Tiber River—a god of a river after all!—from one of its elegant and strategically placed bridges. Never mind the place or moment of your surrender to the embrace of Rome. Just let it happen.

In reality, the question is not whether to surrender but rather how and where to begin. For its part, this book pays due respect to the sensory beauty and immense historical interest of Rome while also setting out to explain and elaborate upon the city's creative forces. Written by college professors who have lived in Rome and specialize in Roman history, religion, and culture, the book introduces readers to the eternal city by turning attention to some of the most interesting people who have contributed to its history and culture. Each chapter is dedicated to a significant historical figure whose life in Rome has left a lasting footprint, be it a monument, a great work of art, or a tangible memory of great ideas and remarkable things accomplished. Men and women are included in the list of biographical subjects, as are important people from all walks of life—artists, writers, politicians, churchmen, and pilgrims. The book takes us as far back as the city's mythical origins with Romulus and Remus and as far forward as the turn of the nineteenth century. Not accidently, focusing in on the lives of some of its most prominent citizens and visitors throughout the ages takes us also to some of the most interesting neighbourhoods and tourist sites of Rome.

This book is a cross between a tourist guide, scholarly endeavour, and encyclopedia. It is written for travellers in search of inspiration and information as they tour the streets, churches, museums, and monuments of the Roman past. Ambitiously, it takes the reader to practically every notable neighbourhood within Rome's ancient walls and many beyond those walls, including Vatican City. It is ambitious, too, in familiarizing readers with virtually every historical epoch in Rome's long and continuous history from ancient through modern times.

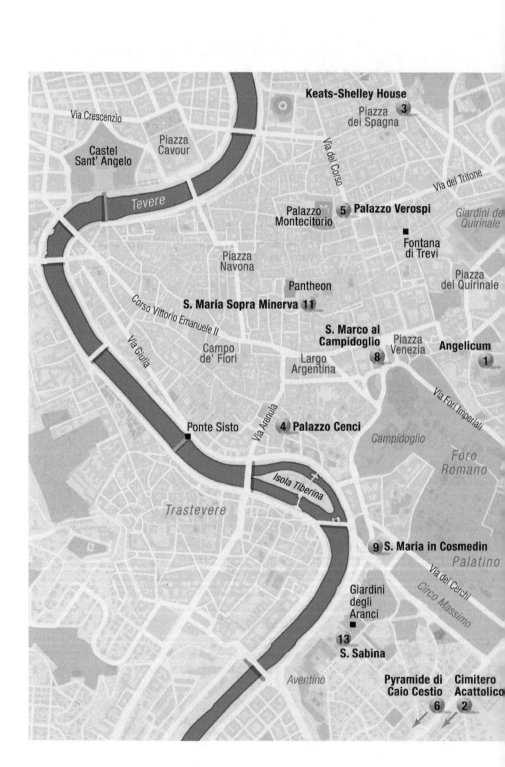

MAP OF ROME FOR CHAPTERS 2–4

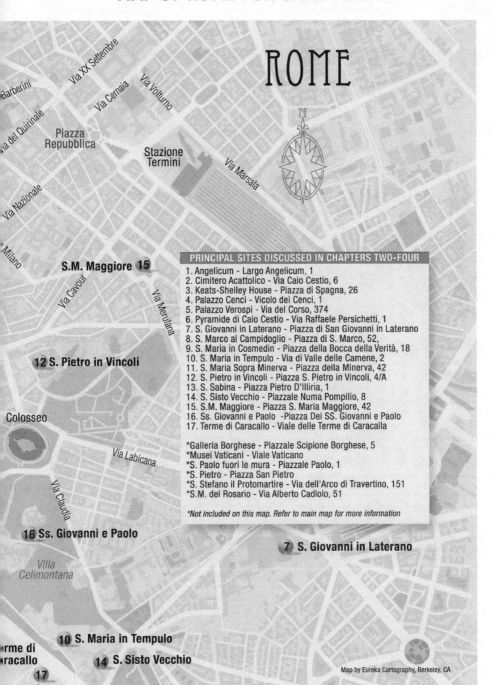

ROME

S.M. Maggiore 15

12 S. Pietro in Vincoli

Colosseo

16 Ss. Giovanni e Paolo

Villa Celimontana

10 S. Maria in Tempulo

14 S. Sisto Vecchio

7 S. Giovanni in Laterano

rme di racallo 17

PRINCIPAL SITES DISCUSSED IN CHAPTERS TWO-FOUR

1. Angelicum - Largo Angelicum, 1
2. Cimitero Acattolico - Via Caio Cestio, 6
3. Keats-Shelley House - Piazza di Spagna, 26
4. Palazzo Cenci - Vicolo dei Cenci, 1
5. Palazzo Verospi - Via del Corso, 374
6. Pyramide di Caio Cestio - Via Raffaele Persichetti, 1
7. S. Giovanni in Laterano - Piazza di San Giovanni in Laterano
8. S. Marco al Campidoglio - Piazza di S. Marco, 52,
9. S. Maria in Cosmedin - Piazza della Bocca della Verità, 18
10. S. Maria in Tempulo - Via di Valle delle Camene, 2
11. S. Maria Sopra Minerva - Piazza della Minerva, 42
12. S. Pietro in Vincoli - Piazza S. Pietro in Vincoli, 4/A
13. S. Sabina - Piazza Pietro D'Illiria, 1
14. S. Sisto Vecchio - Piazzale Numa Pompilio, 8
15. S.M. Maggiore - Piazza S. Maria Maggiore, 42
16. Ss. Giovanni e Paolo -Piazza Dei SS. Giovanni e Paolo
17. Terme di Caracallo - Viale delle Terme di Caracalla

*Galleria Borghese - Piazzale Scipione Borghese, 5
*Musei Vaticani - Viale Vaticano
*S. Paolo fuori le mura - Piazzale Paolo, 1
*S. Pietro - Piazza San Pietro
*S. Stefano il Protomartire - Via dell'Arco di Travertino, 151
*S.M. del Rosario - Via Alberto Cadlolo, 51

*Not included on this map. Refer to main map for more information

Map by Eureka Cartography, Berkeley, CA

Fig. 1: Tomb of Leo I, by Alessandro Algardi, Basilica di San Pietro, Rome.
Photo courtesy of Peter Hatlie.

Chapter Two

POPE LEO I THE GREAT (ca. 400–461, r. 440–61 CE) AT THE BASILICA DI S. PIETRO AND THE BASILICA DEI SANTI GIOVANNI E PAOLO

DAVID DAWSON VASQUEZ

Introduction

The relationship of Rome to the rest of the civilized world was reinvented by Roman Christians in the fourth and fifth centuries as the Roman imperial ideal gave way to a Christian vision. Pope Leo I played an important role in this development. Bishop of Rome from 400–461, Leo articulated a Christian vision of the special status of Rome in the worldwide Church and of the special identity of the city of Rome in relation to its past that was to have far-reaching influence. He took major strides in advancing the development of the role of Rome in the worldwide Church. Leo upheld and extended the growing understanding of the unique role of the pope, seeing this as a natural expression of his role as Vicar of Peter. His actions against various heresies throughout the empire show that he understood his pastoral responsibility to be universal and immediate. His time in office was spent vigorously pursuing this universal ideal, engaging not only in doctrinal disputes but also entering the political realm to protect Rome from the onslaughts of the Huns and the Vandals. These efforts were accompanied by a vision of the Church as rightful heir of the glory of Rome. For him, God had prepared the world for the Church through the Roman Empire, and the Church was duty bound to take up whatever was good in this development.

Background to Leo's Papacy

Hard historical data is difficult to come by on Leo's early years. The *Liber Pontificalis*, a medieval text of a much later date whose historical facts should be taken with a grain of salt, merely records that he was Tuscan and that his father's name was Quintianus. Leo, however, refers to Rome as his homeland. Thus, two possibilities present themselves: either Leo was born in Rome from Tuscan parents or he was born in Tuscany yet called Rome his homeland because he was convinced that he was born to find his way to the Chair of Peter. In any case, the town of Volterra, in modern-day Tuscany, claims him as a native son.

He seems to have been born at the end of the fourth century. If he grew up in Rome, he lived through the sack of Rome by Alaric in 410. He certainly knew Rome during this critical period of its transition from a world capital to a rather modest late-antique city, and for his part Leo was responsible for various rebuilding projects aimed at reinvigorating urban life in the middle of the fifth century. He was ordained a deacon of the Roman Church and was a prominent figure during the episcopacies of Celestine (422-32) and Sixtus III (432-40). Deacons at that time often took on administrative roles, and arch-deacons such as Leo were called upon to act as the representative of the bishop, often being sent as envoys to synods and other meetings. Leo is mentioned as a correspondent of Cyril of Alexandria over the controversy with Nestorius as well as serving Pope Sixtus III in the censure of Julian of Eclanum in the Pelagian controversy. He was also trusted with political duties, including service to the imperial court on a mission to Gaul. He was elected to succeed Sixtus while he was still in Gaul.

Elevation to Pope

When a delegation reached Leo, informing him of his election, he returned to Rome and was consecrated on September 29, 440. Leo's contribution as bishop of Rome can be divided into four areas, all of which were built on the achievements of his predecessors. He developed the authority of the office in order to assure unity in the Church, especially in the West. He spent considerable time and energy defending the faith of the Church, working to suppress various movements at odds with the tradition as he had received it. He continually worked for harmony with the political powers, both the imperial Roman government and those of the northern troops advancing on and occupying parts of Italy. Finally, he was instrumental in reconceiving the relationship between the Church and ancient Rome. Because his work in each of these areas had lasting effect, he has been referred to over the centuries as "Leo the Great." His episcopacy lasted for just over twenty-one years, and when he died on November 10, 461 he was shortly thereafter revered as a saint. In the eighteenth century, Pope Benedict XIV (r. 1740–58) declared him a doctor of the Church, recognizing the enduring doctrinal value of his many homilies and letters.

The Authority of the Bishop of Rome

The role of the bishop of Rome as pope of the universal Church as would be recognized by Catholics today took some time to develop, and Leo played a role in this development. The idea that the Roman Church is in some way set apart from other Christian communities was present already in the first generations of Christians. An early letter of the Roman Church to the Church of Corinth (known commonly today as the biblical 1 Clement) shows that even in the first century, Rome saw itself as concerned with the welfare of other churches, a quality shared by several of the great churches of the time but in Rome particularly connected to the memory of Peter and Paul. In the second century, both Ignatius of Antioch (ca. 35–108) and Irenaeus of Lyons (ca. 140–202) single out Rome as having a certain prominence among the other churches, again connected to the claim that Rome is the place of the death and burial of the greatest of the apostles, Peter and Paul. In the third century, the judgment of the Church of Rome on controversial issues was sought, even if other significant churches, like the Church of Carthage under Cyprian, saw themselves as having equal apostolic status. Rome was seen as one sister church among others, but was emerging as the more important, or elder, sibling. Its importance in the West was always more accepted than in the East.

In the fourth century bishops of Rome began actively fostering the idea that Rome should have an authoritative voice in issues that concerned the universal Church. Pope Julius I (r. 337–52) saw it proper that he review the decisions of synods held elsewhere. By the second half of the century, Pope Damasus I (r. 366–84) was already articulating the principle of the Roman pope's primacy over other Christian bishops. In the lifetime of Leo, the bishop of Rome began to be referred to as "pope" (*papa*), an honorific title referring to his care of the Church at large, and his function as arbiter became more and more articulated.

Leo exercised an important role both in developing a theory of Roman primacy and in putting it into practise. The official word for diocese, "see," is from the Latin *sedes* ("seat"), and refers to the seat of the bishop, in fact the chair of the bishop in the cathedral (also from "seat," *cathedra*, this time from the Greek) of the diocese. For Leo, when a person was called to ascend to the Chair of St. Peter in being consecrated bishop of Rome, he entered into communion with the saint himself and took up Peter's role in the Church. When Leo received word of his election, it seems that he saw this as the culmination of all his previous service to the Church, a calling for which he had been prepared since birth. He seems to have seen himself as created to be the vessel of the Apostle. Thus, he referred to the day of his election as his "nativity," and for many years on this day held a local synod in honour of his "birthday" and addressed those gathered with a special homily reflecting on the continuing role of Peter in the Church.

Leo saw an intimate communion between himself and St. Peter. In his early homilies on the topic (see sermons 2 and 3), he reminded his hearers that Peter's activity continues in the Church through the ministry of the bishop of Rome. Peter continues to live through his successor. He continues to exercise the ministry granted to him by Jesus in being the rock of the Church and in binding and loosing on behalf of Christ. When the bishop of Rome writes to other bishops, it is Peter strengthening his brothers (Luke 22:32). In fact, whatever the bishop of Rome does that is good and that furthers Christ's work in the Church, he does because Peter is acting through him. So strong was this connection in his mind that Leo called himself Vicar of Peter, a title that became a standard title of the pope.

Leo was convinced that he took up the primacy of Peter among the apostles and thus held primacy among all the bishops of the world. He exercised this primacy in varying ways, according to the structure of the Church of his time, always taking care to defend the traditional organization of the Church that he had received, seeing himself as a good caretaker and never as an innovator. In Italy, in the areas over which Rome had direct authority, Leo asserted his full power in bringing bishops in line, criticizing liturgical practices that he found erroneous including, for example, the Sicilian bishops who were baptizing on the feast of the Epiphany rather than at Easter (letter 16). In southern Gaul, he forcefully intervened in disputes among bishops, working both to restrict the aspirations of independence of the bishop of Arles and to reorganize the territory to acknowledge the real leadership of Arles by giving it its own territory. Further away, in Spain, northern Gaul, England, and north Africa, he supported organizational reforms and called for the suppression of heresy through letters and personal support. In the East, where his jurisdictional authority was not recognized, he still worked to affirm and support defenders of the authentic teachings of the Church against innovations.

Defending the Catholic Faith

Leo's age was faced with any number of challenges to the accepted Catholic faith. To name only the most prominent of such movements, Manichaeism was a dualist religion founded in the third century based on Christian, Gnostic, and pagan principles, with a strong following through the end of the fourth century; Pelagianism was a sectarian Christian movement, popular with the aristocracy in fourth- and fifth-century Rome, that regarded human agency and not mere grace as critical to salvation; and Priscillianism was yet another sectarian movement, popular among some fifth- to sixth-century bishops (especially in Spain), and rooted in the idea that severe ascetical practice was an essential component of spiritual authority and renewal. For his part, Leo saw the suppression of subversive movements like these and the clarification of doctrine as a primary pastoral duty. He was particularly zealous in the suppression of Manicheanism, seeking the aid of the imperial government in prohibiting the spread of the sect in Rome and limiting its effectiveness elsewhere. The battle that Augustine of Hippo (354–430) had begun against Pelagianism some years before was still underway. Leo did not hesitate to join it, and also used his influence in Spain against the emergence of Priscillianism. While there is little evidence that Leo was original in his theological approach to these issues, he actively promoted the theology of the great thinkers of the Catholic tradition and of his day.

Most of his doctrinal interventions were directed at the Western Church, but in one area in particular—the clarification of the language regarding the person of Jesus—he acted for the universal Church. While deacon under Pope Celestine, he worked with Cyril, bishop of Alexandria, to convince Celestine to support Cyril in the condemnation of the ideas of Nestorius at the Council of Ephesus (431). As bishop, Leo continued to be vigilant over doctrine in the ongoing dispute. He received an appeal from a monk named Eutyches in Constantinople who sought support for a Monophysite understanding of Jesus, arguing that in the Incarnation, Christ's humanity was absorbed into the divinity. Leo recognized the danger of this teaching and composed a letter to Archbishop Flavian of Constantinople (446–49) that defended the teaching of the Council of Ephesus that the incarnate Jesus has two natures, a full human nature and a full divine nature. This letter, known to posterity as the *Tome of Leo*, was eventually read out at the Council of Chalcedon in 451 and was instrumental in the affirmation of a two-nature Christology that continues to be the official belief of Western Christians today.

Temporal Power

While it was not until much later that the pope exercised a political power of his own, Leo's actions provide important precedents for this development. For instance, Leo fostered a close relationship with the Roman imperial authorities. He was willing to serve as an imperial representative when he was deacon, and when he became bishop, he did not hesitate to solicit political support for his efforts at maintaining unity in the Church, especially in the suppression of heresy. It is in the battle against Manichaeism that Leo went the furthest in this regard, calling on the imperial forces to enforce an old law against the sect so that its presence could be banished from Rome and other cities.

His most memorable political activities are his interventions with the Huns and the Vandals. In 452, he went up to Mantua to meet the army of Attila as part of an imperial delegation. During the meeting, he convinced Attila to abandon his plan to invade Rome. Later, in 455, he took the initiative to intervene in the same way with Gaiseric of the Vandals. This time, he failed to turn back the invaders, but accounts report that he did convince them to use restraint in their "vandalizing." In this action, spiritual authority and political authority united in Leo, foreshadowing what would become the normal course of action among subsequent politically-minded peoples for centuries to come.

Rome as the Patrimony of the Church

The rebuilding of Rome after the sack of 410 provided the opportunity for the bishops of Rome to reimagine the Church's relationship to the city's pagan past. They began to see the heritage of ancient Rome as a divinely-prepared gift and to see the Church as God's instrument in cleansing this gift of its supposed demonic origins. Leo gave voice to this understanding in his homilies and in practice.

While he was deacon under Sixtus III, Leo participated in the building of the Basilica of S. Maria Maggiore and the refurnishing of the Basilicas of S. Paolo Fuori le mura and S. Giovanni in Laterano. At the S. Maria Maggiore, Leo is likely to have been instrumental in its design. At the least, there is evidence that he was behind the idea of decorating the nave with mosaic scenes from the Old Testament, culminating in the scenes of the birth of Christ on the arch that ends the nave. At the Basilica di S. Paolo fuori le mura, Leo is believed to have arranged for biblical scenes along the nave as well. In addition, he likely initiated the placement of an important series of mosaic medallion portraits of the bishops of Rome, starting with that of St. Peter, which form a running frieze around the entire length of the upper walls of the nave just below its clerestory windows. He is mentioned on the triumphal arch commissioned by Galla Placidia, sister of Emperor Honorius, as having effected a renewal of the mosaics there. Finally, at the Basilica of S. Giovanni in Laterano, Leo is thought to have initiated a biblical cycle as well. And since the baptistery was rebuilt by Sixtus III, Leo is likely to have had a significant hand in its octagonal shape.

Beyond the mere fact of building and decorating Christian monuments, the practise of reusing columns and other building materials (or *spolia*) from ancient pagan structures to edify Christian buildings continued strongly apace in Leo's age. Indeed, a new understanding of the relationship of traditional Roman images to Christian images was emerging. Patrons like the bishops of Rome began expressing the idea that Roman symbols could and should be interpreted as foretelling Christian realities. Just as Christians had for centuries interpreted the Old Testament as foreshadowing the New, so now they began interpreting ancient Rome in the same way. For example, the apostolic founders of Rome, Peter and Paul, both martyred in the city in the 60s of the first century, had long been seen as twin patrons of the Church of Rome. It became easy in this new perspective to see them prefigured in the twin founders of Rome, Romulus and Remus, as well as in the heavenly twin protectors of ancient Rome, Castor and Pollux.

Leo expresses the theology of this perspective clearly in a homily delivered on the feast of Peter and Paul (sermon 82). Here he says that God allowed the development of the Roman Empire in order to prepare for the spread of the Gospel. The Romans brought the world together under one ruler and established peace at just the right time so that the Gospel could easily be brought to all corners of the world. Even though Rome was in the grip of demonic forces, the spreading of the Gospel enabled its freedom, and the goodness that was embedded there could be put to the service of the Church. Thus, as Leo saw it, the Church has both the right and the duty to use whatever was good in ancient Rome and to allow that goodness to shine forth in its proper context when used for the glory of God.

Leo's Vision of the Papacy in the Basilica di S. Pietro and the Vatican Apartments

Leo's devotion to and identification with St. Peter led him to choose to be buried within the porch of the Basilica di S. Pietro. He was moved into the basilica itself in the seventh century but his original tomb had to be transformed when the original basilica was completely rebuilt in the sixteenth and seventeenth centuries. Today, he is found in the left transept of the basilica. Because his tomb is tucked away to the side of the main sanctuary, the casual pilgrim may not notice it, but the seventeenth-century relief above the altar is well worth a visit.

Visitors to the Basilica di S. Pietro can find Leo's tomb by walking up the nave to the high altar among brightly coloured marbles and majestic statues that seem frozen in mid-action, passing by one impressive altar after another on either side. Upon reaching the high altar, featuring Bernini's imposing, glorious *Baldacchino* or canopy above, one then proceeds along the left transept until, hidden in the shadows, Leo's tomb is visible (see fig. 1). The sculptural reliefs of this tomb are the work of the high-baroque artist Alessandro Algardi (1598–1654) and on first glance present a massive relief depicting a famous scene of Leo's pontificate: the panicked Hunnic army reacting in fear in his presence. The pope gestures towards the heavens and the Hunnic chieftain Attila (ca. 406–53) looks up to see the heavens opening and the glory of the angels framing two men who descend threateningly toward him. The one to the left, despite being in the rear, is the most defined and thus bends forward to stand out in front of the second figure and the angels. He wields a sword, which stands out of the relief in sharp definition. His short beard and balding head show that he is Peter, and his companion, less defined but also wielding a sword over his head, is Paul, with his long beard blowing back as they descend. These are the patrons of the city and are ready to act should the army advance, the new Castor and Pollux. The Hunnic king is fearful; the men behind seem confused, the horses draw back. Peter is in direct line above Leo, both in equal clarity, showing both that the pope is the successor of Peter and that Peter continues to act in the Church through him. In contrast to Attila's soldiers, who are agitated, those behind the pope are peacefully serene; the young man immediately behind him is even sitting, observing the scene.

The scene, of course, depicts Leo's daring encounter with Attila the Hun in 452. The relief shows viewers two important aspects of Leo's papacy: his assumption of temporal (political) authority in his action with Attila, and his self-identification with Peter.

Fig. 2: Encounter Between Pope Leo the Great and Attila the Hun, fresco by Raphael, 1514,
Stanza di Eliodoro, Musei Vaticani. Photo Credit: Scala / Art Resource, NY.

Visitors familiar with works in this tradition will recognize this 1650 relief by Algardi
as a reworking of the scene painted by Raphael (1483–1520) in the papal apartments,
commissioned by Julius II (r. 1503–13) and completed under the patronage of Leo X (r.
1513–21).

In Raphael's fresco, the scene is broader, and the walls of Rome can be seen in the
background, transporting the historical scene from near Mantua to the outskirts of
Rome. The direct connection between Peter and Leo is not as defined, with both Peter
and Paul in equal clarity. Paul seems to go out in front of Peter here instead of being
overshadowed by him, unlike the depiction of the scene in the Algardi relief. Here Leo
is less majestic, raising his hand in blessing, while two cardinals sit patiently behind
him. Raphael does have the same contrast between the opposing forces: those of the
Church are calm, unaffected, peaceful, while those of Attila are disturbed, their horses
rearing. A dark sky shrouds the Hunnic army and a strong wind blows their banners,
while the bright sun shines behind Peter and Paul and the clothing of the papal retinue
rests unmoved. Here we have a depiction of the disordered and unruly passions of the
Hunnic tribes contrasted with the composure of the life of grace. It is a succinct depiction of Leo's defence of the faith for the betterment of humanity.

The Basilica dei Santi Giovanni e Paolo (John and Paul)

A walk across Rome's Caelian Hill today brings one back to Leo's era. From the valley of the Colosseo, the visitor skirts the edge of the hill along today's wide Via Claudia. The path gets steeper as the road leads up one of the spurs of the hill, where the remains of the aqueduct built by Nero shortly after the great fire of Rome in 64 can be seen. Taking a sharp right, the visitor passes through a narrow gate, the Arch of Dolabella, that was inserted into the Roman city wall in the first century CE. They now find themselves on the ancient Clivus Scauri, today's Via di San Paolo della Croce. Just down the road the façade of a church can be seen. The church, dedicated to saints John and Paul, is in the piazza of the same name (Piazza dei Santi Giovanni e Paolo). There is a majestic medieval bell tower to the right of the church. The bell tower rises from large stone blocks that formed part of the earlier temple to the Divine Claudius (first century CE).

The church was built in the late fourth century on the site of a residential dwelling. Today, it is possible to descend into the excavations below the church to explore a Roman apartment building and a grand Roman house. The church is dedicated to the fourth-century martyrs John and Paul, two brothers who refused to submit to the paganizing legislation of the emperor Julian and were put to death in their home on this spot on June 26, 362 for their public defence of Christianity. The church has been under the care of the Passionists since their founder, St. Paul of the Cross (1694–1775), established the order there in the eighteenth century. Today, the large residence connected to the church is the world headquarters of the order, which is dedicated to preaching about the love of God manifest in the passion and death of Christ.

Fig. 3: Basilica dei Santi Giovanni e Paolo, Rome. Photo courtesy of Peter Hatlie.

The church manifests Leo's passion for defending the truth of Christ and transforming pagan Rome into a Christian city. While he did not build the church, he did renovate it after it was damaged. One can see that it would have been an important church for him, since it drew attention to the continued need to put one's life on the line for the Gospel, even in the face of deadly opposition. Leo likely viewed the heroic martyrdom of John and Paul as an example of the zeal that is needed in defending the faith against the new paganisms of Manicheanism and Priscillianism. The church building itself reinforces this idea, and additions made since Leo's time confirm some of his favourite concerns. Standing in front of the church, visitors can clearly see ancient Rome integrated into the Christian structures. This is therefore a case in point of Christianity's appropriation of paganism rather than its destruction of it. The Claudian temple provides the foundation for the bell tower in the same way that Leo saw the Roman Empire providing the infrastructure for the Church's work. The large stones provide sturdy support for the graceful, arcaded medieval structure. One can also see in the façade traces of the Roman house into which the church was built, and the columns lining the portico, predating the church, show that this house of God has been constructed by redirecting pagan aspirations to the glory of the true God. The portico was reconstructed after another sack of the neighbourhood, this time by the Normans in 1088. It reflects the Romanesque style of the time.

Once inside, visitors see a symphony of medieval, renaissance, Baroque, and contemporary elements. Like all ancient basilicas, the columns lining the nave, like those of the portico, are from earlier, pagan structures. The floor is the typical medieval cosmatesque floor, with its inlaid marble pieces arranged in circular patterns leading from the door to the sanctuary and back. The patterned decoration of the floor may suggest to visitors a parallel between the physical progress down the nave of the church and spiritual progress in the Christian life sustained and made possible by the grace of God, a key principle of the Church's position against Palagianism that Leo defended.

The focal point of the church is the broad sanctuary, reconstructed in the sixteenth century and redecorated in the eighteenth century. The frescoes in the walls of the apse tell the story of the lives and martyrdom of John and Paul. The centre fresco has one of the brothers addressing the emperor and pointing upward to the heavens. Viewers who follow his indication lift their eyes and see in the dome of the apse Christ in glory with choirs of angels, smiling down on the brothers for their fearless testimony. The lower frescoes are later than the upper fresco, which was painted by in 1588 by Niccolò Circignani (1517–96), but Giacomo Triga (1674–1746), who painted the central lower fresco, coordinated his scene with the heavenly glory above. The sanctuary is arranged in the traditional manner; the chair of the presiding priest is in the centre of the apse, with benches for assisting ministers to either side. In the centre of the sanctuary is the altar, a marble table over a purple porphyry sarcophagus that contains the remains of the two saints, placed there in 1724 when the altar was reconstructed. The redesign of the sanctuary can be seen as an echo of Leo's principle of holding to tradition: rather than placing the altar against the wall of the apse, where the presider's chair is (as was customary from the fourteenth century on), those who reconstructed the church preferred to retain the more ancient and more long-standing tradition of a free-standing altar.

Along the right side aisle, what had been a shallow side chapel now opens up into the large chapel of St. Paul of the Cross, built in 1867. The chapel is richly decorated in marble and Egyptian alabaster. The altar contains the remains of the saint within a representation of his body. The deep colours and rich decorations of the chapel reflect the Passionist desire to find in the suffering of Christ the gateway into the richness of human life. The chapel shows that Paul of the Cross has now entered into this richness after a life of contemplation and asceticism. It is a counterpoint to the poignant depiction of the crucifixion just across the church in the second-to-last chapel on the left by Tommaso Conca (1734–1822). The Passionists meditate on Christ's suffering as the key to making sense of our suffering. This interplay in the church of suffering and glory underlines the Christian conviction of the union of humanity and divinity in Christ, in whom all human aspirations are brought to their fulfillment. One can imagine that Leo would be pleased that this church which he helped to embellish continues to present to visitors the mystery of the Incarnation that he helped to clarify.

Conclusion

Leo, the first bishop of Rome by that name, soon came to be known as Pope Saint Leo the Great. His dedication to the Church and his governance of the city of Rome have made a lasting impression. Although a very early pope, his legacy is still felt today. His clarification of the language for the person of Jesus is still professed by all Christians. His dream of the pope as the voice of Peter, preserving unity and truth for the universal Church, is still recognized by Catholics as an authentic vision of the Church. His engagement with the political forces of his day paved the way for more extensive exercise of political power and influence in later generations. His reinterpretation of Roman culture became a principle of Christian engagement with the classical past that is still valid. These concerns are manifest in the works of art associated with his life and memory as well as the churches he had a hand in building. In many ways, to gain a better understanding of Leo is to gain a better understanding of Rome.

Essential Reading

Jalland, Trevor. *The Life and Times of St. Leo the Great.* New York: MacMillan, 1941.

Kelly, J. N. D. "Leo I." In *Oxford Dictionary of Popes*, edited and revised by J. N. D. Kelly and Michael J. Walsh, 40–41. New York: Oxford University Press, 2010.

Krautheimer, Richard. *Rome, Profile of a City, 312–1308.* Princeton: Princeton University Press, 1980.

Wessel, Susan. *Leo the Great and the Spiritual Rebuilding of a Universal Rome.* Leiden: Brill, 2008.

Other Places to Encounter Leo in Rome

- Musei Vaticani, Chapel of Nicholas V: a fresco of Leo is found on the pilaster at the side of the altar.

- Ruins of the Basilica of S. Stefano il Protomartire in the Parco dell Tombe della Via Latina: commissioned by Leo.

- Basilica di St. Pietro in Vincoli: Leo is responsible for receiving the relic of St. Peter's chains, now located in the church, from the Roman Empress Eudoxia (ca. 422–93). A painting by Giovanni Battista Parodi (1674–1730) depicts a miracle of Leo.

Fig. 4: Portrait of St. Dominic, oil painting by Titian, ca. 1565, Galleria Borghese, Rome.
Photo Credit: Alinari/ Art Resource, NY.

Chapter Three

SAINT DOMINIC DE GUZMÁN (ca. 1170–1221 CE) AT THE BASILICAS OF S. MARCO AL CAMPIDOGLIO, SAN SISTO VECCHIO, AND SANTA SABINA

SR. CATHERINE JOSEPH DROSTE, O. P.

A Revolution in Monastic Life in the Middle Ages

On December 22, 1216, Pope Honorius III (r. 1216–27) promulgated the papal bull *Religiosam vitam*, establishing the Order of Preachers, led by its founder, Dominic de Guzmán. The Dominicans, along with the Franciscans who were approved a few years earlier, dramatically changed the face of religious life in Western Europe. While maintaining elements of traditional monastic practice, including the cloistered life, the communal life, and a commitment to praying the Divine Office, the apostolate or work of these new orders brought important innovations. Among the most significant innovations was their approach to poverty. Not only individual members but the entire Dominican Order renounced possessions and received their daily bread from the charity of others, a practice which led to their being called "mendicants" or beggars. In addition, the mendicants renounced a vow of stability binding them to a single monastery or convent, and consequently members were freely sent as needed beyond diocesan, regional, or state boundaries. This freedom of movement facilitated another, more controversial change to traditional modes of monastic life. As the title "Order of Preachers" implies, the Dominican mission was to preach the Word, a role traditionally assumed solely by bishops. The challenge of the Albigensians and other rebellious groups of the twelfth and thirteenth centuries motivated Pope Honorius to endorse this new initiative, with the intention of supporting rather than abrogating the bishop's role as preacher. Dominic and his Dominican brothers were set for the task: a band of preachers living religious vows and, as the original constitutions state, "established from the beginning, for preaching and the salvation of souls." This required a life dedicated solely to study and to preaching the truth, *veritas*, one of the Dominican mottos.

Dominic's Early Life: Of Dogs and Dead Skins

In the year 1169 (possibly 1170), in the small town of Caleruega in Castiglia, Spain, a woman pregnant with child had a vision. She dreamt that the life within her took the form of a dog, running round the globe with a lighted torch in its mouth, setting the world ablaze. The woman was Jane of Aza, wife of Felix de Guzmán. At the time the dream's meaning escaped her, but as the years passed, the life of her son, Dominic, revealed its significance. The dog represented Dominic himself, while the flame became the new gospel which both he and his followers, sometimes nicknamed "hounds of heaven," would preach throughout the world.

At a young age Dominic was destined for religious life. When just seven years old, he was sent by his parents to the nearby town of Gumiel to begin clerical studies with his uncle. Later he would attend the university in Palencia. During his studies there, incidents occurred which began to reveal something of the character of the young man and future founder. Most noteworthy was a simple incident which transpired during a local famine. Although his books were dear to him, not to mention essential to his studies, Dominic nonetheless exchanged them for food to distribute to the needy. His rationale: "I do not want to study dead skins, while people are dying of hunger." This story and others reached the ears of many, including Diego, Bishop of Osma. He sent for Dominic and invited the young man, who was soon to be ordained a priest, to join his chapter of canons. These canons lived a monastic life following the Rule of St. Augustine but were attached to a parish where they administered the sacraments to the faithful.

Dominic joined the canons unaware that this life of contemplative prayer and study in the city of Osma was but a stage of preparation for his future work. The latter revealed itself slowly, beginning in 1203 when the bishop selected Dominic as his companion for a mission to Denmark, entrusted to them by King Alfonso VIII (1158–1214). Lasting two years, the mission entailed negotiating a royal marriage that, in the end, reached an unsuccessful conclusion. Though failing in its primary purpose, this task succeeded as a preliminary step toward the foundation of the Order of Preachers. Their trips to the northern countries had taken Diego and Dominic through Languedoc, a region of southern France noted for its Albigensian heretics. Named for Albi, the town of their origin, the Albigensians were a gnostic sect which claimed to be Christian but posited a dualistic struggle between the good forces of the spiritual realms and the evil forces of matter. Their worldview negated the possibility of a benevolent God becoming man and taking on a physical body, i.e. the Incarnation, thereby violating a principal creed of the Christian faith. Dominic encountered the heresy at an obscure inn in the town of Toulouse. While the rest of the travellers slept, he is said to have spent the night in conversation with the innkeeper. No record of their words remains, but as the sun rose the next morning, the town had one less Albigensian. The town's innkeeper had converted.

Not long after these events, Bishop Diego and Dominic made plans to preach to the Muslims in the East. Accordingly, they headed to Rome in 1206, seeking the pope's approval for their endeavour. Pope Innocent III (r. 1198–1216) willingly authorized a preaching mission, though not in the East but instead back in Languedoc. In accordance with the papal wishes, preaching to the Albigensians of Languedoc began but not without challenges: most notably, the impression among the sectarian Christians that many Catholic bishops, priests, and even religious led scandalously luxurious lives. To counter this perception and demonstrate their dedication to Christ and his poverty, Bishop Diego sent away his horses and entourage, keeping only a few men with him, including Dominic. Then they set out on foot to preach.

The Beginnings of the Order of Preachers and Its First Members

The early years of Dominic's mission to Languedoc were difficult ones. While Bishop Diego was still alive, he and Dominic witnessed some conversions, including a group of women whom they established in a convent in Prouille, France. Following Diego's death in 1207, Dominic continued preaching without full canonical authorization until 1215, when, in a much-needed show of support, Bishop Fulk of Toulouse allowed Dominic and two brothers to establish the first permanent residence of the Order in Toulouse. That same year, Dominic travelled to Rome as Bishop Fulk's companion to the Fourth Lateran Council. This trip occasioned Dominic's request to Pope Innocent that he and his companions be confirmed as an "Order of Preachers." Innocent approved the request under the condition that Dominic and his brothers choose an existing rule of life. They unanimously selected the Rule of St. Augustine, a venerable rule promoting unity, simplicity, and offering a flexibility necessary for reformed preachers.

The year 1216 found Dominic again in Rome to meet a new Pope, Honorius III (r. 1216–27). Honorius would formally approve the order and provide Dominic with necessary documents addressed to bishops in various dioceses. These papal documents not only recognized Dominic and his band as a religious order living a life of poverty, but also gave the *Ordo Fratrum Praedicatorum* the authority to preach in dioceses throughout Europe and eventually the entire world. By 1217 Dominic had already sent his brethren out in small groups to preach in other prominent university cities, including Madrid, Paris, and Orléans. Soon afterwards Dominicans were also to be found in Bologna, Bergamo, Milan, Amiens, Barcelona, Florence, and beyond. In a familiar pattern, they started as university students, then occupied teaching positions, and finally emerged as successful teachers and scholars. Jordan of Saxony (1190–1237), the future Second Master General of the Dominicans, was among the early success stories of this sort.

Dominic and the Nuns of Rome:
San Sisto Vecchio and S. Maria in Tempulo

Dominic's final visits to Rome occurred in the winters of 1219 and 1220. Pope Honorius had earlier entrusted to Dominic the convent of San Sisto Vecchio near the Via Appia as a home for the friars. San Sisto included a newly rebuilt church housing the relics of Pope Sixtus II (r. 257–58). But Honorius had other plans for Dominic and the convent; he wanted Dominic to lead a reform of various convents of nuns in Rome. The plan required bringing several groups of nuns together in San Sisto where they lived the full enclosure, separated from the outside world and their families. Dominic faced opposition both from the nuns' families and from the nuns themselves. A particularly obstinate community was established in S. Maria in Tempulo, a dilapidated medieval church and convent located at the foot of the Caelian Hill across from the Terme di Caracalla and just a few hundred metres from San Sisto. (The deconsecrated building still stands and serves as a hall for civil marriages for the Comune di Roma.) Dominic searched for Roman nuns to help guide the reform but, finding none willing, he resorted to requesting sisters from the original foundation in Prouille. The recalcitrant sisters of S. Maria in Tempulo refused to move to San Sisto. Dominic persisted, both by preaching and spiritual direction, and eventually won most of them over. The abbess renounced her authority and agreed to move on one condition.

Fig. 5: Icon of S. Maria in Tempulo
(detail), Chiesa di S. M. del Rosario,
Rome. Photo courtesy of
Sr. Mary Justin Haltom, O. P.

The convent was in possession of a much-beloved miraculous icon of the Blessed Virgin (see fig. 5). The icon was apparently as attached to the convent as the sisters were to it, for whenever it was moved off the property (stolen or otherwise), it was said to have mysteriously returned to its convent home. The solution the abbess proposed to Dominic was therefore simple: if the icon would stay at San Sisto, so too would the sisters, and if the icon returned to S. Maria in Tempulo, so too would the sisters. The transfer of both nuns and the icon then took place, and both remained at San Sisto for years to come. It is only in fairly recent times that this famous icon has made its way to another community of nuns, that of the monastery of S. M. del Rosario on the northern borders of the city in a neighbourhood called Monte Mario.

Other miracles attributed to Dominic date to these years, as well, including the miraculous healings of a man who fell from scaffolding during construction and the nephew of a cardinal who fell from his horse. But the miracle most beloved by Dominicans, often portrayed in art, is that of the miracle of the bread, an event which occurred while the convent was still the home of the Dominican friars prior to the arrival of the nuns. As mendicants, each day two friars were assigned to walk the streets begging for food and alms from whomever they met. One morning Fra Giovanni and Fra Alberto succeeded in acquiring only a single loaf of bread. Knowing it was pointless to bring home just one loaf, they gave it to a beggar poorer than themselves. Having reported their failure to Dominic, they expected him to notify the brothers of an exceptional fast day. But Dominic, ignoring their entreaties, advised them to call the brethren to the refectory for dinner. After the blessing Fra Enrico began the usual reading from scripture while Dominic sat intent in prayer. To the amazement of all (except Dominic), two angels appeared carrying baskets of bread which they distributed to the friars, beginning with the youngest and ending with Dominic himself. In memory of this miracle, Dominicans preserve the tradition of serving the youngest at table first and ending with the superior.

Miracles, Mercy, and the Basilica di S. Marco al Campidoglio near Piazza Venezia

The Middle Ages saw a marked increase in hagiographical writings, many of which were translated into the art of the Renaissance period. These stories related many insights into the persons, the events, and the culture of the age. While some represented inventions connected with a saint's cult, many recounted actual miracles. Those concerning St. Dominic merit a special note since the many stories of Dominic's holiness and miracles do not solely focus on the person, but rather carry within a message of the mission entrusted by a founder to his followers. So even the hagiography "preached" to the preachers.

One such example of preaching occurred at the Basilica di S. Marco al Campidoglio just off Piazza Venezia in the centre of Rome during Lent of 1220 or 1221. Archaeologists posit that the original fourth-century basilica constructed by Pope Mark in honour of his patron, St. Mark the Evangelist, companion of St. Peter, may be one of the first churches within the heart of the city. Throughout the centuries it witnessed numerous renovations. Dominic was familiar with the medieval version of this church. The reported miracle occurred outside the church where Dominic, having finished preaching a Lenten homily, was making his way back to San Sisto. In her desire to hear Dominic preach, a young mother had left her small sick son at home in bed. When she returned from the preaching, she found the child dead. Wasting no time she picked him up and ran back to St. Mark's where she placed the dead youth at Dominic's feet, begging him to intercede to God for the life of her son. Sister Cecilia, a contemporary and friend of Dominic, relates that, moved with pity for the sorrowing mother, he set himself apart for a moment of prayer, then rose, approached the child, made the sign of the cross over him. He took the youth by the hand, raising him to his feet. He gave the child, fully alive and healthy, to his mother, telling her to speak to no one of what had occurred. A painting in the church above a side altar in the left aisle commemorates both Dominic's Lenten preaching and the miraculous healing.

Santa Sabina—Gem of the Aventino and Generalate of the Dominican Order

Dominic's earlier success with the nuns of S. Maria in Tempulo had repercussions for the brethren. San Sisto was too small to house both friars and nuns, so a new convent had to be found for the men. Made aware of the problem, Pope Honorius agreed to give Dominic some family property—the Savello Fortress on the Aventino, which included the Basilica di Santa Sabina. Santa Sabina holds pride of place among Dominican sites in Rome, both in the time of Dominic and today, since it serves as the Generalate—home of the master general and officials of the order. But Santa Sabina's fame was established even before the Order's founding. Pope Gregory the Great (540–604) long before named it the "gem of the Aventine."

The normal approach to the Aventino and Santa Sabina is from the east, leaving the Circo Massimo at your back and proceeding up the hill to the west by way of the Clivo dei Publici, but a preferred pedestrian incline is the Clivo di Rocca Savello, nearer the Tiber, just southeast of the Bocca della Verità. The latter route passes the twelfth-century outer walls of the Savello fortress and Savello Park or the *Giardino degli Aranci* (Orange Garden). Adjacent to Santa Sabina, the garden offers a magnificent view of the city, including the Vatican. Indeed, contemporary Dominicans recount the story of Pope John XXIII's 1958 visit to Santa Sabina and his pontifical decree that the view from the convent was the most beautiful of Rome. The Aventino has always existed "on the edge" of Rome and throughout the millennia has maintained an atmosphere of peace and calm away from the fray of the congested city centre. Officially it remained outside the pomerium, the religious boundary of the city, even after the third-century CE Aurelian walls encompassed the entire hill. Nonetheless, numerous homes and religious sites have been situated there. Archaeologists have found evidence of pagan temples to many foreign cults in the area, some later incorporated into Christian worship, including early temples to Juno Regina, Venus and Diana. As Rome grew, the Aventino became a refuge for luxurious villas of the wealthy. The Basilica di Santa Sabina was built over one such villa, a typical *domus romana* dating from the first or second century CE. Columns from this building are visible to the right of the side entrance and in the right nave. Some identify the villa as an early "house church," perhaps owned by Sabina, an early Christian martyr for whom the church is named. Though details of the first Christian centuries are scarce, fifth-century evidence is still visible to all who enter the church today.

The church's interior features large clerestory windows whose modern replicas, like the original, are of opaque selenite, allowing the sun's rays to display innumerable themes depending on the season and time of day. Facing the back wall, one views a mosaic dedication resting high above the main doors. This ancient dedication records the foundation of the church. It reads:

> When Celestine held the supreme apostolic dignity and shone as first bishop in the whole world, What thou dost marvel at a priest of the city founded, Peter, of the Illyrian people, a man of so great a name Worthy, nourished from birth in the household of Christ, rich for the poor, poor for himself, who, the goods of life here below fleeing, merited to hope for the future one.

Pope Celestine sat on the Chair of Peter from 422–32, so the church is easily dated. Of interest also is the line, "shone as first bishop of the whole world," a possible reference to Celestine's presence at the Council of Ephesus and testimony to his claim of primacy as bishop of Rome.

The remainder of the nave is relatively stark, bereft of excessive decoration yet betraying a magnificent beauty, a naked simplicity and elegance unmarred by baroque décor. This was not always the case. Like so many ancient Roman churches, Santa Sabina endured baroque transformations in the sixteenth and seventeenth centuries. Fortunately, they covered rather than destroyed her principle treasures, enabling the celebrated art historian and architect Antonio Muñoz (1884–1960), in two separate restoration projects of the early twentieth century, to strip away much of the excess and reveal once again Santa Sabina's austere dignity, a splendid example of classic paleo-Christian architecture. A single measurement—that of the radius of the apse—serves as the mathematical foundation for the whole of the structure. Every measurement—including the height and width of the side aisles, the main nave, the columns (made specifically for this basilica and autographed by a *Rufinus*), arches, windows, and even the distances between each element—is either a multiple or fraction of this measurement. Coupled with the restored *schola cantorum* where the friars still pray, and understated marble decoration in *opus sectile* above the arches of the main nave, the result is an integral whole, pleasing to the eye of the beholder.

The building served its inhabitants well, allowing the history of place and person to intertwine. The tomb of the Dominican order's seventh Master General, Muñoz of Zamora (1285–1300) is still embedded within the floor of the main nave, a mosaic image of him showing the traditional Dominican habit—tunic, scapular, and cappa (the traditional black cloak). As for the order's founder, Dominic, several locations within the church bear his imprint. Gerard of Frachet, an early chronicler of the order, relates the story of St. Dominic and two great stones which still exist in the church: the first, a broken marble slab lying in the center of the *schola cantorum* which once covered the tomb of the martyrs; the second, a large round black stone inconspicuously placed on a small column in the back left corner of the main nave. Similar stones are found in other ancient and medieval churches, including the nearby S. Maria in Cosmedin. They served as weights for market commerce and, to prevent the dishonest from cheating buyers by altering the stone's weight, they were kept in sacred buildings.

As Gerard tells it, one night while Dominic prayed in the church, stretched prostrate over the tomb of Santa Sabina, the devil, who was noted to have attacked Dominic on more than one occasion, hurled the black stone at him. Legend notes that fortunately

Fig. 6: The Crucifixion, wood carving, Basilica di Santa Sabina, Rome.
Photo Credit: DeA Picture Library/ Art Resource, NY.

Dominic rolled quickly off the tomb just as the weight crashed into the marble, breaking it into several large pieces. Gerard also mentions the obscure little window in the back corner of the left aisle, high on the wall connecting the church and convent. On his visits to Rome, Dominic would sleep in a cell near the stairs to avoid waking the friars when he went to pray in the church. Aware of these vigils, more than one friar spied on their founder at prayer in the church below. These spies and others who travelled with Dominic throughout Europe compiled Dominic's "nine ways of prayer"—different modes of Dominic's personal prayer which included lying prostrate on the ground, kneeling, standing with arms stretched to heaven, sitting in silent meditation, or singing as he walked from town to town.

Numerous testimonies state that when Dominic did sleep, whether at Santa Sabina or in other Dominican convents, he had no cell of his own, but used the room of another friar. Be that as it may, the residential and administrative quarters of today's Santa Sabina complex do identify one room as the cell used by Dominic in his lifetime. And another biographical tradition is also associated with this place: an image above the small window of this cell recounts a dream Dominic had one night. In the dream, Christ appeared to him, standing amidst the founders and saints of various religious orders. Dominic searched, but seeing no members of his own order he began to weep, considering it proof that he had failed to assist them in attaining salvation. Noting his sorrow Christ motioned towards his mother, who opened her mantle to reveal numerous Dominicans safe within her protection. In this context, a favourite Dominican title for Mary is "Queen of Preachers."

Before leaving through the narthex, originally a fifth-century quadriportico transformed during construction of the Dominican convent, one finds two other paleo-Christian treasures. The first is a magnificent sculptured door (of conifer, cedar, or cypress), the best-preserved of its kind in the world (two other examples stand in the churches of San Ambrogio in Milan and Santa Barbara in Cairo). While the door is fifth-century, the marble frame may be earlier, perhaps constructed from elements of the villa below or a fifth-century imitation of an earlier work. Ten panels are missing from the door (which was restored in the eighteenth and nineteenth centuries), but from those remaining, one gleans key events of salvation history. Most important of all is the uppermost left corner panel where one sees a simple image of Christ crucified between two thieves, one of the first representations of Christ crucified (see fig. 6). So horrendous was crucifixion that early Christians did not portray it, and non-Christians employed it for ridicule, as recognized in what may be the earliest crucifixion depiction, a second- or early third-century graffito found in a room called the *paedagogium* within the remains of the palace of Domitian on the Palatine Hill. The sketch shows a man crucified on a cross with the head of a donkey accompanied by the Greek words "Alexamenos worships his God." This wood relief panel at Santa Sabina, therefore, represents a grounding move toward casting the Crucifixion in a positive light in Christian discourse, a move that would change Christian iconography forever.

The second treasure—a seventh-century fresco—was uncovered on the same wall as the Crucifixion depiction during a 2010 restoration project. While removing plaster from a wall to the right of the monumental door, archaeologists discovered the fresco picturing the Theotokos—the Blessed Mother holding the Christ child. The classic Byzantine-style image includes Peter and Paul standing on either side of the Virgin, flanked by Sabina and Seraphia (possibly the sister or slave of Sabina). More important historically is a border inscription which identifies the two men in the lower section as Archpresbyter Theodor and Presbyter George, papal delegates to the Third Council of Constantinople held in 680. The square blue halos, a traditional symbol identifying the bearer as alive at the time of the painting, confirms a late seventh- or early eighth-century dating. Also noteworthy is the blue pigment used in the work, which archaeologists identified as of Afghan origin and used during this same period but not later.

Before leaving the narthex, one notes a small circular window facing the convent opposite the great door. Peering through, one sees an ordinary orange tree. Dominican lore associates the tree with the founder. Dominic spent hours in prayer in this convent garden, and also planted trees with orange seeds he brought from Caleruega. Eight hundred years later this tree is said to be the very one originally planted. It merits further acclaim since its flourishing or decline signals a similar thriving or waning of the order itself.

The Order Continues

These brief glimpses of Dominic in Rome do not tell the entire story. A full picture would require retracing his steps up the Italian peninsula through Viterbo and Siena, to Florence and on to Bologna, east to Venice and back to Bergamo and Milan. Dominic's life played out beyond the Pyrenees and into France in places such as Carcassonne, Toulouse, Fanjeaux, Prouille, and finally back to his beloved Spain, to the towns of his youth, Gumiel, Palencia, and Caleruega. These are only a handful of the cities Dominic visited as he travelled throughout Western Europe, preaching, praying, encouraging, and correcting. His last journey ended when he became ill while in Bologna in July of 1221. Trying to preserve him from the intense summer heat, the brothers carried Dominic out of the city and up to the surrounding hills to the Benedictine monastery of S. Maria dei Monti. A few days later, realizing he was dying and aware of a medieval law which constrained burial in the place of death, Dominic requested to return to the Dominican convent so that he could be buried "beneath the feet of the brethren." The friars obliged, carrying him back down the hill to the city, where he died on August 6, 1221. They buried him as he requested, in a simple tomb in the floor of the church. Then they went on preaching, and are still preaching eight hundred years later.

In the Dialogue of St. Catherine of Siena, a fourteenth-century Dominican, God the Father speaks to Catherine of St. Dominic and the Dominican order with the following words:

> Look at the ship of your father Dominic, my beloved son. He governed it with a perfect rule, asking his followers to be attentive only to my honor and the salvation of souls with the light of learning. He wished to build his foundation on this light while not for all that giving up true and voluntary poverty [...] He took up the task of the Word, my only-begotten Son [...] He wanted his children to do nothing else but stand at this table [the cross] by the light of learning to seek only the glory and praise of my name and the salvation of souls. (*Dialogue* 158)

The words of a fourteenth-century hymn sung each night by Dominicans around the world encapsulates Dominic's importance, not only for the order, but for the world:

> O Light of the Church, Doctor of Truth, Rose of Patience, Ivory of Chastity, you freely poured forth the waters of wisdom; Preacher of Grace, unite us with the blessed.

Essential Reading

Berthier, J. J. *L'eglise de Sainte Sabine a Rome*. Rome, 1910.

de Frachet, G., O. P. *Lives of the Brethren*, Vitae Fratrum, *c. 1258*. Translated by P. Conway, O. P. London: Blackfriars, 1955.

Hinnebusch, W., O. P. *History of the Dominican Order*. New York: Alba House, 1966.

Mandonnet, P., O. P. *Dominic and His Work*. Translated by Sr. M. B. Larkin. London: Herder, 1944.

Muñoz, A. *La basilica di Santa Sabina in Roma—descrizione storico-artistica dopo i recenti restauri*. Milan, 1919.

Tugwell, S., O. P., ed. *Early Dominicans: Selected Writings*. New Jersey: Paulist Press, 1982.

Vicaire, M.-H., O. P. Translated by K. Pond. New York: ALT Publishing, 1964.

Other Sites to Encounter St. Dominic and the Dominican Order in Rome

- Monastero e Chiesa di S. Maria del Rosari: a convent founded by Dominic in 1221, housing an important icon of S. Maria in Tempulo left of main altar.

- Angelicum (Pontificia università San Tommaso d'Aquino): from 1575 to 1931 a convent of the nuns founded by St. Dominic, and since 1906 recognized as one of Rome's pontifical universities.

- Basilica di S. Maria Sopra Minerva: the Dominican nun St. Catherine of Siena is buried under the main altar; the Dominican artist Fra Angelico is buried left of the main altar.

Fig. 7: John Keats's Gravestone in the Cimitero Acattolico, Rome.
Photo courtesy of Peter Hatlie.

Chapter Four

JOHN KEATS (1795–1821 CE) AND PERCY BYSSHE SHELLEY (1792–1822 CE) AT THE KEATS-SHELLEY HOUSE AND THE CIMITERO ACATTOLICO

ANDREW OSBORN

Born in England, Buried in Rome

The gravesites of two of the most esteemed British poets of the early nineteenth century, John Keats and Percy Bysshe Shelley, were among the earliest to grace what has been known for much of its three-century history as Rome's Protestant Cemetery, otherwise known in Italian as the Cimitero Acattolico. Neither Romantic poet lived in Rome for long. Having passed through in November 1818, Shelley and his wife Mary returned from Naples to Rome the following March, residing there through the early summer of 1819, then moving north to Livorno. Keats likewise arrived by way of Naples and lived in Rome between mid-November 1820 and his death from tuberculosis a few months later. When Shelley's drowned body washed up on the Tyrrhenian shore in the summer of 1822, a friend arranged a cenotaph to be erected nearby his fellow poet's grave. The fatality of such coincidence, augmenting the deserved regard of these two poets, has secured their stories within the physical memory of Rome and drawn numerous pilgrims to the gravesites. Shelley's long elegiac poem for Keats, which commemorates the only slightly younger poet's final resting place, and the institution of the Keats-Shelley Museum at Keats's rooms on the Piazza di Spagna, are cultural anchors.

A Non-Catholic Cemetery in Catholic Rome

After the Irish writer Oscar Wilde visited Italy in 1877, he commented that the Cimitero Acattolico was "the holiest place in Rome." The sense of this quip should not be ascribed entirely to Wilde's wry wit, however. For as numerous visitors have experienced over several centuries, the pine-and-cypress-shaded site has a special spirit. Two very different tutelary masses rise above each narrow end of the otherwise fairly level rectangular sward. To the east is the geometrically precise Pyramid of Cestius, dating to the first century BCE. To the west is the roughly coeval mound of debris known as Monte Testaccio, a hill built up from fifty million or so amphorae discarded there during the early centuries of the Roman Empire.

At the time of its institution as a cemetery for non-Catholics, the site's most influential recommendation may have been its removal from the city's centre and its pejorative association with the heaped refuse of Testaccio. Rome's ecclesiastical laws prohibited non-Catholics from burial in Catholic churches or consecrated ground. The cemetery's earliest dated grave-marker was a Latin-inscribed lead shield over the remains of the young Oxford graduate George Langton, buried beside the pyramid in 1738. But records indicate that Pope Clement XI (r. 1700–21) granted permission in 1716 for the burial of a protestant medical doctor from Edinburgh who had been exiled to Rome for supporting the Stuart claimant to the British crown. The next known burials occurred in 1723 and at least two of the three were again protestant Jacobites, one a Scottish peer and member of the Stuart court. For several decades, most of those buried in the cemetery were British Jacobite supporters.

By mid-century, however, grand tourists from Britain who had died in Rome and non-Catholics from elsewhere in Europe began also to be interred near the pyramid. Even so, when Shelley buried his son there in 1819, the number of marked graves remained well below a hundred. Shortly after Keats's interment, Pope Pius VII (r. 1800–23) forbade further burial before the pyramid in what thenceforth came to be known as the *Parte Antica* and expanded the cemetery toward the Tiber. The walled "New Cemetery" was enlarged twice, but the dimensions have remained fixed since 1894. The building of non-Catholic places of worship in Rome having been permitted since the end of Papal rule in 1870, a small chapel with a bell tower and mortuary was added in 1898. Today, the cemetery contains graves not only of protestant Christians but also of members of the Eastern Orthodox Church, Jews, Muslims, and atheists. Among the latter is the political philosopher Antonio Gramsci (1891–1937), author of *Prison Notebooks* and founder of Italy's Communist Party. Other well-marked graves belong to the Russian painter Karl Briullov (1799–1852) and American sculptor William Wetmore Story (1819–95), whose Angel of Grief monument may be the site's most arresting. The expatriate American novelist Henry James, who composed a biography of Story, concludes his early novella *Daisy Miller* (1879) by burying his heroine "in the little Protestant cemetery, in an angle of the wall of imperial Rome, beneath the cypresses and the thick spring flowers."

Shelley's Youthful Adventures

Shelley's early rebellions from what he perceived to be unjust familial and institutional strictures represent the revolutionary spirit typical of much of the Romanticism of his time. He was born on August 4, 1792, near Horsham, West Sussex, the eldest son of Timothy Shelley, a Whig member of Parliament who was himself the son of a wealthy baronet. Diminutive and intellectual, Percy Shelley suffered as the object of bullying at Eton. Having entered University College, Oxford in the spring of 1810, he read copiously and published a gothic novel, a romance, and many verses during his first and only year, near the end of which he was expelled for writing and distributing a pamphlet entitled "The Necessity of Atheism." When his father negotiated an opportunity for readmission, Shelley again refused to repudiate the ideas expressed in the pamphlet. The resulting schism between father and son only worsened when, four months later, Shelley eloped to Scotland with sixteen-year-old Harriet Westbrook. Three summers later he abandoned Harriet, who by then was pregnant with their second child, eloping to Switzerland with sixteen-year-old Mary Wollstonecraft Godwin, the future celebrated author of *Frankenstein*. A second summer adventure on the continent was later commemorated in *History of a Six-Week Tour*, which included Shelley's poem "Mont Blanc." Mary's first son and Shelley's first great poem (*Alastor, or The Spirit of Solitude*) came to

Fig. 8: John Keats,
painting by Joseph
Severn, National
Portrait Gallery,
London.
Photo Credit: National
Portrait Gallery.

light in the first months of 1816. In March 1818, at the age of twenty-six, Shelley again
sailed for the continent, this time for Italy, never to return to England.

Remarkable Young Keats

Keats was born three years after Shelley, on October 31, 1795, into much humbler conditions. His father was a horse groomer in central London who died of a skull fracture
when Keats was only eight; his mother succumbed to tuberculosis when he was fourteen. Keats apprenticed as an apothecary and surgeon, which were not so professionally
elevated as they are now, but less than a year after receiving his license to practice, he
announced to his guardian that he would no longer pursue medicine, having set his
sights on poetry. Poet and publisher Leigh Hunt, having printed Keats's first sonnet in
his *Examiner*, grouped him with Shelley in an essay dating to 1816 that recommended
"Three Young Poets" of promise, "a new school." By early 1817, the twenty-one-year-old
had published his first collection of poems, and although he devoted himself to nursing
his tubercular brother Tom, Keats maintained a remarkable pace of literary produc-
tion throughout his few remaining years of health. In 1818, he published *Endymion* and

established an intimacy with Fanny Brawne, the "fair love" he addresses in the late sonnet "Bright Star" and the "thou" he anticipates haunting in "This Living Hand." Keats's *annus mirabilis* was 1819. In the spring months of April and May alone, he composed five of the six odes upon which his canonical status rests most secure: "Ode to Psyche," "Ode on Indolence," "Ode to a Nightingale," "Ode on a Grecian Urn," and "Ode on Melancholy." Before the miracle year was over, he had added to that great store the long erotic dream poem *The Eve of St. Agnes*, two versions of the ballad "La Belle Dame sans Merci," the incomplete epic *Hyperion*, the long narrative poem *Lamia*, and what many critics consider the finest of his odes, "To Autumn." His copious letters to friends and family are a trove of literary theory and critical commentary.

Convergence and Divergences

In early February 1818, one month before Shelley would make his last voyage to the continent, he and Keats met at Leigh Hunt's home for an informal sonnet contest with "the Nile" as their theme. London had been abuzz with Egyptomania since the previous autumn when the British Museum exhibited several major recent finds including the Rosetta Stone and an enormous blue and white granite statue of Ramses II taken from the king's funerary temple at Thebes. Given that they allowed themselves only fifteen minutes for the task, we should not be surprised that the results do not rank among either poet's anthologized favorites. But the differences in their approaches speak to larger-scale characteristics of each poet's style and concerns. Keats, although he was then about to shift to the Shakespearean rhyme scheme, had up to that point composed all of his forty-some sonnets in Petrarchan form, and "To the Nile" is strictly Petrarchan, as well. It begins with two exclamatory epithets—"Son of the old moon-mountains African! / Chief of the Pyramid and Crocodile!"—then devotes the remainder of the octave to questioning whether the Nile deserves its reputation as "fruitful," given that its mention conjures "a desert" in the imagination. The sestet seeks to correct for this skepticism, hoping that it is ill-founded—"O may dark fancies err! they surely do"—and faults "ignorance," which is usually considered to be a condition, as instead an agent "that makes a barren waste / Of all beyond itself." The sonnet concludes by likening that distant river's behaviour and sensibilities to his local waterways:

> thou dost bedew
> Green rushes like our rivers, and dost taste
> The pleasant sun-rise, green isles hast thou too,
> And to the Sea as happily dost haste.

Keats's sonnet therefore concedes his lack of knowledge about its narrow geographic focus to promote a broad ethics of the imagination; the Nile becomes a complex symbol of both his own vast ignorance and of the fruitfulness of empathic generosity toward the unknown.

Shelley's untitled sonnet answers Keats's gentle intimacy with ominous sublimity. It begins with an enumeration of contributors to the eventual flood that is noteworthy for its jarring juxtapositions and personified abstractions: melting snow is said to hang, for example, "from the Desert's ice-girt pinacles, / Where Frost and Heat in strange

Fig. 9: Shelley Writing *Prometheus Unbound* at the Terme di Caracalla, painting by Joseph Severn, Keats-Shelley Museum, Rome. Photo Credit: Scala / Art Resource, NY.

embraces blend." Like Keats's, it opens with a Petrarchan octave and is also addressed, in part, to the Nile. But with a concluding Shakespearean couplet it turns to warn humanity of the very opposite of ignorance: "Beware, O man! for knowledge must to thee, / Like the great flood to Egypt, ever be." A surfeit of otherwise nourishing knowledge will endanger us as readily as the Nile's nourishing waters endanger Egypt when the river floods. With "soul-sustaining airs" come "blasts of evil"; "fruits and poisons spring" from the same rich soil. Shelley had by then not only written but also seen published in Hunt's *Examiner* one of his finest lyric poems on a related subject, "Ozymandias," which deftly suggests that the sculptor's and especially the lyric artist's power to convey an expression is less vulnerable to time's erosions than that of a pharaoh or other tyrant. The dilapidation of the statue does not impede recognition of Ramses's passionate vaunting—his "frown, / And wrinkled lip, and sneer of cold command" all still speak for his character, as it were, albeit silently—and Shelley's disorderly departure from any of the sonnet's normative rhyme schemes in no way undermines his conceit as the pedestal's inscription has been undermined.

If "Ozymandias" succinctly conveys Shelley's triumphal disdain over despotism in all its forms, Keats's defining sensibilities and concerns may be represented by the third, concluding stanza of his "Ode on Melancholy." Keats was a sensualist, and he recognized that all things sensuous are also transient. Whereas Shelley seemed always ready to speak revolutionary truths to power, Keats expressed his courage more intimately. His bargain was neither Faustian nor Satanic—neither a matter of trading the moral soul for knowledge and experience, nor of pretending that the will's autonomy trumps the guidance of any higher authority—but small-*r* romantic: he accepts and even embraces mortality in return for intensity. As Wallace Stevens, the most Keatsian of modernist poets, put it a century later: "Death is the mother of beauty."

Shelley's *Prometheus Unbound* and *The Cenci*

Shelley's first visit to Rome was a stopover as his family travelled from Venice to Naples in November 1818. That he visited what he called "the English burying-place" despite having only a week to tour the city's attractions may indicate the site's already considerable reputation. When the Shelleys returned to Rome in March 1819, the poet enjoyed what were arguably the most productively inspired three months of his life, during which he rapidly composed the second and third acts of *Prometheus Unbound* and began a second verse drama, *The Cenci*.

For this longer stay, Shelley initially took rooms at a fashionable address near the Piazza Venezia. From there he settled into a ritual of strolling daily through the Foro Romano, taking especial interest in the Arches of Titus and Constantine, the symbolic richness of which he would mine in his last, never-completed poem, "The Triumph of Life." In the former arch, which depicts a menorah and other Temple treasures being borne away in Titus's Siege of Jerusalem, and in the nearby Colosseo, which had been completed under that same Flavian emperor's reign, Shelley saw further evidence—for him, mostly hope-inspiring evidence—of institutional mutability. Regarding the Arch of Titus, he noted:

> Beyond this obscure monument of Hebrew desolation, is seen the tomb of the Destroyer's family, now a mountain of ruins. The Flavian amphitheatre has become a habitation for owls and dragons. The power, of whose possession it was once the type, and of whose departure it is now the emblem, is become a dream and a memory. Rome is no more than Jerusalem.

During the previous September at the villa of his fellow poet Lord Byron (1788–1824) near Padua, Shelley had composed the first act of *Prometheus Unbound*. As his walks in Rome took him with increasing frequency beyond the Palatino and the Circo Massimo to the Baths of Caracalla (see fig. 8), he found their "mountainous ruins" and "dizzy arches suspended in the air" a conducive setting for furthering this classical drama about cosmic regime change. What had begun as a recovery in translation became more clearly an adaptation. Although only the first, static tragedy of Aeschylus's Prometheus trilogy remains intact, the few extant fragments of the second and third dramas suggest that the ancient Greek playwright's humanitarian Titan hero is eventually reconciled with Zeus. His Prometheus discloses to Zeus the danger of his mating with Thetis—because her son will be stronger than his father—who is therefore instead married off to mortal Peleus. In return, Zeus allows Herakles to deliver Prometheus from captivity. As Shelley later explained in the preface to his version, however, he balked at this reconciliation of "champion with oppressor": "The moral interest of the fable," he claimed, "which is so powerfully sustained by the sufferings and endurance of Prometheus, would be annihilated if we conceive of him unsaying his high language and quailing before his successful and perfidious adversary."

In April 1819, Shelley considered himself done with *Prometheus Unbound* and turned his artistic attentions away from the classical to refocus on Rome's early baroque. A chance encounter with the Irish painter Amelia Curran (1775–1847) led the Shelleys to move to rooms beside Curran's at the top of the Spanish Steps. In mid-May, having read "a detailed account of the horrors which ended in the extinction of one of the noblest and richest families of [Rome] during the Pontificate of Clement VIII, in the year of 1599," Shelley visited the Palazzo Cenci, "a vast and gloomy pile of feudal architecture [...] near the quarter of the Jews." Several days later he began composing a new tragedy that yet again represented emotionally dynamic responses to tyranny but now within a narrower, domestic scope.

The Cenci's tragic hero is Beatrice Cenci, and at its heart is the horror of incestuous rape. For Beatrice this act's breach of fundamental values is literally unspeakable, and Shelley builds layer upon layer of dramatic tension around the poignant absence of the unsaid, all the more sublime for its lack of boundary or definition. As Shelley explains in the play's "Preface," to represent more directly what was done to Beatrice and her family would be "monstrous":

> The person who would treat such a subject must increase the ideal, and diminish the actual horror of the events, so that the pleasure which arises from the poetry which exists in these tempestuous sufferings and crimes may mitigate the pain of the contemplation of the moral deformity from which they spring.

In act 2, it quickly becomes evident that Count Cenci has threatened his daughter in the night, and by act 3 Beatrice's "brain is hurt." Urged by her admiring stepmother to disclose her sufferings, Beatrice concedes that she cannot imagine their cause; her very thought "is like a ghost shrouded and folded up / In its own formless horror."

With Aristotle, Shelley understood that audiences more readily feel pity for heroes who do not deserve the misfortunes that befall them but who are also sufficiently imperfect as to invite our empathy. To witness the suffering of an utter innocent is more abhorrent than cathartic. Beatrice recommends herself as a tragic figure because, albeit far more sinned against than sinning, she commissioned her father's murder and sought to conceal the act. The drama's denouement follows the historical account fairly closely. In his castle in the Apennines to which the family has ventured, Count Cenci is drugged by his wife then strangled in his sleep by hired assassins, who fail to dispose of the body effectively. When a papal representative, visiting to consult the count, instead finds his corpse lodged in the branches of a pine below his window, the conspiracy is revealed and, although Legate Savella discerns that the murder might be justified as moral self-defence, the surviving family is imprisoned.

Throughout the threat-filled inquest of act 5, Beatrice rhetorically turns the tables on her inquisitors, putting language and the Church's representations of God's will on trial. Rather than denying her guilt outright, she argues that the words with which her guilt is named have ceased to mean what they once did and should. Asked by the judge, "Art thou not guilty of thy father's death?" she demonstrates that formerly secure understandings of both *father* and *Father* have been undermined:

Or wilt thou rather tax high judging God
That he permitted such an act as that
Which I have suffered, and which he beheld;
Made it unutterable, and took from it
All refuge, all revenge, all consequence,
But what which thou hast called my father's death?
Which is or is not what men call a crime,
Which either I have done, or have not done[.]

Beatrice was shortly thereafter publicly executed alongside her brother and step-mother, under papal authority.

Just as he was completing *The Cenci*, Shelley and his wife Mary suffered their own unspeakable tragedy. On June 7, 1819, their three-year-old son William suddenly died and was swiftly buried no more than thirty metres from Testaccio's Pyramide di Caio Cestio. Shrouded and folded up, the living left Rome for Livorno three days later.

Keats's "Posthumous Existence" in Rome and in Shelley's *Adonaïs*

Keats's last great ode, "To Autumn," was composed in the autumn of that same year, 1819. Keats's biographer W. Jackson Bate believes that the poet's tuberculosis had gone "active" by then. Several months later, in early February 1820, he suffered his first severe hemorrhage in the lungs. Although the disease was not understood at the time to be contagious and so he may not have known how he contracted it, Keats's medical training allowed him to diagnose himself immediately and with conviction. By early July, even as his impressive collection *Lamia, Isabella, The Eve of St. Agnes, and Other Poems* was being published, the ever-weakened poet was taken in by Leigh Hunt and examined by a specialist from the Royal College of Physicians, who attested to the severity of Keats's condition and warned him that he would not survive another English winter. Having shown up feverish at Fanny Brawne's house for an impromptu visit in mid-August, he was invited to stay there for what turned out to be a month, during which he exchanged letters with Shelley, who invited Keats to stay with him and Mary in Italy. On September 17, 1820, Keats and the accomplished painter Joseph Severn (1793–1879) embarked in London; on the following evening their ship, the *Maria Crowther*, left for Naples.

Severn had been no more than an acquaintance before this. Indeed, he was approached by Keats's benefactors only four days before the departure and did not have a sense of the severity of the poet's condition. When they finally reached Rome in late October 1820, Keats moved into rooms on the third floor of Piazza di Spagna no. 26, looking out on the grand steps from the southeast side. Keats's friends in England had arranged for the Scottish medic Dr. James Clark, who had recently published a book on the salubrious effects of climate upon disease, to take Keats as a patient. Clark diagnosed Keats's malady as related to the stomach rather than the lungs and encouraged the poet to go horse-riding for an hour daily. When Keats writes in one of his letters to fellow poet Charles Armitage Brown (1747–1842) of November 30, "Yet I ride the little horse," he is not being metaphorical. Severn's biographer William Sharp notes that Keats and Severn would also stroll on the Pincian Hill near the Villa Borghese and on occasion met Prince Borghese's wife, Paulina Bonaparte, sister of Napoleon. They also saw Antonio Canova's

semi-nude sculpture of her as *Venus Victorious*, now exhibited in Rome's Galleria Borghese Museum.

But on December 10, Keats's worst bout of hemorrhaging began and did not cease
for nearly a month. Severn reports to Brown that Keats has vomited "cup-fuls of blood,"
and that Dr. Clark's solution is to bleed him further and, because he still thought the
stomach worse off than the lungs, deprive him of sustenance ("a single anchovy a day,
with a morsel of food"). One of Severn's letters to Brown suggests that he is taking pre-
cautions against a suicide attempt. Others acknowledge deep depressions and paranoia.
When Keats requested the bottle of laudanum that he had brought, Severn initially held
out then confessed his moral quandary to Clark, who removed the bottle from the apartment. During these last days Keats sometimes left his small bedroom in favour of the
larger adjacent room with its books and piano. A week or so before his death, Keats told
Severn that he wished his grave to feature only the simple epitaph "Here lies one whose
name was writ in water." Having asked Severn to visit his burial site, Keats approved of
the description. He became more calm and resigned. Then, in the afternoon of Friday,
February 23, Keats called out to the painter that he was dying. He slipped away around
11 pm, though the date recorded on the gravestone is the 24th. On that day, plaster casts
of Keats's face, hand, and foot were made. On Sunday, Dr. Clark and an Italian surgeon
opened his chest to find that both lungs were so "intirely [*sic*] destroyed" that it was
hard to imagine how Keats had breathed at all during his last months.

Keats was buried on Monday morning, February 26. The gravestone, with its partly
unstrung Greek lyre, was designed by Severn; Keats's phrase was elaborately augmented
by Brown and further altered by Severn (see fig. 7). When Severn's stylistically similar
gravestone was erected beside Keats's over fifty years later, it identified the painter as
the "devoted friend and death-bed companion of John Keats," and acknowledged that
the intervening half-century had sufficed for him to see Keats "number among The
Immortal Poets of England."

Shelley learned of Keats's death in mid-April and immediately launched into the
long pastoral elegy *Adonaïs*. In the poem's preface, he described the cemetery as "an
open space among the ruins covered in winter with violets and daisies" then added, with
ominous prescience: "It might make one in love with death, to think that one should be
buried in so sweet a place." Because his favourite of Keats's works, the abandoned epic
Hyperion, convinced him that Keats was his generation's heir to Milton, Shelley selected
the pastoral elegy as his genre, but whereas Milton's pastoral elegy for his Cantabri-
gian friend Edward King, "Lycidas," rhymes with no set pattern and sporadically punctu-
ates its lines of iambic pentameter with trimeters, Shelley composed *Adonaïs* using the
nine-line stanza that Edmund Spenser had invented for his Elizabethan epic *The Fairie
Queene*, and in which Keats had composed *The Eve of St. Agnes*. By mid-July 1821, Shelley
had completed its fifty-five stanzas.

The poem's titular stand-in for Keats, *Adonaïs*, amalgamates two myths: that of the
vegetable god, Adonis—whom Aphrodite loved and whom another of her lovers, Ares,
gored to death in the guise of a wild boar—and that of the Hebrew Lord, Adonaï. In
its early stanzas, the poem emphasizes Adonaïs's death and the resulting grief. Late in
the poem, however, Shelley alludes to the end of Keats's "Ode to a Nightingale"—"Do

I wake or sleep?"—in bidding us not to mourn as if delight had fled: "Peace, peace! he is not dead, he doth not sleep— / He hath awakened from the dream of life." Shelley cites other hugely talented poets who had died too young, "of unfulfilled renown"—the first-century Roman poet Lucan, for example, and Sir Philip Sidney, whom Spenser had elegized in *Astrophel*—welcoming Adonaïs / Keats "as one of us" much as Homer, Ovid, Horace, and Lucan invite Dante to join Virgil and them in *Inferno*'s Limbo. Then, with a later portion of the *Commedia* apparently in mind, Shelley has them assert that one of the celestial spheres "has long / Swung blind [and] / Silent alone amid an Heaven of song," awaiting its songful genius, "thou Vesper." If one must mourn Adonaïs, the poet asserts, one should seek him beyond our world and "beyond all worlds" at the circumference of the heavens. Or, if one seeks his spirit on Earth, then, with a light heart and rekindled hope, one must

> go to Rome, which is the sepulchre,
> O, not of him, but of our joy: 'tis nought
> That ages, empires, and religions there
> Lie buried in the ravage they have wrought;
> For such as he can lend,—they borrow not
> Glory from those who made the world their prey;
> And he is gathered to the kings of thought
> Who waged contention with their time's decay,
> And of the past are all that cannot pass away.

Shelley distinguishes creative, liberating spirits like Keats from those who impose political and ecclesiastical rules and thus lay waste to life no less than faceless Time does. Unbeholden to tyrannical kings who derive their power from waging wars over land and other material resources, those like Keats pay court instead "to the kings of thought" who contend with transience itself.

In stanza forty-nine, Shelley again recommends the Eternal City as that place on Earth that best envelops contraries. When he and Mary buried little William, Shelley had written to his friend Thomas Love Peacock, "it seems to me as if, hunted by calamity as I have been, that I should neve[r] recover any cheerfulness again." Two years later, he sees Rome's vernal vegetation ornamenting occasions for despair, and he imagines a *genius loci* directing those who would be led to that same Edenic cemetery, a protected place where the joyous levity of innocence defeats death:

> Go thou to Rome,—at once the Paradise,
> The grave, the city, and the wilderness;
> And where its wrecks like shattered mountains rise,
> And flowering weeds, and fragrant copses dress
> The bones of Desolation's nakedness
> Pass, till the spirit of the spot shall lead
> Thy footsteps to a slope of green access
> Where, like an infant's smile, over the dead
> A light of laughing flowers along the grass is spread.

Shelley's Death at Sea

When they learned of Keats's death, the Shelleys had been living near Pisa, where they had recently become acquainted with the young retired East India Company lieutenant Edward Williams and his wife, Jane. A year later, having been joined there in November by Byron, Shelley was at odds with the far more famous poet and yearned to spend the spring and summer on the coast. His adventurous friend Edward John Trelawny (1792–1881) had also been with them since January and had encouraged Shelley and Byron to buy sailing vessels. In April 1822, the Shelleys moved northwest to a house on the shore near Lerici with the Williamses. Two weeks later Shelley took possession of a custom-made schooner. Black letters on the mainsail declared the name of Byron's hero: *Don Juan*. Shelley rechristened his *Ariel*.

Toward the end of a May full of sailing with Williams, Shelley wrote, in a fit of inspiration, over five hundred lines of what would be his last, unfinished poem, "The Triumph of Life," in which the life force itself is presented as an imperial juggernaut. Albeit far from complete, the poem shows great promise; critics as discerning as T. S. Eliot have called it his best work. Nevertheless, by mid-June 1822, when Mary suffered a miscarriage and another Byron visit disturbed lives, Shelley was showing signs of psychological vulnerability. Among other things, he was taken with a desire for Jane Williams and in the meantime acknowledged in confidential letters that Mary no longer sympathized with him, leaving him with "the curse of Tantalus." He wrote to Trelawny about procuring various poisons and admitted that, although he was not at present suicidal, "it would be a comfort to me to hold in my possession that golden key to the chamber of perpetual rest." Mary wrote to a friend that Shelley had screamed in the night and come rushing into her room, speaking of gory and murderous visions.

On July 1, Shelley sailed south to Livorno to meet with Leigh Hunt and Byron regarding a new journal, *The Liberal*, they planned to co-publish. One week later, on the 8th, Shelley set out from Livorno in the early afternoon. Edward Williams and an English youth whom they had hired to help crew were with him in the small schooner. As they headed north for Lerici, a storm arose from the southwest around 6:30 pm. An Italian captain later gave an account of having sought to take the three aboard; failing that, he had advised them at least to lower their sails. But the *Ariel* went down under full sail.

When Shelley's eaten-away body washed ashore near Viareggio ten days later, Trelawny recovered Leigh Hunt's copy of Keats's poetry from the jacket pocket and temporarily buried the remains with quicklime as the quarantine laws dictated. On August 15, he exhumed the body from the sand and, as Hunt and Byron looked on, cremated it in a small iron furnace. The ashes were held by the British Consul for several months until they could be interred at the cemetery. Trelawny then had them moved to Rome, to a second plot beside the back wall of the Cimitero's "new" section. The horizontal tombstone is inscribed with Shelley's name, the Latin phrase "COR CORDIUM" [heart of hearts], the dates of his birth and death, and three lines from a song with which *The Tempest*'s spirit Ariel ushers shipwrecked Ferdinand to Miranda for their love-at-first-sight encounter:

> Nothing of him that doth fade,
> But doth suffer a sea-change
> Into something rich and strange.

In their original context, these words from Shakespeare's last drama suggest that the living should take heart from the thought that what passes is never truly lost; even drowned bodies may be transformed into maritime marvels like bony coral and pearls as round as eyes. They more obliquely imply that there may be something of each of us that does not fade, even with death. For irreligious Shelley, who wrote of the poetic mind "as a fading coal which some invisible influence [...] awakens to transitory brightness," that something was his Romantic verse, his ever-protesting-but-not-doctrinally-protestant art, which his readers, like Keats's, keep alive and pulsing with their breath.

Essential Reading

Bate, W. Jackson. *John Keats*. Cambridge, MA: Harvard University Press, 1963.

Holmes, Richard. *Shelley: The Pursuit.* New York: Penguin, 1974.

Keats, John. *John Keats*. Edited by Elizabeth Cook. Oxford: Oxford University Press, 1990.

Shelley, Percy Bysshe. *The Letters of Percy Bysshe Shelley*. Edited by Frederick L. Jones. 2 vols. Oxford: Oxford University Press, 1964.

——, *Shelley's Poetry and Prose.* Edited by Neil Fraistat and Donald H. Reiman. New York: Norton, 2002.

Other Places to Encounter Keats and Shelley in Rome

- Piazza di Spagna: Keats-Shelley Museum.
- Palazzo Verospi, Via del Corso 374: a Shelley residence.
- Via Sistina 65: another Shelley residence.
- Terme di Caracalla: where Shelley drew inspiration for his *Prometheus Unbound*.
- Palazzo Cenci: the setting for Shelley's *The Cenci*.

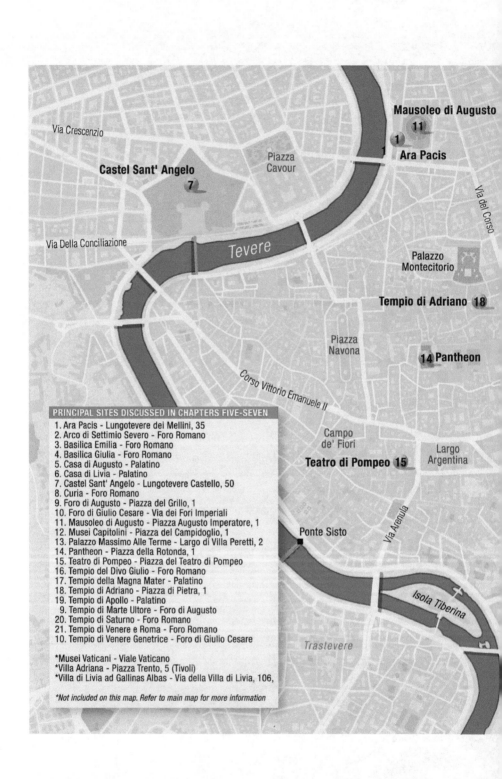

Via Crescenzio

Mausoleo di Augusto
11

1

Ara Pacis

Piazza
Cavour

Castel Sant' Angelo
7

Via del Corso

Via Della Conciliazione

Tevere

Palazzo
Montecitorio

Tempio di Adriano 18

Piazza
Navona

14 Pantheon

Corso Vittorio Emanuele II

Campo
de' Fiori

Largo
Argentina

Teatro di Pompeo 15

PRINCIPAL SITES DISCUSSED IN CHAPTERS FIVE-SEVEN
1. Ara Pacis - Lungotevere dei Mellini, 35
2. Arco di Settimio Severo - Foro Romano
3. Basilica Emilia - Foro Romano
4. Basilica Giulia - Foro Romano
5. Casa di Augusto - Palatino
6. Casa di Livia - Palatino
7. Castel Sant' Angelo - Lungotevere Castello, 50
8. Curia - Foro Romano
9. Foro di Augusto - Piazza del Grillo, 1
10. Foro di Giulio Cesare - Via dei Fori Imperiali
11. Mausoleo di Augusto - Piazza Augusto Imperatore, 1
12. Musei Capitolini - Piazza del Campidoglio, 1
13. Palazzo Massimo Alle Terme - Largo di Villa Peretti, 2
14. Pantheon - Piazza della Rotonda, 1
15. Teatro di Pompeo - Piazza del Teatro di Pompeo
16. Tempio del Divo Giulio - Foro Romano
17. Tempio della Magna Mater - Palatino
18. Tempio di Adriano - Piazza di Pietra, 1
19. Tempio di Apollo - Palatino
 9. Tempio di Marte Ultore - Foro di Augusto
20. Tempio di Saturno - Foro Romano
21. Tempio di Venere e Roma - Foro Romano
10. Tempio di Venere Genetrice - Foro di Giulio Cesare

*Musei Vaticani - Viale Vaticano
*Villa Adriana - Piazza Trento, 5 (Tivoli)
*Villa di Livia ad Gallinas Albas - Via della Villa di Livia, 106,

*Not included on this map. Refer to main map for more information

Via Arenula

Ponte Sisto

Isola Tiberina

Trastevere

MAP OF ROME FOR CHAPTERS 5–7

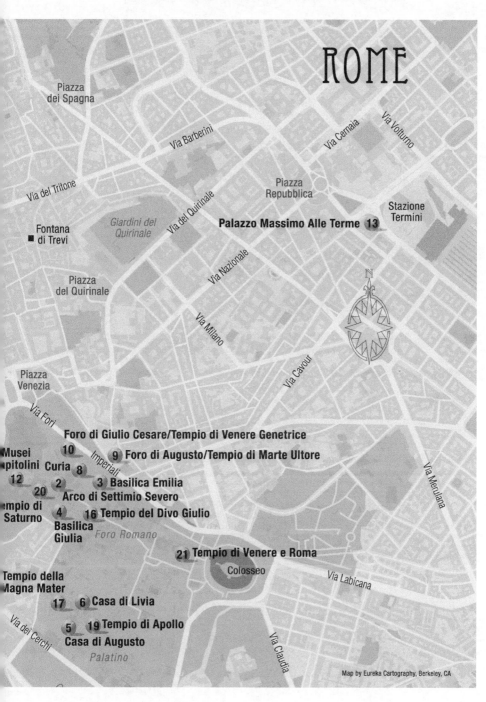

ROME

Piazza dei Spagna

Via Barberini

Via Cernaia

Via Volturno

Via del Tritone

Piazza Repubblica

Stazione Termini

Fontana di Trevi

Giardini del Quirinale

Via del Quirinale

Palazzo Massimo Alle Terme 13

Piazza del Quirinale

Via Nazionale

Via Milano

N

Piazza Venezia

Via Cavour

Via Fori

Via Merulana

Foro di Giulio Cesare/Tempio di Venere Genetrice

Musei ipitolini Curia 8

10

Imperiali

9 Foro di Augusto/Tempio di Marte Ultore

12

20 2

3 Basilica Emilia

Arco di Settimio Severo

mpio di Saturno

4

16 Tempio del Divo Giulio

Basilica Giulia Foro Romano

21 Tempio di Venere e Roma

Colosseo

Via Labicana

Tempio della Magna Mater

17 6 Casa di Livia

Via dei Cerchi

5 19 Tempio di Apollo

Casa di Augusto

Palatino

Via Claudia

Map by Eureka Cartography, Berkeley, CA

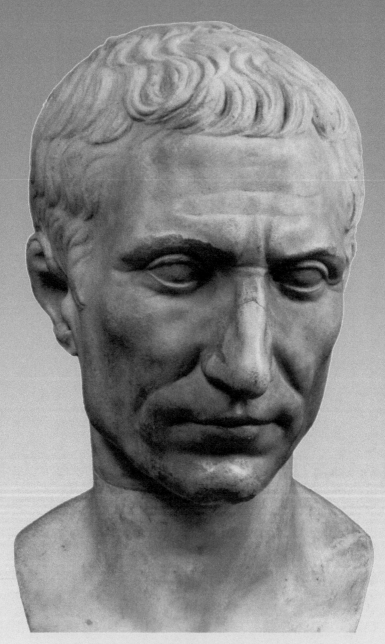

Fig. 10: Marble Bust of Julius Caesar, Museo Pio-Clementino, Musei Vaticani, Rome. Photo Credit: Scala / Art Resource, NY.

Chapter Five

JULIUS CAESAR (100–44 BCE) AT THE TEATRO DI POMPEO, ROSTRA, TEMPIO DEL DIVO GIULIO, AND BASILICA GIULIA

DAVID SWEET

From Republic to Empire

Julius Caesar was a singular individual of rare gifts who made a single decision that changed the course of history. That decision was his crossing of the Rubicon River in 49 with his army headed for Rome, a crossing that chased his more powerful rival, Pompey the Great, from the city and initiated a civil war that would make him, against all odds, the sole ruler of Rome. It had been 450 years since Rome had come this close to having a king, and it is Caesar who can be considered the proximate cause of the conversion of an ostensibly democratic republic into an autocratic empire. Such a series of events undertaken and accomplished by such an individual raises many questions, near and far. Readers of history who wish to speculate upon the relationship between individuals and historical action have much to reflect upon in regard to Caesar's life and actions. Student of politics should take note as well if they wish to understand political regimes and how they transform themselves under the influence of extraordinary individuals and circumstances.

Caesar was surely extraordinary. He was a man of unusual intelligence and audacity, a skilled and far-sighted politician, and a general perhaps never matched for his tactical and strategic acumen. Rarely have the statesman and the soldier coalesced to such a degree in one person. For this to have happened Caesar had to have many virtues and, from an early age, it became apparent that he did. He was born in the year 100 into the distinguished Julian family that traced its lineage back to the regal period and claimed to trace the origin of its name centuries earlier than that of Iulus, the son of the Trojan hero, Aeneas. The family, however, had left little trace of itself in the consular records and only recently was emerging from obscurity. But Caesar would change all of that and much more. In life and legend, there is arguably no one in Roman history who has attracted as much attention as he has.

Gifted Youth in a Hurry

The power the consulship had of elevating its holders and their families to the nobility may help us understand part of what motivated Caesar, a young man driven by ambition, for himself and for his family. Not long after he reached maturity, he married Cornelia (97–69), the daughter of Lucius Cornelius Cinna (ob. 84). Marriages for aristocratic Romans were family alliances, and this alliance reveals something about the political sympathies of Caesar. How so? By marrying Cornelia he threw in his lot with the *popu-*

lares, a political faction in Rome, that stood for the average people's—or "popular"—rights as embodied in their representatives, the tribunes, over and against the *optimates* who supported the senate and its resolutions. For most of the first century BCE, these two factions struggled ruthlessly with one another for power and advantage. The history of the late Roman republic can be read as the conflict between these two polarized and often violent groups, not unrelated to earlier struggles between patrician and plebeian orders. Arguably Caesar could have joined either party, but in the end he chose the *populares*.

He became a member of the popular party when he married Cornelia, the daughter of Cinna, a man with an ancient patrician pedigree who held the consulship illegally for four years in succession, during the turbulent days of the 80s when the populares under him and their hero Marius (157–86) seized control by force of arms and purged the state of their enemies. The pendulum swung the other way shortly after Caesar married Cornelia, leaving him with the first of many big challenges in his eventful life. The general, Sulla, an *optimate* and staunch supporter of the senate, retaliated against Cinna's popular movement, assuming the office of *dictator* and conducting the first of the proscriptions in 82. Among his many acts suppressing the popular party was his requirement that Caesar divorce Cornelia. At great risk to himself Caesar refused and became a fugitive, narrowly avoiding being killed. He saved himself from Sulla's agents by bribing them, while his aristocratic relatives interceded with Sulla himself, who very reluctantly granted him a pardon, warning that "they should know that [...] there were many Mariuses in Caesar." Sulla recognized the fibre that was in the nineteen year old boy, who was so resolutely loyal to his wife, the future mother of his only legitimate child, Julia.

In the next year, when it was time for Caesar to begin his political career in the traditional way, he joined the staff of the pro-praetor of Asia, who was conducting a siege of Mytilene, a Greek city on the island of Lesbos that had supported Rome's enemy, Mithradates VI of Pontus (ca. 119–63). In the course of the siege Caesar won the civic crown of oak leaves, awarded to a soldier who in combat had saved the life of a Roman citizen. The crown was a distinct medal of honour. When a recipient wearing it appeared at a public festival, the audience would stand in admiration of the hero, who could take his seat in the section of the stands reserved for senators.

In these early years, not only did Caesar demonstrate his ability to act on his own initiative and to lead men in battle, he also perfected his skill as a speaker. His training in this field came from the famous rhetorician, Apollonius Molon (fl. 50), who was also a teacher of Cicero (106–43). Subsequently Caesar and Cicero became the most famous orators of their era and the principal models for two approaches to public speaking and writing: the ample, copious, periodic "Asian" manner of Cicero and the lucid, spare, stringent "Atticism" of Caesar. Each of them admired the other. Caesar wrote a two-volume treatise on oratory, entitled *de Analogia*, a text which unfortunately does not survive. In it, apparently, he argued for simplicity and clarity by eschewing archaic or recondite words or phrases. He dedicated the work to Cicero, who returned the compliment. In the latter's dialogue, *Brutus*, the speakers praise Caesar's *De Bello Gallico* ("Commentaries on the Gallic War"), and Cicero remarks that only the inept would attempt to improve upon Caesar's annual accounts: "They are like naked statues, standing upright, beautiful, stripped of all the adornments of rhetoric.... In writing history there is nothing more agreeable than brevity, pure and perspicuous." Ever since, Caesar's *Commentaries* have served as a model for those who would write Latin prose, from schoolboys to Bacon and Hobbes.

Caesar's talent at judicial rhetoric showed itself early in the prosecution of some ex-Sullans, and he used his skills at speaking to enhance his popularity by delivering two funeral orations in 69, one for his aunt Julia (130–69), the widow of Marius. On this occasion he celebrated her ancestry, which was his own, by tracing it back through the Marcii to Ancus Marcius, the fourth king of Rome, and through Iulus, the son of Aeneas, to the goddess herself, Venus. He also caused a stir by having the effigies of Julia's husband, Marius, and son, also a Marius, carried in the funeral procession—their first appearance in public since Sulla's prohibition of them. In this year his wife, Cornelia, also died. It was not customary to deliver a public oration on behalf of a young woman, but Caesar gave one, and as a demonstration of his affection for her it also won the approval of the people. Several years later he is credited with delivering a stirring speech in the Senate in defence of Lucius Sergius Catilina (108–62), who was charged with conspiracy in an episode that has come to be called the Second Catilinarian Conspiracy (63). The impact of the speech on its audience was great, even though Caesar's plea—to reduce the conspirator's penalty from death to a house arrest and loss of property—failed. Remarkably, however, Caesar was outdone on that day only by two of Rome's very best orators, Cicero and Cato the Younger (95–46). This famous debate, which took place in 63 BCE when Caesar was thirty-seven years old, highlights just how accomplished and how highly regarded he had become by this time.

Cursus Honorum

By this point in his career Caesar had manifestly shown his feats of military heroism along with his political skills in the power of his oratory, in his success in winning elections, and in his ability to negotiate the swirling rapids of political life, pursuing a policy as a popularis but not failing to maintain his position as a member of the class of the optimates. In 73 he had been co-opted into the college of priests (*pontifices*) on the basis of his aristocratic connections. In 63 the position of *pontifex maximus* became open, now an elective office, no longer determined by co-option. Caesar sought it, despite his youth and the eminence of the two other aristocratic candidates. Depending on a combination of enormous bribery and the affection of the voters, he was elected, a startling and unexpected victory.

In the year 63 Caesar was nearing the top rungs of the *cursus honorum*. He had begun his ascent by being chosen one of twenty-four military tribunes in 72. In 69 he was elected a *quaestor*. Holders of the quaestorship were admitted into the senate, and as a member of this body he delivered his orations for his aunt Julia and his wife Cornelia. In 67 he was made *curator* of the Via Appia, another post which enabled him to add to his popular approbation by using his own resources for its maintenance. By this time he had already earned the reputation of living extravagantly. He was said to have bought a pearl of incomparable value for his mistress Servilia, the mother of the Brutus (85–42) who was one of his assassins in 44, and he confirmed this reputation in his service as curule aedile, a post to which he was elected for 65. Curule aediles were responsible for maintaining various public services in Rome, but for political purposes the office could be used to advance one's career because an aedile was charged with sustaining some of the most important religious festivals, in particular for producing games and gladiatorial contests. His colleague as curule aedile that year complained that although he too had spent great sums on the contests, Caesar was the only one to receive the credit. This was understandable. On his own, Caesar had celebrated games in which an unprecedented number of pairs of gladiators had fought, as many as 320 gladiators. On the strength of this office and his growing alliance with Rome's wealthiest citizen, the leader of the optimates Marcus Licinius Crassus (115–53), Caesar's ascent up the political ladder continued with his election as *praetor* in 62. As praetor that year he was given Hither Spain as his pro-praetorial province. Once there he quickly demonstrated his brilliance as a commander in the field. By military as well as diplomatic means he subdued an area of Spain that had been resistant to the prior attempts of his predecessors. He rewarded his soldiers, himself, and the Roman treasury with the income produced by these victories, which were so successful that he was now in the position to run for Rome's highest political office: that of *consul*.

First Triumvirate and Ascent to Superpower Status

It was a clash of interests within Rome's dominant popular party in the years 62–60 that ultimately delivered Rome's highest office to Caesar. Two of Rome's most powerful politicians, Pompey and Crassus, had fallen out of favor with their fellow optimates senators over the course of the years 62–60 BCE. The Senate had snubbed Pompey as he returned from his successful military campaigns in the East (70–62), and it had coldly overturned some tax legislation favoured by the wealthy Crassus around 63. The formation of what became known as the First Triumvirate ("Rule By Three Men") was an unconstitutional agreement among Pompey, Crassus, and Caesar to work together quietly in promoting their own interests and careers against the optimate party in the senate. The condition of the triumvirate was that none of the three would promote any political proposal that was not supported by the other two. In 60, Caesar's popularity and the critical support of Pompey and Crassus in the background carried him to victory in his run for the consulship for 59. The other consul elected that year was Marcus Calpurnius Bibulus (102–48), an optimates stalwart and bitter enemy who opposed Caesar at every step during their shared consulship of 59. Although many of his initiatives were sabotaged by his rival, Caesar did manage to please his two allies in the triumvirate by pushing through laws in support of Pompey's military veterans and a renegotiation of certain commercial contracts favouring Crassus. He also succeeded in forcing through the democratic process some laws that addressed long-standing problems, including a wide-ranging agrarian reform which up to that point had been opposed by the optimates, that carved out new farms in the Roman provinces for under- and unemployed citizens in search of a new start. Finally, Caesar managed to introduce an important law bearing his own name— the *lex Julia repetundarum*. This was a long and complex document circumscribing the activities of Rome's provincial governors and stipulating penalties for infractions, notably those which enriched these politicians and their staffs at Rome's expense. The legislation was so comprehensive and effective that it seems to have remained in force permanently and, generally speaking, gave great credit to Caesar's consular year.

During his consulship Caesar had succeeded in passing legislation that was manifestly beneficial and long-needed, but he faced two threats once his year of office ended. Would his legislation be rescinded and would he himself, on various legal grounds, be indicted and very likely condemned? The only way to defend himself against these threats was with money and military power. It had long become clear that the best way to acquire both was through a pro-consular (i.e. provincial governor's) command over an area in which there was a probable need for Roman armed intervention. Stirring victories in this very office had brought Pompey his power, as it had his predecessors, Marius and Sulla. Now the combined forces of the First Triumvirate gave Caesar what he required: the pro-consulship of both Nearer and Further Gaul, a region that was on the immediate northern border of Italy and that had sent armies of devastation into the peninsula in the recent past. Gaul was also unstable. Within it were many Celtic peoples that strove with each other for dominance, thus a perfect area into which to introduce Roman law and political stability. The opportunity was there, and over the next eight years (58–51) Caesar exploited it, conducting a series of extraordinary military campaigns that culminated in the conquest of all the land to the west of the Rhine, the area that is now France, Belgium, and Holland. After it was over, he published his *De Bello Gallico* ("Commentaries on the Gallic Wars"), one of the greatest military narratives ever written.

By the conclusion of the Gallic Wars, Caesar possessed a formidable fighting force, the like of which had rarely ever been assembled in antiquity and one that was passionately devoted to him, ready for him to deploy elsewhere if needed. He had also acquired incalculable wealth, some of it from tribute imposed on conquered nations, some from the plunder of towns and sanctuaries, and some from the sale of captives, perhaps as many as one million. With this wealth he rewarded his troops generously, he filled the treasury in Rome, and he protected his home front by funneling enormous sums into the pockets of influential Romans who became indebted to him for the future. Each of the above developments alone and in combination soon began to alarm Caesar's allies in the triumvirate. Pompey and Crassus had received what they wanted during Caesar's consulship, but now they both recognized that to keep pace with him as his popularity and power accelerated would be difficult. Soon enough, the partnership unravelled. One feature of the alliance disappeared in 54 when Caesar's daughter Julia, who had married Pompey in 59 as part of the triumvirate's formation, died in childbirth. Another element was removed with Crassus's death at the disastrous Battle of Carrhae (53) against the Parthian Empire. These losses left Pompey and Caesar to deal with one another directly in order to determine whether a new strategic alliance could be formed.

Caesar and Pompey at War

In the years leading up to the final standoff between the two men and their respective supporters, there were many attempts at mediation. Caesar remained at his military command north of the Alps during the whole period of negotiation during the years 53–49, while Pompey stayed in Rome to cultivate his growing alliance with the Senate. Fear of a brutal civil war and an awareness of the unusual strengths of each party kept negotiations going early on, only to see them harden in 52 when the Senate declared Pompey sole consul and thereafter proceeded with a series of measures to deprive Caesar of his arms and punish him and his supporters for presumed abuses during his governorship of Gaul. By the close of 50 the positions of both sides had hardened, leaving only Cicero (106–43), the person who regarded both Caesar and Pompey as close friends, to try to pull them back from the brink. Shortly after this negotiation too failed, the Senate passed its "ultimate decree" (*senatus consultum ultimum*), enjoining Pompey, the consuls, and other magistrates to take whatever measures were necessary to keep the state from suffering harm. Caesar's tribunes were prevented from vetoing the motion and immediately left Rome to join Caesar in Cisalpine Gaul. There he was confronted with a choice: either to capitulate totally to the Senate's demands and to leave himself at the mercy of the courts or to cross the Rubicon. At that point, complaining of the unacceptable outrage done to his dignity, he made his decision. On the night of January 10, 49, he quietly crossed the river, saying that the die had been cast. He made his statement not in Latin (*iacta alea est*) but in Greek (Ἀνερρίφθω κύβος), citing a line from a play by one of his favourite authors, the Greek comic poet, Menander.

Lone Consul, Dictator, and de facto King of Rome

Just over four years, many battles, and tens of thousands of casualties later, Pompey was defeated and dead while Caesar was Rome's sole recognized authority. The final battle of his civil war with Pompey and his supporters, the Battle of Munda (Spain) in March 45 against Pompey's sons Gnaeus (75–45) and Sextus (67–35), was reportedly the most difficult of his campaign. By that point, his veterans were exhausted, having followed their leader through so many lands and seas. At one point in the final encounter, they hesitated. Caesar, now a middle aged man of fifty-five years old, left on his own and unprotected by his troops, rushed into combat with his shield in front of him and took a volley of spears from the enemy (numbers vary as to how many). Then, out of shame that they had exposed him to fight alone, his loyal legions joined him. "As he was going away after the battle," reports the historian Plutarch, "he said to his friends that he had often striven for victory, but now first for his life" (573). That was his final battle.

Ever since his initial victory over Pompey at Pharsalus in northern Greece (August of 46) Caesar had been the ruler of Rome and all it possessed. He ruled as consul or as dictator, all the while maintaining the appearance of the structure of the ancestral Roman constitution, filling the offices with appointments of his own choosing, many of them from among the former senatorial opposition. The policies he pursued in the years from 48 to 44 were similar to those that marked his consulship in 59. He continued his agrarian policy of land redistribution to reduce the urban population of recipients of the dole, reducing the number from 350,000 to 170,000. He continued his policy of constraining the avarice of provincial governors by stipulating how they could govern and how much they could extract from their subjects. His most lasting initiative was, as it turned out, his reformation of the calendar. He converted it from a lunar calendar of 360 days a year to a solar calendar of 365 and a quarter days, inserting an extra day every four years. This is the calendar the Western world lived with until 1582 CE, when Gregory XIII stipulated that the leap year's extra day not be observed when it falls on a century year (unless that year can be 400).

Whether Caesar, as dictator, had plans to restructure Roman political institutions is not known. It appears that he meant to continue the constitution in its traditional form, but the question of his own position was paramount. Many suspected that he intended before long to reintroduce monarchy with himself as king. But it seems that he intended to postpone a decision on the constitutional issue and pursue a policy that had worked well for him. In the year 44 he made preparations for a war against Parthia, with the aim of recovering the standards lost by Crassus at Carrhae. His thought may have been that, while he was gone, he could maintain control over the government in Rome through his political appointments and while abroad he would achieve the kind of successes that he had in Gaul. That would bring him reaffirmation as Rome's first citizen and justify his constitutional pre-eminence. In February of 44, however, he had allowed himself to be declared dictator in perpetuity, an office that had always had a specific termination. This step upward was viewed as essentially a restoration of the monarchy and as monarch therefore he would remain, all the while he was on campaign against Parthia.

That prospect finally brought together the conspirators. They determined that they had to strike before he left for the East and, on the Ides of March in 44, they acted. That day, as it happened, Caesar had arranged to meet with the Senate in an audience hall attached to the Teatro di Pompeo. Suetonius gives a full description of what happened. He reports that Caesar received twenty-three knife wounds on that day, only one of which, according to post-mortem reports, was fatal. His last words, if indeed he spoke them, were addressed to Brutus, and were not the Latin "et tu Brute" that modern audiences know, but the Greek, "καὶ σὺ, τέκνον" (you, too, my child). In one of history's infinite ironies, he fell at the foot of a statue of Pompey. From there his body was removed and several days later cremated in the Foro by an outraged populace. When he died, he left to his grand nephew and adopted son, Octavian, the task of completing the conversion of the Roman Republic into the Roman Empire.

The Tempio del Divo Giulio

The historian Dio Cassius (155–235 CE) reports that, while still alive in 45–44, Caesar was granted the privilege of being buried within the Foro Romano, of being addressed in divine terms as Jupiter Julius and "the unconquered god," and of having a temple dedicated to him in Rome (xliv.6–7 and xliii.45). If true, these types of representations would have placed Caesar on the same footing as so many Hellenistic rulers of the age who sought recognition as divine (or quasi-divine) kings as an instrument of power. Not all modern historians agree with this ancient source; it is therefore not to be excluded that

Fig. 11: Tempio del Divo Giulio, Foro Romano. Photo courtesy of Peter Hatlie.

Dio Cassius was projecting backward in time a status that Caesar would only earn many years after his death. Be that as it may, Caesar does represent a turning point in Roman history by being recognized as divine most certainly after his death. The Senate granted him such honours two years after his death in 42, and the construction of the Tempio del Divo Giulio (*Aedes Divi Julii*) followed in 29 (see fig. 11). The rather barren concrete core of this once impressive building is today still located in its original position in the Foro Romano.

The temple is thought to have been built on the very spot where Caesar's body was brought after his assassination and cremated, after a rousing funeral oration delivered by his longstanding aide and the elected priest of his personal cult, Marc Antony (83–30). Cicero, who was undoubtedly there that day, publicly rebuked Antony later for his role in the chaotic funeral proceedings:

> Mark Antony, you were the one who shamelessly presided over the funeral rites of Caesar—if you can call chaos a ritual. You delivered the eloquent funeral oration, the moving lament, you provided the incitement to riot: in a real sense, you lit the flames by which the great Caesar was half-burnt (Cic. *Phil.* 2.90–1).

After the crowd had spun out of control and cremated Caesar on the spot, an altar was established on site with a twenty foot column of Numidian marble nearby bearing the inscription "To the Father of Our Country." Caesar's great-nephew and adopted son Octavian Augustus, Rome's first emperor, inaugurated the new building as one of the very first of his public acts after obtaining sole rule. Augustus would himself be divinized after his own death in 14 CE, but it was this full public recognition of his adopted

father's apotheosis that initiated a tradition of subsequent emperors being unapologeti-
cally honoured with divinity and granted temples. Among the special features of Caesar's
temple was its cult statue, which pictured him with a star on his head, representing the
comet that reportedly appeared after his death to signal that he had become a god.

Julian Civic Monuments in the Foro Romano

During his tenure as Triumvir, Caesar ordered that a large amount of the spoils of his
Gallic War be used for works in and around the Foro Romano. To this extent he was
responsible for giving final definition to the constantly evolving Foro of Republican
times and for starting the shift of political life from that Foro to the nearby Imperial
Fora—dedicated to him and Rome's future emperors. Defining the perimeter of the
original Foro Romano are structures either associated with or built by Caesar, perhaps
explaining why the Roman public appreciated Caesar's contribution to the city so fondly.

On the south side he erected the Basilica Giulia, an enormous five-aisled, three-sto-
ried structure faced lavishly with dazzling white marble and used especially for judicial
and economic functions (see fig. 12). Of it almost nothing remains except the brick column bases marking the aisles, but these are of modern making. The site itself, however,
is of historic interest. Archaeologists have found beneath it the remains of the earlier
Basilica Sempronia, built by the father of the tribunes Tiberius (164–33 BCE) and Gaius
Gracchus (154–21 BCE), who started the land reform movement, and beneath that the
house of Scipio Africanus (236–183 BCE), the victor over Carthage in the Second Punic
War. By all accounts, this was one of the most busy areas of the Foro Romano after Caesar's intervention here.

On the Foro's west side, Caesar reconstructed and rearranged two of Rome's most
important monuments. First, he moved the republican Rostra (or "Speaking Platform")
from in front of the old Senate House, the Curia Hostilia, to where it now stands between
the Arch of Septimius Severus and the Tempio di Saturno. In addition, after the old Senate
House was destroyed by a mob riot in 52 BCE, Caesar replaced it in 44 BCEwith his own
Curia Julia, which is the structure that we now see at the northern corner of the forum. As
in the case of so many other ruins in Rome, the reconstructed remains are from late antiquity, in this instance from a rebuilding by the emperor Diocletian (284–305 CE). Because,
however, the Romans were conservative in their architecture, as in so many other
respects, they tended to preserve the older structure in the new, and what we see today of
the Curia Julia is likely to be quite similar in size and shape to what Caesar erected.

Adjacent to the Curia Julia, stretching to the east along this entire side of the forum,
lies the Basilica Paulli, once one of the most celebrated buildings of ancient Rome. In his
Natural History, Pliny the Elder (23 BCE–79 CE) described it as one of Rome's gems and
singled out its pale yellow Phrygian marble columns as particularly fine. Also referred
to as the Basilica Fulvia et Aemilia, it owes its origins to a vast sum of money that Caesar gave to Lucius Aemilius Paulus (fl. 50 BCE), so that he could finish the building that
still bears the family's name. Like the Basilica Giulia, its functions were judicial and economic. When it was stripped and destroyed in the sack of Rome by Alaric the Goth in
410 CE, coins still visible today melted into the pavement.

The Foro di Giulio Cesare: His Last Act

Fig. 12: Basilica Giulia, Foro Romano, Rome.
Photo courtesy of Peter Hatlie.

From the vantage point of either the Campidoglio or the northeast corner of the Palatino, one has a view of the entire rectangle of the Foro Romano, so much of which bears the imprint of Julius Caesar. From at least 54, however, he had been planning to construct another Foro. In that year he engaged Cicero as his agent to purchase from private owners a large tract of land north of the Curia Julia. Here he placed the Foro di Giulio Cesare (the *Forum Iulium*), a long rectangular open courtyard, lined on three sides with a double colonnade and on the fourth side closed by the Tempio di Venere Genetrice, three of whose columns have been re-erected. Caesar made a vow to build this in 48 on the eve of his victory over Pompey at Pharsalus. He took Venus to be his divine parent, through Aeneas's son Iulus, the eponymous ancestor of his family. In the centre of the courtyard was an equestrian statue of Caesar, aligned with that of Venus in the *cella* of the temple. Here he summoned the Senate in 44, sitting in front of the temple and remaining in his chair without paying the senators the honour of rising to greet them. The notion that he was starting to consider himself a god was in many people's minds. Within a month he was dead but shortly thereafter he was indeed divinized as Divus Julius.

Essential Reading

Caesar, Julius. *Civil War*. Translated by Cynthia Damon. Cambridge, MA: Harvard University Press, 2016.

Caesar, Julius. *The Gallic Wars*. Translated by H. J. Edwards. Cambridge, MA: Harvard University Press, 1917.

Cicero. *Second Philippics*. Edited by Albert Curtis Clark. Oxford: Oxford University Press, 1918.

Coarelli, Filippo. *Rome and Environs*. Translated by James J. Clauss and Daniel P. Harmon. Berkeley: University of California Press, 2007.

Gelzer, Matthias. *Caesar: Politician and Statesman*. Translated by Peter Needham. Cambridge, MA: Harvard University. Press, 1968.

Gruen, Eric S. *The Last Generation of the Roman Republic*. Berkeley: University of California Press, 1974.

Plutarch. "The Life of Julius Caesar." In *Lives*, translated by Bernadotte Perrin, 443–608. Cambridge, MA: Harvard University Press, 1911.

Scullard, H. H. *From the Gracchi to Nero: A History of Rome, 133 B.C.–68 A.D.* 5th ed. London: Methuen & Co., 1988.

Suetonius. "Julius." In *The Lives of the Caesars*, translated by J. C. Rolf, 5–119. Cambridge, MA: Harvard University Press, 1914.

Syme, Ronald. *The Roman Revolution*. Oxford: Oxford University Press, 1939. Reprint, Oxford: Oxford University Press, 2002.

Weinstock, Stefan. *Divus Iulius*. Oxford: Oxford University Press, 1971.

Other Places to Encounter Caesar in Rome

- Teatro di Pompeo: where Caesar was murdered, near the modern Largo Argentina.

- Saepta Julia: ancient voting halls rebuilt by Caesar in the Campus Martius, near the modern Piazza Navona but current location unknown.

- Tempio di Marte Ultore: erected by Augustus in his own imperial forum after he had slain the last of Caesar's assassins.

Fig. 13: Portrait of Livia, Museo Nazionale Romano / Palazzo Massimo alle Terme, Rome.
Photo Credit: Vanni Archive/ Art Resource, NY.

Chapter Six

EMPRESS LIVIA (58 BCE–29 CE) ON THE PALATINO

ELIZABETH C. ROBINSON

Rome's First Empress

Livia was a pivotal figure in ancient Rome and the Roman Empire in general. Her unique role as the first Roman empress is reflected in the series of honours she received and tasks she accomplished, many of which had never been possible for a Roman woman and some of which would only ever be achieved by her. Her life ushered in several historical changes and many firsts, particularly after her second husband Octavian ended the Roman Republic and founded the Roman Empire. Octavian then became Rome's first emperor and officially took on the title Augustus while Livia, as his wife, became empress and Augusta. Despite her long life, it is difficult to formulate a well-rounded picture of Livia. This is partially a result of the nearly two thousand years that have elapsed since her death. Another contributing factor is that ancient authors often pay little attention to women, and when they discuss them they often provide stereotypes and few personal details. In Livia's case, she is repeatedly overshadowed by the accomplishments of her second husband, the emperor Augustus, and her son, the emperor Tiberius. Even when we do find references to her, some are inherently biased, making it difficult to separate the real story from the spin. Nevertheless, Livia's biography yields important insights into the early period of the Roman Empire. Although many of the places associated with her can no longer be seen, visits to areas such as the Palatino that were significantly associated with Livia provide a deeper connection to her and to the world that she inhabited.

Early Life and First Marriage

We know very little about Livia Drusilla's early life. She was born on January 30 of 59 or 58 in Italy, perhaps in Rome. Her father's family was very distinguished: he came from the Claudius family and was adopted into the Livius family. The Claudii boasted such ancestors as Appius Claudius Caecus, the commissioner of Rome's first aqueduct and its first consular road. The Livius family, on the other hand, included Marcus Livius Drusus, famous for his defence of the plebeians' rights in Rome at the time of the Gracchi. In contrast, Livia's mother Alfidia likely came from a wealthy family that had not participated in Roman government. Livia was probably their only natural child.

Livia grew up at a time of great unrest in Rome. It was likely shortly after Caesar's assassination in 44 that she celebrated her first marriage to Tiberius Claudius Nero, a relative from another branch of the Claudii. Livia was probably fifteen or sixteen, while Tiberius Nero was likely in his late thirties. The exact year of their marriage is uncertain, but it may have been 43 since their first son, the future emperor Tiberius, was born on

November 16, 42. The historian Suetonius reports that Tiberius was born on the Palatino, presumably in Tiberius Nero's house. In the meantime Octavian, the adopted son
of Julius Caesar, had become one of the main contenders for power in Rome following
Caesar's death. As leading Romans took sides in the power struggle between Octavian
and his chief rival Mark Antony, Livia's husband sided with Antony. She and her family left Rome for Perusia (modern Perugia), the centre of opposition to Octavian. When
Perusia fell in early 40 the family was forced to flee to Praeneste, then Naples, then Sicily.
In Sicily Tiberius Nero tried to align himself with Sextus Pompeius, and as a result was
proscribed by Octavian. He was declared an enemy of the state and banished but was
not executed. Although she herself was not exiled, Livia followed her husband to Athens
and Sparta, bringing her son with her.

Marriage to Octavian

Circumstances changed for Livia in 39 when a treaty granted amnesty to those associated with Sextus Pompeius. She and her family returned to Rome and at some point
that year she met Octavian for the first time. She was still married to Tiberius Nero and
pregnant with their second child. Octavian, a promising young politician, was married
to Scribonia who was expecting their first child, a daughter Julia, who would be born
in October. Octavian divorced Scribonia shortly after Julia's birth, and Livia (still pregnant) secured a divorce from Tiberius Nero around the same time. It is likely that by late
autumn 39 Livia and Octavian were betrothed. Livia's powerful and prestigious family
offered Octavian a status that he could not attain on his own. The couple also seems to
have been mutually attracted to one another.

Thus it happened that Livia and Tiberius Nero, who had fled from Octavian and
his army the previous year, arranged to give her to Octavian in marriage. After their
betrothal Livia moved into Octavian's residence on the Palatino. It is there that Livia
and Tiberius Nero's second son, Drusus, was born on January 14, 38 BCE. After waiting just three days Octavian and Livia were married on January 17. The historian Cassius Dio says that Tiberius Nero not only sanctioned the union, but also officiated at the
ceremony, assuming the traditional role of the father in giving away the bride. Almost
immediately after the wedding an important event occurred at the Villa di Livia ad Gallinas Albas at Prima Porta. This villa, a country estate that belonged to Livia, was located
just north of Rome. According to tradition, when Livia was returning to her villa after
her wedding, an eagle dropped into her lap a white chick with a laurel branch in its beak.
Livia kept the bird, which grew to produce several white chicks, and she planted the laurel, which produced a famous grove from which victory crowns were made for members
of the imperial family. This omen was taken as a sign of the future offspring of Livia and
Octavian, as well as the important role that Livia would play in Octavian's career.

The Wife of the Princeps

Despite the politically loaded conditions of her second marriage, Livia largely stayed out
of the limelight. Octavian, on the other hand, became the chief protagonist of this period.

His rivalry with Mark Antony culminated in the Battle of Actium in 31, where Octavian and his general Agrippa defeated Mark Antony and Cleopatra. This left Octavian as the sole ruler of the Roman world. At this point he had to make a decision about the type of government that would follow. A return to the Republic was nearly impossible for a number of reasons, while a monarchy was unadvisable and even feared. Over the next few years Octavian carefully avoided the mistakes of his adoptive father, Julius Caesar, but gradually led Rome into a new form of government, even as he claimed he was restoring the Republic. In 27 he handed over his powers to the Senate, and they granted him others, including the title of Augustus, which would be handed down to his successors. From that time on, Octavian (Augustus) ruled as Rome's first emperor, preferring the title *princeps*, or "first citizen."

The role of princeps was a new one for Augustus and for Rome, and Livia's role as the princeps's wife was equally new. She needed to display the traditional Roman virtues of a good wife, including modesty and fidelity, and she and Augustus needed to produce heirs. Suetonius reports that they succeeded in conceiving a child together, but this child was stillborn, and throughout their marriage Augustus and Livia had no natural children together. Before Tiberius Nero died in late 33 or 32 BCE, however, he named Octavian as guardian to both Tiberius and Drusus. Augustus would eventually adopt Tiberius in 4 CE.

Augustus spent considerable time outside Italy during the next fifteen years, alternating his trips with visits to Rome. How often Livia accompanied him on these journeys is unknown, but she is recorded as having joined him in both the West and the East, implying that she may have travelled to Spain and Gaul, as well as Sicily, Greece, and Syria. In celebration of Augustus's safe return from Spain and Gaul the Senate voted to erect the Ara Pacis Augustae, or Altar of Augustan Peace. This monument was built on the Campus Martius and was dedicated on Livia's birthday, January 30, 9 BCE. The altar displayed elaborate sculptures, both allegorical and historical, promoting Augustus's reign by linking it to Rome's legendary past and suggesting a promising future. The friezes on the north and south walls surrounding the altar depicted a state ceremony, one where Livia certainly would have been present. There is some debate as to which figure represents the empress, but she was undoubtedly depicted along with the important members of Augustus's immediate and adoptive family.

In the same year as the Ara Pacis's dedication, tragedy struck Livia's family. Her younger son Drusus had been fighting successfully in Germany when he broke his femur in a riding accident and became seriously ill. By September he had died at the age of only twenty-nine. Livia was unable to see Drusus before his death, and was understandably devastated by the loss, but she is reported to have maintained a respectable level of grief, befitting her status as a Roman matron. As compensation for her loss she received a series of honours that allowed her to assume a greater public role in Rome. Until this point she had been the devoted wife of Augustus and a dedicated mother to her sons; with Drusus's death she stepped out of the shadows for the first time.

Around 9 the decision was made to build a porticus in her honour. The Porticus Liviae is best known from ancient authors and fragments of the *Forma Urbis Romae*, the Severan-period marble plan of Rome. It was erected by Augustus in Livia's name and dedicated in 7 by Livia and Tiberius. The Porticus Liviae was located on the northern slope of the Oppian Hill (Colle Oppio), and was probably a large open area measuring about one hundred twenty metres by seventy metres surrounded by a double colonnade. It contained a garden and a collection of paintings, and also probably housed a shrine to the goddess *Concordia* (Harmony), built by Livia to celebrate her harmonious marriage with Augustus.

Owing to confusion amongst ancient authors, it is difficult to understand Livia's role in the last years of Augustus's life. It appears that he was already in declining health in 12 CE, and a journey he took in southern Italy with Tiberius and Livia in 14 would be his last. He became ill during the voyage, and at Beneventum Tiberius continued on but Augustus and Livia decided to return to Rome. Augustus was too sick to continue, so they stopped at his family estate at Nola, where on August 19, 14 CE, he died. Suetonius claims that Augustus's last moments were spent with Livia, and his last words were "Livia, be mindful of our marriage and goodbye."

The Mother of the Princeps

Ever the devoted wife, at Augustus's funeral Livia remained on the spot for five days of mourning before gathering up his ashes and placing them in Augustus's mausoleum, the Mausoleo di Augusto. On September 17, 14, Augustus was deified and his worship became an official part of Roman state cult. He became known as *Divus Augustus* (Divine Augustus), and received the right to a temple and a priesthood. Livia and Tiberius paid for and oversaw the construction of the Tempio di Augusto on the Palatino, begun in 14 CE and completed under Tiberius's successor, Caligula. Livia was appointed as the first priestess of Divus Augustus, a great honour and an important role.

Augustus's will named Tiberius as his successor, passing to him the title of Augustus. Livia's role changed from the wife of the princeps to the mother of the princeps, but Tiberius's rule was quite different from Augustus's. While Tiberius's accession had been anticipated, Augustus's will transformed Livia's role in an unexpected way: he posthumously adopted her as his daughter, bringing her into the Julian family. He also passed on to her the title of Augusta, making her known from that point onward as Julia Augusta. There was no precedent in Rome for the transfer of such an honorific title from a man to a woman, and Augustus's decision to honour Livia in this way became a source of great tension between Livia and Tiberius. This discord arose in part from the ambiguity of Livia's position, and in part from Tiberius's views on the exclusion of women from affairs of state.

It is likely that Augustus's will also bequeathed to Livia the use of part of his house until her own death, a common practise in Roman society. In 14 CE, then, Livia may have moved from the main imperial residence on the Palatino into a smaller part of the house. Some scholars have identified the quarters in which she lived at this time with the Casa di Livia. Tiberius built himself a palace, conventionally known as the *Domus Tiberiana*, on the western side of the Palatino closer to the Foro Romano. Mother and son were now living in close proximity to one another, yet their relationship was in a poor state. In 26, motivated by a series of factors in Rome, Tiberius withdrew to the island of Capri. Livia may have been one of the many causes behind his disappearance, as their relationship seems to have soured: Tiberius would never return to Rome alive, and would only meet his mother once more before her death.

Death and Legacy

Livia is credited with a passion for natural remedies, including daily drinks of a small amount of wine from Pucinum, and daily doses of elecampane, a type of sunflower. Despite her home cures, she fell seriously ill both in 22 and in 29. This second illness led to her death that year. Tiberius remained absent not only from her deathbed but also from her funeral. Her funeral oration was given by her great-grandson, Caligula, the future Roman emperor. After her cremation her ashes were placed inside the Mausoleo di Augusto.

After Livia's death the Senate ordered an official year-long mourning period for women in Rome and voted to erect an arch to her in recognition of her acts of kindness and generosity. This was the first and last time that such an arch was voted for a woman. The arch was never realized, however, as Tiberius promised to fund it himself but then neglected to build it. The Senate also voted divine honours for Livia, to make her the first woman to be consecrated and worshipped officially as a goddess in Rome. She was allowed a temple and priesthood in the city. Tiberius refused this honour for her, however, noting that she would not have wanted it. His refusal is in keeping with his general attitude toward the role of women in public life. Livia would eventually become the first woman to receive divine honours, however, under the rule of her great-grandson Claudius. He made her a goddess on January 14, 72 CE, the anniversary of her wedding to Augustus. Her statue was erected in the Tempio di Augusto, and inscriptions referring to a *Tempio del Divo Augusto* (Temple of Divus Augustus) and Diva Augusta on the Palatino prove that the joint worship of Augustus and Livia occurred there.

Another important element of Livia's legacy is the role her descendants played in the future of Rome. These included her son Tiberius, but it was her second son, Drusus, whose offspring ruled Rome until 68. Drusus's son Germanicus was the father of both Caligula and Claudius, and Germanicus's daughter Agrippina the Younger gave birth to Nero. Throughout the first one hundred years of the empire, Rome would thus be ruled by Livia's husband, son, great-grandsons, and great-great-grandson. There is even speculation that Galba, who ruled briefly in 68, was related to Livia.

The Casa di Augusto on the Palatino:
A Residence from the Time of Livia and Augustus

After Livia's betrothal to Octavian she moved into his house on the Palatino, where she would live for more than fifty years. The Palatino was a popular place of residence in the Late Republic (people like Cicero lived there), but when the later imperial palaces were built many of the earlier buildings were destroyed. Fortunately, two sets of rooms dating to the time of Livia, known as the Casa di Augusto, have been preserved on the southwestern corner of the Palatino. They are located between the Tempio di Apollo Palatino and the precinct of the Tempio della Vittoria and Tempio della Magna Mater.

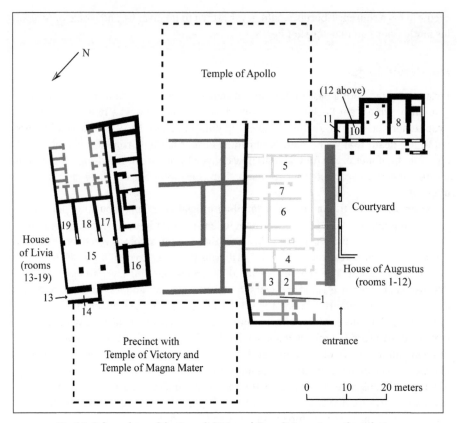

Fig. 14: Colour plans of the Casa di Livia and Casa di Augusto on the Palatino.
Drawn by author. Based on Figs. 51 and 54 from Amanda Claridge,
Rome: An Oxford Archaeological Guide. Oxford: Oxford University Press, 2010.

Although these rooms are conventionally known as the Casa di Augusto, many scholars reject this identification. This has in no way slowed down the number of visitors to
this area, though. The decorations of these rooms have paintings that date to 50–30 BCE,
about the time that Octavian and Livia began to live together. The rooms are also located
near the Tempio di Apollo Palatino that Augustus built. While a visitor to the Casa di
Augusto is most likely not walking on the floors that Livia and Augustus trod for half a
century, he or she still has the chance to experience the atmosphere of a first-century
BCE aristocratic house on the Palatino, complete with its wonderful frescoes.

The surviving rooms (see fig. 14) flank the northern and eastern sides of what
remains of an open-air courtyard. One must imagine away the large piers in the courtyard, as well as the long wall (in blue) in front of the northern rooms, since these formed
supports for post-Augustan-era buildings. The first block of rooms on the north side of
the courtyard contains both a small suite of rooms on its northernmost side (in red) that
seems to have been used for more private functions, and others (in yellow) that may

have served more public purposes. The more private rooms have floors made of black and white mosaics and are all connected via a narrow hallway (1). The well-preserved frescoes in this suite include: the *Pine Room* (2), which portrays simple painted columns with pine-branch garlands strung between them; and the *Room of the Masks* (3), which depicts elaborate multicoloured architecture of vibrant reds, yellows, and purples, with theatrical masks resting on cornices halfway up the walls. Panels depicting painted landscape scenes showing rural sanctuaries, framed by the illusionistic architecture, occupy the centres of the walls in the *Room of the Masks*. The more public rooms, on the other hand, had marble floors, as seen from the impressions left behind after the removal of the marble. Two of these rooms (4, 5) are identified as libraries or rooms for displaying artworks, owing to shallow niches on their sides. Two of the other rooms (6, 7) have architectural and decorative schemes that seem incomplete. Room 7 provides an excellent example of a painting of a two-storey building rendered in perspective in vibrant blue, red, yellow, and white.

The rooms on the eastern side of the courtyard are preserved on two different levels and contain examples of exquisite fresco paintings. Many of these paintings had fallen off the ceilings and walls and broken into tiny pieces, and can only be viewed today thanks to their painstaking reassembly. The first room, the *Ramp Vestibule* (8), is decorated with brightly painted frescoes depicting stone blocks in a masonry style. At the top of the walls are architectural elements leading up toward a trompe l'oeil ceiling of painted coffers. The next room is a large hall or *oecus* (private dining room) (9). The four pedestals on the floor, once covered in marble veneer, would have held columns that supported a false ceiling. The wall paintings with their vivid reds, blues, and yellows display an illusionistic architecture of columns, platforms, and framed panels. The last interior room on this level is a *cubiculum* (a multi-purpose room) (10) that again displays wonderful frescoes of illusionistic architecture in red, blue, and yellow, with scenes of landscapes and human figures set behind the architectural elements. Just beyond this room, but visible only from the outside, is a small fountain room (11) with a well and two niches decorated with shells. The final room to visit on this eastern side, located on the second story, is accessed via a modern stairway. From the upper platform visitors look into a small cubiculum (12) with beautifully decorated walls and ceilings. Here the scheme is again based on illusionistic architecture, and the vibrant red, yellow, and black colours highlight all of the various elements, including the panel paintings set between the false columns. The ceiling is made of white stucco with coloured insets.

Although Augustus and Livia most likely did not reside in this house, a visitor to these rooms has a chance to experience a dwelling that was in use during Livia's lifetime. The architecture and wall paintings of these rooms provide a glimpse into the world of aristocratic dwellers of the Palatino in the Late Republic, perhaps making it easier for visitors to imagine the lifestyle of the most famous couple of that period, Octavian and Livia. At the time of this book's printing, the Casa di Augusto was recently reopened to the public (only via a guided tour together with the Casa di Livia) after extensive renovations that have done a remarkable job of restoring these rooms, with particular attention paid to the frescoes.

The Casa di Livia on the Palatino:
A Possible Residence for Livia after Augustus's Death

As controversial as the identification of the Casa di Augusto may be, the Casa di Livia has even more doubt concerning its ownership. It sits north of the Casa di Augusto and east of the Tempio della Vittoria. It has been suggested that this is the part of the imperial residence that Augustus left to Livia in his will to use until she herself died. Evidence for this theory comes chiefly from its close proximity to the Casa di Augusto, and from the discovery of a lead pipe stamped with the name "Julia Aug," denoting it as the property of Julia Augusta, the name given to Livia in Augustus's will. While this evidence is compelling, the fact that later imperial women also bore this name means that the pipe cannot be taken as secure proof that this house was Livia's.

Nevertheless, this house dates to the time of Livia's residence on the Palatino and represents an excellent example of an aristocratic household. It has undergone significant changes over time, but certain elements from Livia's day can still be appreciated by visitors. The house (see fig. 14), built in 75–50 BCE, had its original main entrance on the southeastern side (in green). Today, one enters through a secondary entrance (13) on the northern side, probably created around 30–20 BCE at a time of modification and redecoration of the house. This entrance leads through a narrow hallway (14) to an underground level where pieces of the original black and white mosaic pavements can still be seen in the rooms. The hallway empties into a rectangular courtyard decorated with frescoes depicting green and black panels surrounded by red frames and bordered on the top and bottom by yellow bands (15). The bases of the columns that supported the roof are still preserved. In this room and others in the house the frescoes have been detached from the walls.

A finely painted room, traditionally identified as a dining room (16), opens off the southwestern corner of the courtyard through a small doorway. This southernmost room contains frescoes of large panels framed by ornamental illusionistic columns. The panels depict landscapes and sacred elements. Returning to the courtyard, a series of three rooms, perhaps reception rooms, open onto its eastern side and display excellent examples of paintings and mosaics from this period. The right room (17) is painted with garlands of fruit, leaves, and flowers hanging in front of white panels, set behind an illusionistic colonnade. Above these panels is a yellow band painted with scenes of daily life in Egypt. Further above this band is another set of panels depicting winged figures, grape clusters, and candelabra. The leftmost room (19) is decorated in a style somewhat reminiscent of the right room: it displays a number of red panels (without garlands) set behind an illusionistic colonnade (see fig. 15), topped by a series of panels again depicting winged figures, grape clusters, and candelabra. The central room (18) was especially well-decorated and each of its walls featured large central mythological panels framed by illusionistic columns on high bases. The central panel on the back wall, visible at the time of excavation, has been severely damaged. Some sense of its colours has been brought back by the recent restorations but it is difficult to tell that it depicted the story of Polyphemus and the nymph Galatea. The central panel on the right wall, in comparison, has been revived by the recent restoration work. It depicts the story of Io, the lover of Jupiter, sitting on a rock in front of a sacred column while being guarded

Fig. 15: Casa di Livia, fresco with garlands / Room 17.
Photo Credit: Scala / Art Resource, NY.

by Argus. Mercury arrives from behind the rock to free Io. Toward the back part of the right wall is a painted panel that opens onto an architectural vista with human figures, and both walls display small painted panels resting on the cornices. The upper surfaces of the walls are populated with various decorative motifs of winged divinities, grape clusters, and candelabra.

The three lead pipes mounted on the left wall of the central room were found connected to each other on the eastern side of the house, running between this building and the later imperial palace. Each pipe bears a different stamp: one names Domitian; one Julia Aug[usta]; and one L. Pescennius Eros (associated with the Severan emperors). These reflect the long history of the imperial family's use of this part of the Palatino.

While there is no undisputable evidence to link this house to Livia, visitors can still gain an appreciation for the style of house that existed on the Palatino in Livia's day, and can stand in a house that Livia herself most likely visited, and perhaps used as her residence. At the time this book was at press, the Casa di Livia was recently reopened to the public (only via guided tour with the Casa di Augusto) after extensive renovations that have done a remarkable job of preserving and enhancing the frescoes.

Conclusion

Livia Drusilla (Julia Augusta) left an important legacy both in Rome and throughout the Roman Empire. Despite her popularity, however, her reputation has suffered from accusations of meddling in politics to promote herself and her sons. These allegations even went so far as to suggest that she was responsible for poisoning multiple members of the imperial family, including Augustus himself. Most modern scholars chalk these stories up to the kind of bad publicity that tends to accompany women of power in general and Livia in particular, and have therefore exonerated her. In looking past the accusations of conniving conduct it is possible to see a side of Livia that has endured through the ages. She represents the connection between Augustus and Tiberius, the two emperors whose rule would set the course for the government of Rome for the next three hundred years. Her conduct, her modesty, and her intelligence would make her worthy of emulation by future empresses, and a subject of worship and admiration for much of the history of the Western Roman Empire.

Essential Reading

Barrett, Anthony A. *Livia: First Lady of Imperial Rome*. New Haven: Yale University Press, 2002.

Bartman, Elizabeth. *Portraits of Livia: Imaging the Imperial Woman in Augustan Rome*. New York: Cambridge University Press, 1999.

Claridge, Amanda. *Rome: An Oxford Archaeological Guide*. Oxford: Oxford University Press, 2010.

Coarelli, Filippo. *Rome and Environs: An Archaeological Guide*. Translated by James J. Clauss and Daniel P. Harmon. Berkeley and Los Angeles: University of California Press, 2007.

Purcell, Nicholas. "Livia and the Womanhood of Rome." *Proceedings of the Cambridge Philological Society* 212 (1986): 78–105.

Treggiari, Susan. "Women in the Time of Augustus." In *The Cambridge Companion to the Age of Augustus*, edited by Karl Galinsky, 130–47. New York: Cambridge University Press, 2005.

Other Places to Encounter Livia in and near Rome

- Tempio di Augusto e Livia on the Palatino: after Livia's deification in 42 CE, Claudius erected a statue to her in the Tempio di Augusto. The remains of this temple have not been found.

- Porticus Liviae: this building's entrance was probably near the Chiesa di Santa Lucia in Selci on the modern Via in Selci. The structure probably extended south to the Via delle Sette Sale. The pavement of the Porticus was found around six metres below modern ground level but nothing is visible today.

- Ara Pacis: the most common identifications of Livia on the monument's frieze are either the first female figure on the southern side behind Agrippa, or the female figure on the northern side near the end of the procession between the youngest boy and a slightly older boy. Both are labelled in the museum at the small-scale model of the altar.

- Mausoleo di Augusto: the final resting place of Livia, Augustus, and several other members of the Julio-Claudian dynasty. Completed in the 20s BCE, this concrete drum, circa 89 metres in diameter, was once faced with travertine and capped by a mound. The Mausoleo is currently not open to the public but can be viewed from the outside.

- Villa di Livia ad Gallinas Albas at Prima Porta: a country estate just north of Rome. The well-known statue of *Augustus of Prima Porta*, now in the Musei Vaticani, was discovered here.

- Palazzo Massimo Alle Terme, upper floor of the museum: the fresco from Livia's *Garden Room* from the Villa di Livia ad Gallinas Albas at Prima Porta. The beautiful painting depicts a garden full of a great variety of scientifically accurate birds and plants.

Fig. 16: Statue of Hadrian, second century CE, Musei Capitolini.
Scala / Art Resource, NY.

Chapter Seven

EMPEROR HADRIAN (76–138, r. 117–38 CE) AT CASTEL SANT'ANGELO, THE PANTHEON, AND THE TEMPIO DI VENERE E ROMA

TYLER TRAVILLIAN

An Emperor of the People and For the People

Hadrian was a complex man who inherited a complex empire. Upon becoming emperor in 117, he faced a series of both short-term and long-term challenges to successful rule. In the shorter term, memories of the civil wars that arose after the death of Nero (r. 54–68) were still fresh in his subject's minds, and there was still considerable antipathy felt by the upper orders at what they had perceived to be their domination by the victors in those wars—the Flavian dynasty, consisting of emperors Vespasian (r. 69–79), Titus (r. 79–81) and Domitian (r. 89–96). As a result, after Domitian's death, the Senate hastily named one of its own number, the elderly Nerva (r. 96–98), as a corrective to the military rule of the Flavians. Nerva, perhaps forced by his own Praetorian Guard, soon named the general Trajan (r. 98–117) as his successor. Trajan recognized the tension between the Senate and the army and, after consolidating his power on the German frontier, he set out to win the hearts of the Senate while expanding the empire's borders in the East. For this, the Senate named him the *optimus princeps* ("best prince"). Hadrian's prospects for a successful reign therefore depended upon his ability to rule with authority, yet without alienating the Roman upper classes as the Flavians had done. A long-term challenge faced him as well, concerning the peculiar way imperial power itself had been structured and exercised for over a century prior to his reign. It was Octavian Augustus (r. 27 BCE–14 CE) who created Rome's system of rule after the collapse of the Roman Republic and his imposition of what we today call the Roman Empire. Governing the empire required retaining power over four basic institutions of Roman society and politics: the army; the magistrates in general and above all the Senate; the people as a whole and, more specifically, the tribunes who represented their interests; and various powerbrokers of provinces. No emperor after Augustus had been quite as successful in dominating these four constituencies and thereby retaining the political right to be Rome's *princeps* ("first citizen") and *imperator* (emperor) as he had been. Hadrian was among the more successful of those who came before and after him, however, because of his ability to control at least two of Rome's principal institutions—people and provinces—while neutralizing the potentially destabilizing influences of the army and senate. The fruits of his success are to be seen in his relatively long reign (117–38), an impressive list of building and infrastructure projects, and his decisive impact on the relationship between Rome and its provinces. He is grouped together with four additional emperors (Nerva, Trajan, Antoninus Pius and Marcus Aurelius) who come down to us as the "five good emperors." Without exaggerating his case too much, it is probably true that he was the most resourceful and dynamic of these "good emperors."

Groomed to Rule

Born on January 24 or 26, 76 CE in Rome, Hadrian was the son of Afer, a senator who had only obtained the rank of *praetor*. His family traced its ancestral roots to Italica, a Roman colony in the Spanish province of Baetica. His stock, however, was purely Roman, and like any upper class Roman from a family with aspirations, he was raised and educated in Rome. His father died in the year 85 when Hadrian was only nine. The boy passed into the protection of two men: the future emperor Trajan, at the time a praetor, and Publius Acilius Attianus, a close friend of Trajan's.

The young Hadrian's education continued. In 90, at age fourteen or fifteen he assumed the *toga virilis* and seems to have visited Italica for the first (and perhaps the last) time. His career marked him for greatness from the beginning. He held successive posts under Trajan's patronage, including three military tribunates in Moesia (in the Balkans) and Germany (95–97). In 100 he married Sabina Augusta, Trajan's great-niece (a match suggested by Pompeia Plotina, Trajan's wife), became quaestor in 101, and fought the Dacians with Trajan in 101–2. His career crested as he was named consul in 108 and archon of Athens for 112/13. Hadrian's last honour under Trajan was to be named consul-designate for 118, yet Trajan took ill and died on August 8, 117 while on campaign in Cilicia (in modern day Turkey). Hadrian was at his side at the time. Pompeia Plotina, Trajan's wife, announced Hadrian's adoption on August 9, withholding news of Trajan's death for two more days. Hadrian's accession would never escape the suspicions occasioned by this timing but there was no one to oppose him.

Ruling Rome and Living Elsewhere

Hadrian's first act as emperor was to pull out of Trajan's military expansions in Armenia, Mesopotamia, and Assyria. Trajan had won his battles, but he had failed to conquer: the regions were quagmires, draining resources without benefit to the Roman state. The move, as astute as it was unpopular, distanced Hadrian from his predecessor. As he journeyed from Cilicia back to Rome, Hadrian, intending to keep the imperial threads tight, swore not to use his powers to attack the Senate. By the time he reached the city, however, four senators, all former consuls, had been killed. This was an inauspicious beginning. The affair has come to be known as the "Conspiracy of the Four Consulars," because P. Acilius Attianus, the praetorian prefect and Hadrian's former childhood guardian, claimed that these men had conspired against the new emperor. The truth is as obscure now as it was then. Hadrian sought to mollify the Senate by removing Attianus from his position as praetorian prefect, but as Attianus was allowed to retire with all the rights and privileges of a senator, the act did little to satisfy. Hadrian had earned a lifetime of enmity from the Senate, one of the chief institutions behind successful imperial rule.

The new emperor arrived in Rome on July 9, 118. Though his time there would be brief, amounting to just three years during this visit, he wasted no time in restoring the city's buildings. As part of his extensive campaign to benefit the city, he rebuilt Agrippa's Pantheon, a casualty of fire, and erected the Tempio di Venere e Roma (see below). He was later to build a new imperial mausoleum (the modern Castel Sant'Angelo) and the

Pons Aelius, a bridge by which to approach the mausoleum (the Ponte Sant'Angelo). Hadrian's building initiatives beautified the city and restored integral structures from Augustus's own building campaigns. We can see from these projects that Hadrian envisioned himself as a new founder of a unified empire in much the way Augustus before him had been a new founder of the city.

After inaugurating the Tempio di Venere e Roma, Hadrian departed to tour the provinces. He would spend the majority of his reign away from the imperial city. His goal seems to have been to repair the defects of his predecessor, Trajan, who had sought to expand the empire militarily at the cost of attention to its people and unity. Hadrian would, in fact, embark on what seems to have been a program of unity, integrating Rome and its provinces into a greater, more cohesive whole.

His first tour took him to Gaul, Germany, Britain, and Spain, where he firmed up the borders, the most famous of which is known now as Hadrian's Wall in northern England. In 123, his tour of the West was cut short by impending war with Parthia in the East. For the next several years he travelled to Athens and throughout Italy in order to confirm his power and influence in these places. Among other actions, he divided Italy into four provinces, all with equal powers, a bold move that set in motion a completely new vision of the relations between the city of Rome and its provinces. Two centuries later Emperor Constantine (312–37) would complete this move to decentralize Roman government, but for Hadrian it further spoiled his relations with a Roman aristocracy that was not ready to see itself reduced to one province among many, equal beneath a single emperor.

Perhaps because he did not feel at home there anymore, Hadrian would not stay long at Rome. He began his tour of the East in 128, travelling to Asia Minor via Sicily and Africa. On the way he stopped in Jerusalem, which had been destroyed in 70 by Vespasian's son Titus. Surveying the destruction, Hadrian decided to rebuild the site, including the Jewish Temple, as he had so much else. However, he re-established the city as a Roman colony: *Aelia Capitolina*. He continued on to Athens but soon found his march halted. The Jewish people were in revolt: they were incensed both by the news that Hadrian intended to dedicate a temple to Jupiter on the site of the Jewish Temple and, likewise, by an earlier decree forbidding circumcision (an edict against mutilation). This marked the Third Jewish War, known as the Bar Kokhba Revolt for its leader, Simon bar Kokhba, and lasting from 133–35. Hadrian supervised the first year of military operations himself. Bar Kokhba was thought by many to be the Messiah, a military leader who would throw off the oppressive Roman regime, but he was not supported by Christian Jews. The revolt contributed to a sharper distinction between Christianity and Judaism. It also sparked an attempt by the Romans to wipe out the Jews as a people: 985 villages were laid waste, Judaea was renamed Syria Palestina, and Jews were banned from Jerusalem, their diaspora intensified. Hadrian had sought to wipe out the Jewish people whose monotheism (and so outright rejection of the imperial cult) was seen as a threat to unity in the empire. Their persecution would continue until his death in 138 and the accession of Antoninus Pius.

Exhausted and in poor health, Hadrian returned to Rome in 133. He lived another five years, long enough to celebrate his *vicennalia*, twenty years as emperor. In 138, after his first choice for succession predeceased him, Hadrian adopted Aurelius Antoninus under the condition that he in turn adopt the young Marcus Aurelius and Lucius Verus. The emperor died on July 10, 138. He barely escaped the fate of Domitian: the Senate longed to issue a *damnatio memoriae*, wiping his name from all official monuments. His successor, Antoninus, convinced the Senate instead to grant his adopted father divine honours, and for this he earned the name "Pius" ("dutiful").

An Architectural Emperor at the Tempio di Venere e Roma

Numerous monuments and works of art with Hadrian's signature on them can be identified today in England, Athens, central Egypt and many other locales within the former borders of the ancient Roman Empire. The city of Rome alone has several commissions, some of which still stand today in the open air and museums, while others are known mainly through written sources. A late-Roman source, the *Scriptores Historiae Augustae* or *Augustan History*, gives the following account of the emperor's main building projects in the city:

> At Rome he restored the Pantheon, the Saepta, the Basilica of Neptune, very many sacred buildings, the Forum of Augustus, and the Baths of Agrippa, and dedicated all of them in the names of their original builders. He also built a bridge named after himself and the tomb next to the Tiber, and the shrine of the Bona Dea. With the help of the architect Decrianus he also moved the Colossus, held in an upright position, from the place where the Tempio di Venere e Roma is now—so vast a weight that he provided twenty-four elephants for the work. When he had consecrated the statue to the Sun after removing the face of Nero to whom it had previously been dedicated, he undertook to make another one of a similar kind, for the Moon, under the direction of the architect Apollodorus. (19.10–13)

As the above passage indicates, Hadrian was not a mere royal patron of arts, buildings, and infrastructure projects. In addition, he frequently took a personal hand in designing and developing a commission, even to the point of functioning as an architect. His reign was glorious from this point of view and his attention to this particular exercise of imperial power reveals a great deal about him and his priorities as emperor.

While Augustus had been venerated alongside the goddess Roma in the provinces, Hadrian was the first to introduce that cult to Rome. His new temple, dedicated jointly to the goddesses Venus and Roma, was inaugurated or consecrated on the April 21, 121 CE during the *Parilia*, a festival in honour of the founding of the city. The building itself was not completed until 135 and it was restored by Maxentius in 307 after its destruction by fire. It stands on a raised platform on the southeastern end of the Foro Romano and overlooks the Colosseo from the northern side of the Via Sacra and the Arco di Tito. The temple has been difficult to reconstruct due to confusion between the Maxentian and Hadrianic remains. Hadrian's temple, however, seems to have had seven steps leading up to a rectangular structure supported by twenty columns along its length and ten across its width. Inside were two cellae, back to back, which housed the images of Venus and Roma. The interior space was surrounded by a porticus thirteen metres deep on the north side and eleven metres deep on the south side.

Hadrian had studied architecture as a true amateur—that is, one motivated by love of the discipline, and he was quite skilled in its application. It is very possible that the

Tempio di Venere e Roma, which became the largest temple in Rome and showed a great deal of Greek influence in its style, was truly of Hadrian's own design. An anecdote from the historian Dio Cassius (69.4) reports that Hadrian himself determined the site for this temple, drew up architectural plans (possibly by hand), and planned interior decoration, including the statues to be installed there. The same source alleges that Hadrian fiercely clashed with the most famous architect of his times, a certain Apollodorus, over this and other commissions. More likely, Hadrian merely traded ideas with the elder and more experienced Apollodorus over this massive project, resulting in the emperor having to give some ground. The bigger lesson of Venus and Roma, however, is the role of the emperor-cult in unifying the empire. Augustus had allowed and even encouraged the provinces to worship the princeps alongside the goddess Roma. Together they gave the disparate peoples of the empire a single figure around which to rally: Roma and the emperor as one. Subsequent emperors continued the practice but it did not penetrate Rome, where the emperor's *genius* (guardian spirit) was worshipped but the emperor himself remained a single, mortal man among many. Venus, however, was not just a divinity within the city; she had a close link to the imperial household, as the direct ancestor of Julius Caesar and Augustus. This made Venus a safe and compelling substitute for direct worship of the emperor in the city. And in fact the temple would be adopted by later emperors in direct connection with their divinity: Philip the Arab (244–49) and Probus (276–82) both depicted themselves as gods on coins with the temple stamped on the back. Introducing the temple (and thus the cult) to the city seems to have been part of Hadrian's broader egalitarian project to equalize the empire: Italy and its chief city Rome were to hold the same status as the other provinces—parts of the greater whole—and so they would hold the same cult, the same relationship to their emperor.

Daring Experiments in Architecture at the Pantheon

The original dedication of the Pantheon (see fig. 17) is a mystery. The name seems to indicate a sanctuary to "all the gods." Yet temples to more than two gods were forbidden in Rome, since the state wished to avoid confusion about which gods were due sacrifice in any given place. Whatever its origin, Agrippa dedicated a temple in 25 BCE as part of Augustus's building campaign in the Campus Martius and Pliny the Elder (*Nat. Hist.* 38.4.38) tells us that this temple quickly came to be known by the nickname "Pantheon." Any official designation was forgotten. The shape of Agrippa's Pantheon is unknown, in part because the building burned down at least twice: in 80 CE and again in 110. The dedication of the version now extant reads, "Marcus Agrippa, son of Lucius, consul for the third time, made this." Hadrian honoured the original dedicant, and history believed this pious lie until the early 1890s when the French architect Georges Chedanne analyzed the brick stamps. The bricks that could be dated were manufactured from 114–24—during the end of Trajan's reign and into Hadrian's. Chedanne concluded that Hadrian had rebuilt the structure in the early years of his reign using existing stockpiles of bricks, and most archaeologists agree. In truth, Hadrian not only rebuilt the Pantheon but he likely also designed the structure personally.

Fig. 17: The Pantheon Dome. Photo courtesy of Peter Hatlie.

The Pantheon displays an architectural perfection that, aided by an almost unequalled preservation, deserves to be described in some detail. The building has a north-south orientation with its entrance from the north. The dome is constructed of poured, molded concrete with the interior forming a perfect hemisphere. Its diameter is 43.3 metres (one hundred fifty Roman feet) and it is raised up on the interior by a cylindrical drum of 21.65 metres (seventy-five Roman feet) tall so that a 43.3 metre diameter sphere would fit exactly beneath the dome and just rest upon the floor. The rotunda room is lined with niches in which statues of divinities could have stood; these were relieved by arches built into the brickwork and hidden by marble cladding. The dome itself is decorated by rings of coffers. In antiquity these were covered in bronze tiles which may have depicted stars, constellations, or other images. As well as being decorative, the coffers reduce the weight of the dome itself. On the outside, the dome is thicker at the bottom, thinning toward the top, with each successive layer made of lighter materials. The uppermost layer is composed of concrete mixed with pumice. Empty internal chambers lighten the load; thus the weight decreases as the dome grows more fragile. At the top, the oculus serves a dual purpose: as the only source of natural light and for the purpose of removing what would have been the weakest, most vulnerable portion of the dome. The Pantheon was the world's largest dome until the Renaissance and it remains the largest unreinforced concrete dome.

The portico forms a rectangle on the north side. It was meant to be sixty Roman feet high (fifty foot columns with ten foot capitals) but due to construction difficulties, it had to be resized at the last moment to four-fifths of its original dimensions (forty foot columns with eight foot capitals). This preserved the perspective but unfortunately exposed the pediment above the portico. The whole structure is built around the fundamental units of geometry: the interrelation of square and circle. The Pantheon was restored (perhaps merely cleaned) in 202 by Septimius Severus and his son Caracalla but we owe its preservation to Pope Boniface IV (r. 608–14), who converted it to a Christian church, the Basilica di S. Maria della Rotonda (or S. Maria ad Martyres), in 608. The Pantheon remains in good repair despite being despoiled periodically throughout the Middle Ages. Emperor Constans II (641–68) removed the bronze cladding of the dome in 663 and, in the seventeenth century, Pope Urban VIII (r. 1623–44) pilfered the bronze girders from the portico roof to make cannons for the Vatican.

As it stands now, the Pantheon is magnificent; with its original decoration, it must have been glorious. That Hadrian chose this building to restore is no doubt ideologically significant. With it, he restored—and more importantly, improved—Augustus's legacy in the Campus Martius. By choosing to omit his name, attributing the building only to its original builder, Marcus Agrippa (63–12 BCE), close friend and son-in-law of the legendary Emperor Augustus, Hadrian also invited comparison between himself and the latter's regime. His own legacy, he seemed to say, was so secure, so inevitable, that it needed nothing so mean as another inscription to maintain it.

Hadrian's Villa and New Empire

Then as now, Rome could quickly feel crowded and, in the summer, sweltering. Hadrian, like all of Rome's emperors, had several getaways for when he needed a respite, including villas on the Palatino and in the Horti Sallustiani (east of where the Villa Borghese is now). The best preserved of his villas is his Tiburtine Villa, which we know now as Hadrian's Villa and which lies in Tivoli (ancient Tibur), twenty-eight kilometres northeast of Rome. This was far enough away to be a retreat from politics but close enough to allow convenient access to the city should the need arise. Tibur's favourable landscape and climate had already made it a favourite place for imperial villas, having hosted also Augustus, Claudius, and possibly even Julius Caesar. Hadrian's Villa seems to have been one-half of a square mile (over one square kilometre) in area. Its excavation was begun by Pope Alexander VI (r. 1492–1503), but a generation later in the latter half of the sixteen century, the villa was pillaged for materials and decorations by the pope's grandson, Cardinal Ippolito d'Este (1479–1520), who modelled his own Villa d'Este after it. Despite the despoliation, the villa retains a remarkable amount of decoration and statuary.

Rome was becoming something new—an idea rather than a city—and Hadrian's Villa reflects this conception, unique for the time, of the empire as a whole, single entity for which the emperor was totally responsible. But how to render such an idea in reality and communicate it to one's subjects? In constructing his villa, Hadrian went about this task, in the words of one source (*Scriptores Historiae Augustae* 26.5), "in wonderful fashion, in such a way that he inscribed the most famous names of provinces and places there, and called them, for example, Lycium, Academia, Prytanium, Canopus, Poecile, and Tempe. So that he might omit nothing, he even made a Lower World."

Fig. 18: Serapeum and Canopus, Villa Adriana, Tivoli. Photo courtesy of Peter Hatlie.

The villa was constructed in two distinct stages, the first from 117–25 and the second from 125–33, and it is composed of a series of self-contained complexes. Some scholars have attributed these complexes to the staged nature of the building process, but they may equally be meant to represent the nature of the provinces of the Roman world: relatively independent units welded into a single greater whole overseen by a single *dominus* (lord). The villa was serviced by extensive underground passageways, some large enough for oxen-drawn carts to pass. The villa was primarily a summer haunt: water is present throughout and ice houses have even been found to store snow that could be used to cool drinks.

Among the villa's more striking features are the Canopus and Serapeum, together representing Egypt. The Canopus, named for a port city on the Nile delta near Alexandria, is a long rectangular pool (120 by 19 metres) flanked by a row columns with Corinthian capitals. The columns themselves are caryatids, larger than life statues of female figures inspired by Greek art. The Canopus and its colonnade lead toward the Serapeum, a half-domed reclining room so named because of its similarity to shrines to the Egyptian god Serapis. The room is a semi-circular, domed apse with another small, rectangular pool in front perpendicular to the Canopus. It was heavily frescoed and had smaller rooms to either side along with a second story now lost. The area was filled with sculptures arranged to remind the viewer of Hellenistic Egypt. The Serapeum seems to have been used as a dining area to entertain guests.

The villa reveals the fundamental tensions Hadrian faced, or perhaps it shows us how he thought about those tensions. As part of his reign's political reforms, he sought to integrate Rome the city into Rome the empire by turning Italy into provinces, each one equal to the rest, and also by trying to bring the provinces of Rome into closer contact with Rome the city. Essentially, the villa was a bridge between city and provinces in this sense and thereby allowed Hadrian to be in Rome even though he was "abroad."

Final Years, Death, and Castel San Angelo

The emperor needed a fitting burial site, but Augustus's tomb, which contained the Julio-Claudians, their families, and Nerva, was full. A new site would have to be found. Hadrian found it beyond a bend in the Tiber, in an undeveloped plot of land near today's Vatican City. Hadrian's Mausoleum, now known as Castel Sant'Angelo, was begun sometime between 123 (the date of the earliest brick stamps) and 134 (the dedication of the Pons Aelius, which led to the Mausoleum), but it was left to Antoninus Pius to complete in 139. The plan of Hadrian's Mausoleum resembled Augustus's in general shape: both were rotundas, but Hadrian's was grander and set on higher ground to avoid the nuisance of flooding. The entire structure sits 800 metres downriver from Augustus's mausoleum. Any traveller would be invited to comparison: first Augustus, now Hadrian. Where the former surrounded his mausoleum with an account of his deeds, the latter let the elegant lines of his architecture speak for him. Hadrian did not leave us completely wordless, however. According to his biographer (*Scriptores Historiae Augustae* 25.8), he composed his own epitaph on his deathbed, a brief poem:

ANIMULA, VAGULA, BLANDULA	My charming little soul, my beloved vagrant,
HOSPES COMESQUE CORPORIS	You've been with me, my body's friend and companion,
QUAE NUNC ABIBIS IN LOCA	But now you will go your way to some new place,
PALLIDULA, RIGIDA, NUDULA,	There too the light will be thin, the air stiff, and a little cold,
NEC, UT SOLES, DABIS IOCOS!	And your usual fun, that too will be gone.

The mausoleum's basic shape was of a marble drum perhaps sixty metres tall, with a diameter of slightly less than eighty-four metres resting on a square foundation of equal size. The interplay of circle and square so elegantly employed in the Pantheon is again visible here. A spiralling interior stair led up to the cella, which held the ashes of the emperor and family. It is uncertain what decorated the roof the structure, but it may have been a monumental equestrian statue or quadriga (a statue of a four-horse chariot). To approach the mausoleum, Hadrian constructed a new bridge, the Pons Aelius (modern Ponte Sant'Angelo). The bridge, dedicated in 134, aims directly at the centre of the mausoleum, leading the eye and the foot to the tomb of Caesars. The ancient bridge, much like the Bernini reimagining that we see today, was lined with statues, and the original plinths may even have been the architect's inspiration.

The mausoleum has had a mottled afterlife. It housed the remains of the emperors who followed Hadrian (the last being Caracalla in 217), as well as their families. It was looted by Alaric the Goth's armies when he sacked Rome in 410. It was likely then that Hadrian's ashes were lost. In 590 a plague beset Rome, which only lifted after a reported vision of the archangel Michael standing atop the mausoleum, sheathing his sword. It is from this legend that it earned its new name, Castel Sant'Angelo; following this legend, Pope Leo X had the sculptor Raffaello da Montelupo in 1536 add a statue of an angel to the top (replaced by a bronze in 1753). The Mausoleum had already been converted to a papal fortress and prison by then. In 1277 Pope Nicholas III (r. 1277–80) had built the *Passetto di Borgo*, a bridge, approximately 800 metres long, from the Vatican directly to the Castel along which popes could escape to safety. The Castel has since been converted into a museum. Once a tomb, the mausoleum and its bridge stand now as monuments to Rome's epochs: ancient, medieval, Renaissance and modern, each superimposed upon the last.

Conclusion

In the "good emperors" we can see special affinities to the institutions that upheld the Roman Empire: in Nerva, the Senate; in Trajan, the military; in Hadrian, the people and the provinces; in Antoninus Pius, the city Rome. Hadrian, however, had the longest vision. He saw that the empire was no longer the conquest and possession of a single city, but rather it had become a much larger whole that, in order to survive, needed to see itself in a new way. He tried to reimagine the empire as a collection of provinces held together by a single bureaucracy controlled by the emperor, not the city, of Rome. As a result, much of his reign was spent travelling, visiting his constituencies across the empire. What time he spent in Rome involved bringing his vision to the aristocracy there: a new plan that redefined Italy as a series of provinces, an imperial villa that represented all the provinces of the empire as a whole, and a building program in the city that set himself up as a successor and rival to Augustus. It is not hard to see how his vision would alienate the Roman aristocracy, who had been opposed to him almost from the first day of his reign. Although the redistricting of Italy would be dismantled after Hadrian's death, his vision was ultimately proven correct: "Rome" had become something more than a city. Just what that would be and how to run it effectively would plague emperors, rebels, and usurpers alike until Constantine founded a New Rome in the East, fulfilling a conception of the empire that had begun, however imperfectly, with Hadrian.

Essential Reading

Birley, Anthony R. *Hadrian: The Restless Emperor*. New York: Routledge, 1997.

Boatwright, Mary Taliaferro. *Hadrian and the City of Rome*. Princeton: Princeton University Press, 1987.

Dio Cassius. *Dio's Roman History*. Translated by Earnest Cary. Cambridge, MA: Harvard University Press, 1961.

Lives of the Later Caesars. Translated by Anthony Birley. Baltimore: Penguin Books, 1976.

Perowne, Stewart. *Hadrian*. New York: Norton, 1960.

Syme, Ronald. Various studies on Hadrian collected in *Roman Papers*, vol. 4, 295–324; vol. 5, 546–62, vol. 6. 103–14 and 57–81. Oxford: Oxford University Press, 1988–91.

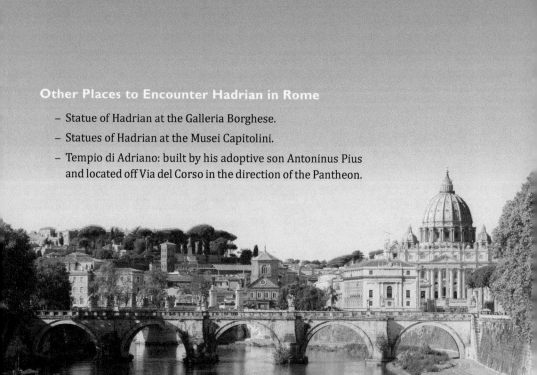

Other Places to Encounter Hadrian in Rome

- Statue of Hadrian at the Galleria Borghese.
- Statues of Hadrian at the Musei Capitolini.
- Tempio di Adriano: built by his adoptive son Antoninus Pius and located off Via del Corso in the direction of the Pantheon.

MAP OF ROME FOR CHAPTERS 8–9

ROME

Via Cernaia

Piazza
Repubblica

Stazione
Termini

Via Marsala

Via Cavour

PRINCIPAL SITES DISCUSSED IN CHAPTERS EIGHT-NINE

1. Arco di Costantino - Via di San Gregorio
2. Arco di Giano - Via del Velabro, 5
3. Basilica di Massenzio - Foro Romano
4. Battistero lateranense - Piazza di S. Giovanni in Laterano, 4
5. Carcere Mamertino - Clivo Argentario, 1
6. Musei Capitolini - Piazza del Campidoglio, 1
7. S. Clemente al Laterano - Via Labicana, 95
8. S. Giovanni in Laterano - Piazza di S. Giovanni in Laterano, 4
9. Ss. Quattro Coronati - Via dei Santi Quattro Coronati, 20

*Musei Vaticani - Viale Vaticano
*Palazzo Barberini - Via delle Quattro Fontane, 13
*S. Lorenzo fuori le mura - Piazzale del Verano, 3
*S. Paolo fuori le mura - Piazzale San Paolo, 1
*S. Pietro - Piazza San Pietro, 1
*S. Sebastiano - Via Appia Antica, 136

*Not included on this map. Refer to main map for more information

Colosseo

Via Labicana

7 S. Clemente al Laterano

9 Ss. Quattro Coronati

Via Claudia

Battistero lateranense

4   8 S. Giovanni in Laterano

Villa
Celimontana

Fig. 19:
The Glory of St. Clement,
painting by Giuseppe
Bartolomeo Chiari,
Palazzo Barberini,
Rome. Photo Credit:
Mondadori Portfolio /
AKG Images.

Chapter Eight

POPE CLEMENT I OF ROME (ca. 35–99 or 101, r. 88–99 or 101 CE) AT THE BASILICA DI SAN CLEMENTE

JOHN NORRIS

An Elusive Saint of Great Renown

Clement of Rome, traditionally the fourth pope and third successor to Peter, is a mysterious figure whose historical traces are as slight as his reputation and fame are great. His authentic letter to the Corinthian Church from 96 is of great importance; his legend and cult have grown great over the centuries, notably in connection with the Basilica di San Clemente in Rome. Excavations underneath the current twelfth-century basilica led to the discovery of an original fourth–fifth-century church, and beneath it are Roman buildings of the first and second centuries. At this site, visitors can journey back in time from the present day street level, through twelfth- and fourth-century strata, all the way down to the first-century Roman level. Such a journey takes the visitor through a series of complex historical realities, matched in their complexity by the history and narratives surrounding Clement himself. A study of Clement's legends, his writing, and the historical context in which he carried out his priestly life reveal much about the early Church in Rome, allowing us to make contact with a colleague of St. Peter himself.

Contextualizing Clement in Rome

Although his biographical information is elusive, Clement is sometimes linked to the Roman patrician Titus Flavius Clemens (50–95) and his wife Domitilla. Titus was a nephew of the former emperor Vespasianus (69–79) and as such a great nephew of the emperor Domitian (81–96), who nonetheless put Titus to death and exiled his wife in 96 on the grounds of godlessness and deviation into Jewish practices. Legend has sometimes associated Clement with Titus Flavius Clemens himself, though more frequently with a freedman of his household. Scholars now argue that the source of their treason would have been a refusal to sacrifice to the cult of Domitian's divine genius.

Though Titus Flavius Clemens is not now considered to have been Christian, many hypothesize that his wife indeed was of the Christian faith. Returning from exile after the death of Domitian, she may have been responsible for the donation of lands to the Christian community that eventually formed the Catacombe di Domitilla on the Appian Way. Her influence may also have led to the property that lies under the current Basilica di San Clemente, first given to a group of Christians and later to the Church in Rome. Frequently, Clement has been identified as a freedman of the house of Titus Flavius Clemens, taking the name of his former owner upon being freed. However, the custom of the time would have meant taking on the name Flavius, not Clemens. Nevertheless, we encounter some elements here which fit general patterns of conversions to Christianity in the first and second centuries CE. If Clement is somehow related to the Titus Flavius

Clemens household, it follows that this was the conversion of a relatively well-educated, Greek-speaking Jew who played a leading role in the Roman Church. As for Domitilla, we can similarly propose that she was a Latin-speaking Roman matron who had some relation to Jewish practices before converting to Christianity. Persecution of these figures is related to a refusal to worship the divine genius of the emperor, which was linked to treason. The support of the Christian faith of these Latin and Greek converts eventually led to the establishment of a thriving community in Rome.

Clement's *Letter to the Corinthians*

Lists of the leaders of Rome traditionally place Clement as the third successor to Peter. Second-century references, such as that of the theologian and bishop Irenaeus (130–202), acknowledge his closeness to the apostles, i.e. as a person who had seen and heard them directly. Another testimony of Clement is a *Letter to the Corinthians* bearing his name and sent to the Church in Corinth from the Church in Rome, addressing an uprising against the council of elders that had occurred and urging them to return their elders to power. In a number of early codices, it stands in a place of honour alongside the likes of Paul's letters and the other epistles. Though the final New Testament canon did not include the letter, its importance and reputation in the early Church led to a longstanding cult and a legendary expansion of the narration of his life and memory, including his miracles and a martyrdom which, though likely spurious, reveal much about the early Church as well.

Clement's letter reveals a man of subtle diplomacy and deep humility. His vision of the Church seeks peace and unity through humility and obedience to divine authority. Writing from Rome to a Corinthian community that is embroiled in divisions and rebellions, he focusses primarily on the vaguely indicated quarrels in the Church in Corinth. Subtly, Clement addressed the whole community, not merely the individuals overthrown or the wrong-doers. He reminds them first of their great reputation prior to this "unholy schism" when their good name was renowned throughout the Christian community. His praise reminds them of their better selves, when they paid more attention to their own faults than they did to the faults of others. Clement offers a psychological analysis of prosperity: prayerful and brotherly unity in Corinth first brought popularity and growth, but then such successes ironically led to strife, envy, and the overthrow of the Church leaders. He roots his critique of this division in the Old Testament's own stories of rivalry and envy, beginning with Cain and Abel and ending with the near present day and the times of the heroes of his own day, Peter and Paul. Such examples are meant to appeal to all groups within the divided community, works and heroes respected by all members of the Church in Corinth. Clement does not stand in judgment above the community, but admits that the Church in Rome must also be admonished to avoid such powerful urges towards sin. The lynchpin of Clement's argument, of his spirituality, and of his Christian faith, is the example of Christ. Clement's vision of ecclesial leadership is founded on his understanding of the incarnate Lord, whose humility is exemplified by his lowering himself to become one of his flock, not lording his authority over them. Clement draws, strangely enough, not from stories of Jesus from the Gospel, but from Old Testament passages messianically interpreted to refer to Christ: Isaiah 53 and Psalms 22. Christ sets an example for the Corinthian leaders, not rising up against any unjust treatment but suffering it in silence even to the point of death. The point Clement wishes to convey to the Corinthians is that whatever injustices the young usurpers may have suffered at the hands of their presbyters, such actions do not justify their overthrow of the council of presbyters.

Clement propounds a vision of the Church that is based upon mutual respect, humble service, and a clear vision of order. Clement's vision of the stability of order strongly reflects the Greco-Roman world view of his times. For example, he compares the Church to the marching orders of a military general, where the ranks must each submit to their superior. Yet Clement here exhibits the Christian limits of his world view, too: his description of ranks in the army does not reflect current Roman imperial reality, but reflects the military ranks of Pharaoh's army in the book of Exodus. Diligent labourers are rewarded, while lazy workers are not. Influenced by St. Paul's analogy of the body, Clement emphasizes both the merit and individual importance of every part of the body, yet also notes that all must be united in a single obedience to the head. God's establishment of the Church reflects the same hierarchy of the universe, the empire, and the social order. The Lord established the rites, rules, and ministers of the Church in an order that cannot be transgressed. The scriptures, sacred and binding upon all members of the Christian community, confirm this vision of the unchangeable and divinely inspired order of the Church. Clement, true to his humble character, does not call upon the authority of the Church in Rome or upon any of his own authority to correct the Corinthian community. Instead, he calls them to a truer obedience to their own faith, to the scriptures, and to God Himself, in order to resolve their rebellion and to reestablish a healthy Christian community.

A few more insights into Clement and his world can be drawn from an analysis of the Church in Rome at his time. As noted above, Clement exhibits such a pervasive understanding of the Greek Old Testament that some conclude that he may have been a convert to Christianity from gentile "god-fearers," a term used in both ancient scripture (e.g. Acts 13:16 and 13:26) and by modern scholars to refer to those who were in sympathy with the Greek-speaking Jewish populations. Such a hypothesis fits with the general description of the Christian community in the mid-first century. St. Paul's letter to the Christian community in Rome clearly acknowledges the Jewish-Christian character of the community and justifies Paul's own support for gentile Christian presence in the Church. Though later patristic sources tie Clement to the colleague of Paul of the same name mentioned in Philippians 4:3, most scholars hold that the Clement mentioned there has nothing to do with our Clement. Later tradition also portrays Clement as the single bishop of Rome, third in succession after Peter. However, his letter itself seems to indicate that the leadership in Rome involved bishops in the plural, as does the early second-century author of "The Shepherd of Hermas." Clement is likely to have been one of the most important of the council of elders in Rome, perhaps the one assigned to relations with other Christian communities. His letter indicates a certain sophistication in style that indicates at least a level of education in grammar and rhetoric, though not a higher level of education in philosophy.

Clement in Legend

Clement's *Letter to the Corinthians* was regarded highly enough that it was included in early versions of the New Testament. Such a heritage seems to indicate that Clement's arguments were successful in reuniting the Corinthian community. By the second half of the second century, Clement is already listed with reverence in the list of bishops of Rome by Irenaeus. As happens frequently in the second and third centuries with narrations about the apostles, missing historical details are eventually filled in by pseudonymous legends. Clement acquires a martyrdom, a number of miracles, and a series of letters, homilies, and narratives through such legends, which in turn become an inseparable part of his reputation and cult. His iconography eventually depends more upon legend than history.

Clement was given a romantic and perilous backstory, one which clearly attributes God's providential care for him. According to this legend, he was presumed to have been orphaned as a child when his mother and brothers were lost at sea, only to be miraculously reunited with the entire family later through the miraculous agency of St. Peter. From there he went on to study philosophy and took a particular interest in the immortality of the soul. Encountering St. Barnabas, he was, at first, one of the philosophers who mocked Barnabas's preaching, but quickly was moved to faith and even headed to Judea to study under St. Peter himself.

Clement's miracles reflect many of the elements of saint stories of the day. In one of the miracle stories involving the conversion of a certain woman by the name of Theodora (see fig. 20), the latter's husband Sisinnius objected to his wife's conversion and entered

Fig. 20: Legend of Clement and the Couple Theodora and Sisinnius, fresco from the Basilica di San Clemente. Photo Credit: Scala / Art Resource, NY.

into the Basilica di San Clemente (an anachronism, as churches were not constructed until the fourth century) intending to remove her. Upon entering, however, Sisinnius was struck blind and deaf and had to be led out by his servants. At the request of Theodora, Clement then cured Sisinnius of his blindness and deafness. But Sisinnius, rather than reacting with gratitude, had his servants seize Clement and his colleagues, with a view to throwing them in the river. Miraculously, the bodies of Clement and his fellows were freed, and columns and trees were thrown into the river instead, a deserving sign since the pagan Sisinnius worshiped idols made of wood and stone. Eventually St. Peter appeared to Theodora in a dream and predicted that she would be the instrument of her husband's conversion. Sisinnius was then duly cured and converted by Clement himself.

In another story, pagan consternation at Clement's power and influence led him to be tried by the emperor Trajan for being a Christian and not sacrificing to the genius of the emperor. Judged guilty, he was sent into exile on an island in the middle of the Black Sea. There he continued to preach and perform miracles. Working as stonecutters in a quarry, the enslaved Christians there had to travel six miles for water. Clement prayed to the Lord for his blessings and a lamb appeared. Clement struck that exact spot with a pick-axe and a fountain of water gushed forth, just as it had done for Moses in the desert and likewise for St. Peter in Rome's Carcere Mamertino.

The same legends that speak of Clement's success in preaching the faith and encouraging Christians in exile eventually led to his martyrdom. Clement was taken into the middle of the sea, an anchor was tied around his neck, and he was thrown overboard. This anchor thus became indelibly associated with his iconography. Miraculously, his remains were preserved by angels in a small temple at the bottom of the sea. Every year, on the anniversary of his martyrdom, the sea would roll back to reveal the temple so that Christians could venerate his remains and celebrate Clement's feast day. His miraculous power for intercession continued after his death. One year, a young boy was left behind at the temple and believed lost after the waters covered the temple once again. However, on the anniversary of the feast day the next year, the child was discovered by his mother miraculously alive by the saint's protective power. Clement's remains were disinterred by saints Cyril and Methodius and brought to Rome when they visited the city in the 860s. Even now, his remains are held to be contained under the current high altar of the Basilica di San Clemente.

The Basilica di San Clemente: Early Christian Foundations

The present day Basilica di San Clemente is rooted in the times of the historical Clement and reflects his cult and the growth of his legend up to the present day. Like Clement himself, our knowledge of the earliest history of the site is obscure and becomes better known as time passes. Like Clement, too, our knowledge of the site has been explored with greater accuracy since the advent of the historical-critical era. Archaeological discoveries of the mid-nineteenth century by Irish Dominicans, who have been caretakers for the church since the seventeenth century, led to the excavation of the original fourth-century church underneath the current church constructed in the twelfth century. Buildings from the first–second century CE were further excavated underneath

that building, and the remains of structures destroyed by Nero's fires are partially excavated below. Visitors can explore all of these levels today.

Two major buildings from the late first century—one an apartment building and
the other a warehouse—lie two levels below the current church, separated by a narrow Roman road. Underneath the church proper is a two-story warehouse whose
top story was knocked down to build the first fourth-century edifice. This building is
associated with land belonging to the family of Titus Flavius Clemens. The construction of large tufa blocks in *opus quadratum* indicates the high quality of this building.
As with many Roman buildings, the outer two stories frame an open courtyard which is
situated underneath the current nave of the church. Travel literature often misleadingly
describes this building as an aristocratic house-church in which Clement once exercised
his priestly duties. If this reading of the site is to be accepted, then it can be imagined
to have been a continuous place of Christian worship from before the death of St. Peter
up to the present day. Scholars now are less sure of the use of the building, however,
holding that it more likely functioned as a type of warehouse. Only small sections of the
building have been excavated and are open to the public. In those spaces, visitors can
see barrel vaults of cement still bearing the marks of the wood that formed the mold
for the ceiling. In some areas, visitors can look down through grates to the rubble from
the buildings destroyed by the fire of Nero. Water can still be heard flowing underneath
the ruins, one of the major obstacles for the Dominicans in their excavation of the area.
Intricate Roman brickwork of the period, *opus reticulatum*, where the square ends of the
brick work are laid like diamonds, and *opus spicatum*, where small thin bricks are laid
in a continuous "w" pattern, form the walls and floors. In some rooms, the wall stucco
remains and some fresco images can still be seen, though a century and a half of humid
air since the time of the last excavations has almost completely obliterated any traces of
what was likely an elaborate scheme.

From this building, one can cross the very narrow Roman road, which in its day must
have been fairly dark and malodorous. Here one finds a brick building from 92–96, with
a central nymphaeum-grotto surrounded by rooms on two levels. This building seems
originally to have functioned as an apartment building. Visitors have a similar experience here as to Pompeii and Herculaneum, seeing ancient Roman housing with stucco
details decorations on the walls and walking in rooms where ancient Romans lived
nearly two thousand years ago. Sometime in the second century, the first floor began
to be utilized as a Mithraeum, a centre for the worship of the pagan god Mithras. The
worship of Mithras became popular in Rome in the second century CE, though it has
origins in Rome from about 80. In one room, an ancient *triclinium* (or dining room) with
benches on three sides, one can see a marble altar with a relief of Mithras slaying the
bull. This altar was not original to the room but has been placed there for visitors.

The First Basilica di San Clemente:
Fourth–Eleventh-Century Construction

The ancient Roman two-story apartment building that lay under the current church
of Clement remained in use from the second century until the beginning of the fifth

century CE. Sometime during the fourth century, when Christianity had not only been legalized but had become the favoured religion of the emperors, the Christian community took the space over, filled in its first floor, and constructed a large, three-nave basilica on top. This church was twenty-five per cent larger than the current church and was dedicated to Clement, according to fourth-century references. We see in this story a clear indication of the cosmopolitan religious character of fourth-century Rome, where Christianity existed alongside other religions. However, when the late fourth-century emperors began to favour Christianity over all other religions, Christianity soon began to dominate Roman public and private life. By the time of the Roman emperor Theodosius (r. 379–95), paganism had been outlawed and economically sanctioned. Sometime in the early fifth century, when Mithraism had been outlawed, the apartment building was destroyed. It was filled in to form the foundation of the new, enlarged apse of the early Christian basilica. The destruction of the Mithraeum shows an increasing uniformity of religion in Rome at the beginning of the fifth century.

When visitors examine this church, the first dedicated to Clement on this site, its original size and shape are not easily determined. This church suffered severe damage during the fires that engulfed the area around 1084 when the Norman troops of Robert of Guiscard sacked the city after attempting to rescue Pope Gregory VII (r. 1073–85) from the troops of Henry IV (r. 1056–1105). When a new church was constructed on top of this building in the twelfth century, the population of Christians in the area had decreased in number as medieval Rome shrank significantly from earlier times. The earlier church was filled with rubble up to the level of the tops of the columns and the new church only covered the left and the main nave of the original church. Irish Dominican excavations opened up the naves and narthex of the first church. Since the floor of the twelfth-century church was installed in the previous working space of the earlier church at a vertical level roughly midway up the old walls, we are currently able to see only about half the church from floor to roof. Furthermore, nineteenth-century brick arches were put in place to uphold the weight of the church above, and these obstruct our full view of the original church even further.

Despite our inability to see all of its original architecture, the fourth-century church nonetheless demonstrates that there was prominent financial funding for the Christian community in the area. It could not match the levels of patronage known for imperially sponsored commissions (such as those of S. Pietro and S. Giovanni in Laterano) but it was still impressive. The columns were borrowed from a variety of pagan buildings, a typical scavenging practise in Rome in the fourth century for both pagan and Christian buildings. The floor is a rather primitive piecing together of precious marbles from other Roman buildings, not the magnificent geometric designs one finds in the church above. The narthex and the central left and right naves all retain fresco decoration dating from the building's beginning until near the time of its destruction. This church preserves rare examples of Roman wall frescoes which otherwise would have been destroyed as the churches were remodelled to fit the changing liturgical and artistic styles of the centuries.

In the narthex, we discover some lively frescoes from the tenth and eleventh centuries. One depicts Christ accepting the ninth-century saints Cyril and Methodius into paradise with the approval of Clement, with the miracle of the salvation of the boy lost and recovered in Clement's underwater chapel beneath the Black Sea. Another represents the procession of the presentation of the body of Clement to Rome by saints Cyril and Methodius in the 860s. Cyril and Methodius had discovered the remains of a body with an anchor near the Black Sea and believed the remains to be those of Clement himself; they brought them to Rome when they came to visit Pope Adrian II (r. 867–72). This fresco exhibits the lively manner of the Roman painting, with thurifers swinging their incense madly in the air. Such imagery differs radically from the stiff hieratic Byzantine painting of the Eastern Church. Later Roman painters, like the thirteenth–fourteenth-century Pietro Cavallini (1250–1330) are clearly indebted to these painters for their lively style of Roman naturalism.

In the main nave of the church, one finds a fresco, partially destroyed by a later altar, which depicts the ascension of Jesus, painted during the time of Leo IV (847–55). Leo's head bears a square nimbus, indicating he was still alive when the painting was made. The apostles surround Mary and together they behold Jesus ascending on a rainbow with an angel on either side. An alternative reading of this painting identifies the fresco with the Assumption of Mary, and more specifically, a depiction of Mary ascending to a stationary Christ who is already in heaven. Scholars who support this reading of the fresco draw attention to that fact that Leo IV was the first to give the Feast of the Assumption a special liturgical status, called an *octava*.

We also find in the nave some eleventh-century frescoes of the life and miracles of Clement, donated by a certain Beno and Maria de Repiza. The first on the left depicts the life of Alexis, an Eastern saint whose legend became popular in Rome after the ninth century. The next wall fresco depicts the story of Clement and Sisinnius recounted above (see fig. 20). Language scholars have been intrigued by the use of colloquial Latin in the fresco. Though Clement is depicted speaking in Latin, "*Duritiam cordis vestris. Saxa trahere meruisti*" ("Your heart is hard. You deserve to carry stones"), Sisinnius speaks Italian: "*Fili de la pute, traite, Gosmari, Albertel, traite. Falite dereto colo palo, Carvoncelle!*" ("Sons of whores, pull! Gosmari, Albertello, pull! Carvoncello, pull it upright with the pole!"). Just as the later legends of Clement depicted him from the point of view of contemporary standards of the papacy, so these frescoes portray Clement dressed like an eleventh-century pope, presiding over liturgical services as such. However, we can also gain some insight into early Christian times from both the legends and the frescoes. Note that in this story it is the wife who is first leading the family into the Christian Church, and that there is opposition by the paterfamilias. This opposition is overcome only through miraculous intervention.

The Twelfth-Century Church

The current upper-level church was constructed in the twelfth century and has been remodelled many times since. Just as the fourth-century church below drew upon elements of an earlier structure, so too does the twelfth-century building respect some of the elements of its predecessor, including artistic themes, liturgical witness, and even some architectural elements. The twelfth-century portico may stand over a portico from the original church, but this has not been excavated. Many elements from the fourth-cen-

Fig. 21: Interior of the Upper Church, Basilica di San Clemente, Rome.
Photo Credit: Scala / Art Resource, NY.

tury church were moved up to the twelfth-century church (see fig. 21) when the rebuilding took place. In particular, the marble choir chancel and screen around the altar from the sixth century were originally located in the earlier church. They have been reused here in the twelfth-century church, but have been cut in size to fit the diminished space. The candlestick was also moved from the fourth century basilica to its present location here. The *Baldacchino* stands over the altar, marked with Clement's anchor. Underneath are believed to be preserved the remains of both St. Ignatius of Antioch, martyred in Rome in the early second century, and the bones of Clement, brought to Rome by Cyril and Methodius, and then transferred to the upper church when it was rebuilt. The great treasure of the upper church is the glorious mosaic apse, whose multi-angled golden tiles glimmer and gleam in both daylight and candlelight. The design perhaps imitates the design from the fourth-century basilica. Much of the mosaic imagery is traditionally found in mosaics from this earlier period, including representations of the Tree of Life, the hand of God, the lambs, the evangelists, the doves, hart, phoenix, and the saints of the Old and New Testament. The crucified Christ is certainly a later medieval addition to the iconography, as a major Cross without the crucified Christ would have been rare in the twelfth century. In the mosaic imagery, the Cross emerges from the fronds of a Tree of Life, which is positioned on a green plain above the four rivers of paradise. Twelve doves representing the apostles rest on the Cross while Mary and John the Apostle stand on either side. Saints Peter and Paul, their names written in Greek, sit on either side of the apse, Peter accompanying Clement and his anchor and Paul accompanying another famous Roman holy martyr, St. Lawrence with his grill. The complicated geometric designs of the *cosmatesque* floor, common in many medieval churches in Rome, match the quality and beauty of the mosaic apse.

Alongside this twelfth-century construction, the church bears witness to artistic and liturgical history from the twelfth century to the present day. As the result of repairs and redecorations throughout the centuries, one finds many different small chapels and altars in the church. In the back of the church on the left nave, there is a chapel dedicated to St. Catherine of Alexandria. There Masolino (1383–1447), the great early Renaissance master, painted a cycle of frescoes between 1428 and 1431 representing the legendary story of Catherine's life. She protests against the persecution of Christians; she is then questioned by fifty philosophers of Alexandria, and the emperor Maxentius incarcerates her. After being imprisoned, Catherine converts the empress. Maxentius has his wife beheaded, and sentences Catherine to death on the wheel. Catherine is freed by angels before finally being beheaded. Angels then fly her body to Mount Sinai. Up above, one finds the traditional representatives for the four vaults: the four evangelists and the four doctors of the Church, Ambrose, Gregory, Augustine, and Jerome. In the upper walls of the central nave of the church, eighteenth-century frescoes depict the life of Clement to the left and St. Ignatius to the right.

Conclusion

The reverberations of a person's life, however indistinct the details, can exert an extraordinary influence over a community. The memory of Clement has inspired the universal Church and a neighbourhood in Rome for nearly two millennia. His letter is still read for spiritual guidance and his corporeal remains are still revered. Clement's gentle humility lives on as an example of Christ-like behaviour and worshippers still gather around his remains on his feast day to celebrate his life and memory. The spot where he may once have celebrated the liturgy maintains a living history that is one of the most remarkable in all of Rome.

Essential Reading

Clement of Rome. "The Epistle to the Corinthians." In *The Epistles of St. Clement of Rome and St. Ignatius of Antioch*, translated by James A. Kleist, 3–50. New York: Newman Press, 1946.

Cunningham, John M. *The Basilica of St. Clement*. Rome: Basilica di San Clemente, 2015.

de Voragine, Jacobus. "St. Clement." In *The Golden Legend*, translated by William Granger Ryan, 170–78. Princeton, NJ: Princeton University Press, 2012.

Dempsey, Luke, L. E. Boyle, and Eileen Kane, eds. *San Clemente Miscellany II: Art and Archeology*. Dublin: Dominican Publications, 1978.

Fuellenbach, John. *Ecclesiastical Office and the Primacy of Rome: An Evaluation of Recent Theological Discussion of First Clement*. Washington, D.C.: Catholic University of America Press, 1980.

Guidobaldi, Federico. *San Clemente: Gli edifici romani, la Basilica paleocristiana e le fasi Altomedioevali*. Rome: Collegio San Clemente, 1992.

Hagner, Donald Alfred. *The Use of the Old and New Testaments in Clement of Rome*. Leiden: E. J. Brill, 1973.

Lloyd, Joan Barclay. *San Clemente Miscellany III: The Medieval Church and Canonry of S. Clemente in Rome*. Rome: San Clemente, 1989.

Osborne, John. *Early Mediaeval Wall-Painting in the Lower Church of San Clemente, Rome*. New York: Garland Press, 1984.

Pseudo-Clement. "The Second Epistle of Clement." In *The Ante-Nicene Fathers*, vol. 9, edited by Allan Menzies and translated by John Keith, 249–56. Peabody, MA: Hendrickson Publishers, 1995.

Other Places to Encounter Clement in Rome

- Musei Vaticani, Constantine Room: features a fresco of Clement as one of the founding popes of the Church in Rome.
- Palazzo Barberini, Room 33: houses a large series of sixteenth- and seventeenth-century paintings of the life of Clement (see fig. 19).

Fig. 22: Fresco of Constantine Handing over Imperial Insignia to Pope Sylvester,
Basilica dei SS. Quattro Coronati, Cappella di San Silvestro, Rome.
Photo courtesy of Peter Hatlie.

Chapter Nine

EMPEROR CONSTANTINE (ca. 277–337, r. 324–37 CE) AT THE ARCO DI COSTANTINO, THE BASILICA DI SAN GIOVANNI IN LATERANO, AND THE BASILICA DEI SANTI QUATTRO CORONATI

PETER HATLIE

The Last Pagan and First Christian Emperor

Constantine is one of history's most influential figures. His world was that of late antiquity and the early Christian centuries, an interesting and complex world that he made more interesting still. For it was Constantine who gave Christianity the support and tools needed to be transformed into a world religion. It was he who put a definitive stamp on an outline of European political geography, where east became East and west became West in a way that seems obvious today even if it was not in his own day. One of the essential things that made Constantine influential within both the city of Rome and the Roman Empire at large was his rare ability to anticipate challenges and opportunities before others did. Not only was he consistently ahead of friends and rivals alike in his plans for war, politics, religion, social reform and much else, but he would also stop at nothing in order to get his way, even when the personal costs and risks to himself were immense. Not unlike the emperor Augustus of some centuries before, his reign was long and assertive enough to be truly transformative. And not unlike Augustus, he made a massive contribution to the heritage of the city of Rome, as well.

Birth and Upbringing in a World of War and Politics

Born in the 270s to the future co-emperor Constantius I Chlorus (ca. 250–306) and his common-law wife Helena, Constantine likely spent his early years in the Balkans, where his father held the post of provincial Roman governor. The lives of both parents had changed dramatically by their son's fifteen birthday and perhaps even earlier. By 288 Constantius had accepted a new post in the western province of Gaul, a career move that turned out to be permanent as he climbed the military and political ladder of the later Roman Empire to become junior emperor of Rome's western provinces in 293. Helena did not join Constantius in his move westward. Indeed, as early as the year 288 but certainly by 293, she was abandoned in favour of his new wife, the politcally connected Theodora. In the meantime, the couple's son, Constantine, spent his adolescence and early adult years in the court of one of Rome's two senior emperors, Diocletian, whose realm stretched from the Balkans through Asia Minor toward Mesopotamia and southward into Palestine and Egypt. The nature of Diocletian's rule required that his court, although officially centred in the city of Nikomedia (Iznik, in modern Turkey), was often on the move. As one of the court's most prized courtiers and aides, the young

Constantine travelled with Diocletian throughout the 290s and early years of the 300s, learning the skills required for military and political leadership that would serve him for years to come. By the late 290s he was old enough and experienced enough to play an active role in Diocletian's regime, both as a government official and top military commander.

Political Marriages, Murder, and Career Ascent

In the year 305, while still in his late twenties or early thirties, Constantine's life and career took a dramatic turn. Leaving the East, he now headed to the western parts of the empire to join his father and seek his future there. Constantine had married his first wife, Minervina, by this time and together they had produced a son by the name of Crispus. Whether this union was political in nature cannot be confirmd; Minervina was possibly a relative of Diocletian and thus a pledge of security for closer ties between the otherwise unrelated families of Constantine and Diocletian. Still, the fact that we lose any trace of Constantine's first wife as of 305 to relegation or death just as a new and critical phase of his political career was opening may be telling. By 307 Constantine took up another marriage, this time for purely political ends. Her name was Fausta, and she was the daughter of Rome's just-retired senior emperor Maximian (286–305) and sister to the just appointed junior emperor Maxentius (306–12). Both Maximian and Maxentius were emperors of the West, and it was Constantine's ambition to gain a solid foothold in the western provinces that propelled him into Fausta's embrace. For years Fausta served as a true icon of his regime's self-representation through her depictions in art and on coins, until sometime around the year 326 when Constantine astonishingly ordered her execution under circumstances that are as unclear as they are depressing. Fausta's father Maximian and brother Maxentius proved useful to Constantine for even less time; both were dead at her husband's hand within a few years of Fausta's marriage to Constantine. Whether in alliance or in opposition—and they tried both on Constantine—neither the elder Maximian nor the younger Maxentius could help but succumb to their in-law's stunning rise to sole political power between 305 and 312, culminating with his uncontested claim to the position of senior emperor of the West on October 28, 312 after defeating Maxentius at Rome's Battle of the Milvian Bridge.

Two critical developments help explain Constantine's impressive rise to power between 305 and 312. First, shortly after Constantine joined his father in the western provinces, Constantius himself passed away, leaving his army in his son's hands. Seizing upon this opportunity, Constantine took control of his father's army, trained them, and fought shoulder to shoulder with them in a series of mostly successful campaigns in Britain and northwestern Europe, including the defeat of two Gallic kings whom, with great spectacle, he proceeded to throw to wild animals in the arena at Trier. When Constantine finally marched on Italy in the year 312, he stood at the head of a battle-hardened and loyal army, largely recruited from beyond the Alps and yet ready to follow their commander all the way to the gates of Rome. In a second crucial development of the years 305–12, Constantine embarked upon a long and intense spiritual journey that would bring him to Rome a converted Christian, convinced of his invincibility. By the year 310 Constantine had developed a particularly strong devotion to Apollo and the closely related cult of Sol Invictus ("The Unconquered Sun"). Dreams and visions followed in the years 310–12, reinforcing a belief that he was favoured by the highest and greatest god. By 312 that god had become the Christian God in Constantine's eyes, and it was this God who inspired and encouraged him during his march to Rome. Was this a conversion in the modern sense of the word, something akin to a "born-again" experience? Scholars continue to debate just how profound and sincere Constantine's conversion was but it remains clear that he emerged from his conquest of Rome as an emperor sympathetic to Christianity.

Pagan Rome Has a Christian Emperor

The arrival of a conquering Christian emperor to Rome in 312 would hardly have impressed a city that still had strong pagan affinities and deep local traditions. The city's ruling class may indeed have been apprehensive of Constantine, given that he was not only suspicious in religious terms but also an outsider and usurper who had visited the city at most once in this life, otherwise displaying northern origins and affinities. Constantine went immediately to work in making his imprint. One of his first acts was to raze the neighbourhood associated with his opponent Maxentius's imperial bodyguards and replace it with the foundations of a Christian church, the future Basilica di S. Giovanni in Laterano. This was a clever act of *damnatio memoriae* and re-appropriation that was quickly followed by others, including the renaming of Maxentius's recently constructed and grand Basilica di Massenzio (also known as the Basilica Nova) into the Basilica di Costantino, along with his appropriation of a colossal statue, probably of Trajan (98–117) or Hadrian (117–38), to be refigured in the image of himself and placed in the very same basilica.

The new emperor left Rome for urgent business in the north within a matter of months after these bold interventions in local affairs. He would be back to visit a mere three times over the next twenty-five years of his reign. The very fact that he came back so infrequently reveals a certain level of disinterest on Constantine's part, of course, but it also demonstrates how well he managed to govern Rome from afar. None of his later visits were for the specific purpose of putting down a rebellion or fixing a crisis brought about by his appointed governors, for example, and it is noteworthy that his probable visit in 315 was for the purpose of celebrating his reign through the inauguration of the Triumphal Arco di Costantino. Rome did not love Constantine the emperor any more in later years that they did Constantine the usurper in 312, but they certainly came both to respect him and accept his changes to their way of life. In terms of buildings alone, roughly ten large churches and five major civic projects can be attributed to his age.

By the time that Constantine left Rome for the north in the winter of 312–13, he was approaching forty years old, still married to his young wife Fausta, and still full of projects for the future. Fausta bore him five children between 316 and 323, including the future senior emperors Constantine II (r. 337–40), Constantius II (r. 337–61), and Constans (r. 337–50). Constantine must have taken pride in his growing family and there is even good reason to believe that he had a genuinely close personal bond to his wife for a time. His sense of family was enriched, too, by the return of his mother Helena, who was reunited with him after his ascent to power and honoured with the title of *Augusta* (empress). Whatever satisfaction Constantine may have realized in his personal life in the decades after 312, it still remained true that a man in his position of power, living in dangerous and uncertain times, could ill afford to indulge himself in private affairs. Constantine understood this truth all too well. So it comes as no surprise that he was perfectly ready to make cold calculations about those closest to him if necessary, as he did most dramatically in ordering the executions of his in-laws Bassanius (316), Licinius I (324), and Licinius II (324), and then even more painfully when he condemned to death his eldest son Crispus (326) and the young Fausta herself (326). The motives for such drastic action against family members were slightly different from one case to another. What these murders reveal collectively, however, is the emperor's fixation with public affairs in general and his own political survival and success in particular, whatever the personal cost. His ostensible Christian faith failed to move him to mercy at these and other decisive moments in his reign, prompting questions about how sincere his attachment to the imperatives of Christianity may have been.

Move to Constantinople and Expansion of Christian Rome

These public and political concerns consisted first and foremost of expanding his empire into the East, a feat he accomplished with victory over his fellow senior emperor and brother-in-law Licinius (r. 308–24) in 324. With this victory Constantine claimed absolute control over the entire Roman Empire and proceeded to relocate its main capital to the city of Byzantium, now renamed Constantinople. From this time forward Constantine increasingly devoted his energies to governing his empire. Hundreds of communications emanated from his chancery during the years 312–37. Religious reform and governance were issues he held in high regard and to which he returned regularly. Most memorably, perhaps, Constantine met with his fellow emperor Licinius in Milan in the early months of 313 to formalize the legalization of Christianity across the whole empire, an accord that was finally announced in the city of Nikomedia June 313 and has come to be called the Edict of Milan. Constantine's convocation of the Council of Nicaea (325), a council that produced a new doctrine of the Trinity, was another demonstration of his deep involvement in the empire's religious life. The emperor went on to produce a large body of practical guidelines for the Christian faithful and Church, some of which touched upon the delicate issue of relations between Church and State. Social issues of various sorts interested him as well, including setting up protections for the poor, regulating slavery, and sustaining women's and family rights.

Death and Legacy

Constantine died at age sixty-five on May 22, 337 as he prepared for an ambitious campaign against the Sassanian Persians. His body was then transferred to Constantinople and buried in the Church of the Holy Apostles there. After a bloody palace reorganization, his three sons Constantine II, Constantius II, and Constans I succeeded him as sen-

Fig. 23: Bronze Columns of the Altare del SS. Sacramento,
Basilica di S. Giovanni in Laterano, Rome. Photo courtesy of Peter Hatlie.

ior emperors. Constantine's life had taken him far from Rome for a very long time by the time of his death and yet his name lived on there for centuries in the form of an authoritative legend called The Donation of Constantine. According to the Donation, which began as an invented story as early as the fifth century and then became officialized by the so-called Constitution of Constantine in the ninth century, the emperor accepted baptism in Rome at the hands of Pope Sylvester (r. 314–35) and then proceeded to confer unusual honours and powers on him and on successive popes. Although no part of the Donation was true (except for the existence of Constantine and Sylvester themselves), it remained an influential document legitimizing papal temporal power throughout the Middle Ages.

Constantine's Christianity at the Basilica di S. Giovanni Laterano

Constantine's monumental church architecture in Rome consisted of nine buildings corresponding to Christian Rome's most important and historic churches. Among them are the basilical churches S. Paolo fuori le mura, S. Pietro, S. Lorenzo fuori le mura, S. Sebastiano, and S. Giovanni Laterano. Not all of these were completed before Constantine's death and, in the case of the realization of the Basilica di S. Pietro, the emperor played almost no part. The Basilica di S. Giovanni Laterano was an entirely different story. The first of Constantine's buildings, it was also arguably his most significant. By the time of its inauguration by Pope Sylvester somewhere between the years 318 and 324, it was both a landmark work of ecclesiastical architecture and, practically speaking, the spiritual and temporal home of the newly legalized Church.

Although Constantine did not supervise the actual building of the Lateran, there is good reason to believe that he played a decisive role in choosing the church's initial design and monitoring construction from afar. The Lateran's design was innovative, bordering on revolutionary. Constantine avoided the showy exterior display of pagan religious architecture as well as the intensely private, irregular, and small-scale floor plans of early-Christian house churches. Instead, in his new basilica design he embraced a monumental church plan, adapted from Roman civic architecture in general and imperial building traditions in particular. The church's massive exterior façade was soberly crafted of mere plain brick, while its roomy interior, big enough for 3,000 worshippers at a time, was a grand celebration of light, precious materials, and lavish furnishings. As one modern art historian has put it, the Lateran was conceived of as an audience hall of Christ the King. The first of its kind, this quickly became the prototype of church architecture in all of Western Christendom.

Multiple remodelling programs and additions in later centuries—notably Francesco Borromini's complete reworking in ca. 1645–60—have considerably altered Constantine's original church. Yet upon entering the Lateran today, one can still catch exquisite glimpses of the original church and its furnishings. Four massive bronze columns dating to the second century, which were re-employed by Constantine to support the church's original *fastigium*, still stand in all their brilliance. The fastigium was a magnificent, colonnaded triumphal arch or screen separating sanctuary and nave. Pope Clement VIII (r. 1592–1605) ordered that this massive monument to the Constantinian church be preserved and moved from the nave to Altare del SS. Sacramento, where it is visible today (fig. 23). Moving to the central nave of Borromini's church, one still finds the forty-two columns of beautiful Thessalian *verde antico* marble which adorned the side aisles of the original church. These columns now function as elegant frames for the dramatic, early eighth-century statues of the apostles which now occupy niches in the nave.

In light of what we know about Constantine's activity at the Lateran, it becomes clear that the emperor regarded it as one of his most important endeavors. He initiated construction within weeks of his conquest of Rome in October of 312 and endowed the church with riches that included both the sumptuous architecture and furnishings themselves, along with annual revenues of a minimum 400 gold *solidi*. In his choice of the type of building, the basilica, we see furthermore the very beginning signs of Constantine's move to join the interests and activities of the Roman state with those of the emerging Christian Church. Although such a plan may have seemed absurd (if not impossible) at the time of the Lateran's construction, by the time of Constantine's death, he had worked hard to cement this new configuration by empowering Christians and their clergy in public life and by extending a heavy hand over the Church itself as it emerged from a persecuted to fully legal institution.

Legitimacy and the Arco di Costantino

Like so many other imperial hopefuls of his age, Constantine had a legitimacy problem. In contrast to the best years of the Roman Empire, the people and Senate of Rome could not be easily convinced anymore that pretenders to the imperial throne had either the qualifications to rule well or the best interests of Rome in mind. The previous century had seen emperors come and go in droves, each with a different and often self-serving agenda. Over the course of one particularly bad stretch of the later third century, a new emperor came to power on average every two years, most of them overthrowing one reigning emperor only to be overthrown themselves. The senior emperor Diocletian joined up with his counterpart Maximian to stabilize things during the years 284–305. But upon their joint retirement in 305, the same old problems returned: too many ambitious imperial hopefuls competing for personal power with too little time to govern the Roman people properly. By 312 Constantine finally emerged as one of two emperors to be able to claim uncontested rule in his domain. But neither Constantine in the West nor Licinius in the East could count on the Roman people to readily embrace them. The Arco di Costantino was a hopeful response to Constantine's legitimacy predicament. Dedicated in 315 by the Senate, this was a public monument that broadcast several messages at once about the emperor. One of its messages was about power and prestige, another communicated Constantine's closeness to the gods, still other messages affirmed his kinship with great emperors of old and his ability to be a Rome-friendly emperor. These were visual messages that Constantine, the primary force behind the arch's construction, wanted to put on full public display.

The arch is a visually impressive structure located at the crossroads of three important centres of power in Rome: (1) the Palatino, with its historical association with Rome's foundations as a monarchy under Romulus and an imperial monarchy once

Fig 24: Constantine Addresses the Roman People in the Foro Romano,
Detail of North Façade, Arco di Costantino, Rome. Photo courtesy of Peter Hatlie.

again under Augustus (r. 27 BCE–14 CE); (2) the Via Sacra, a sacred road leading into
the Foro Romano; and (3) the Flavian Valley, home to both a colossal sun statue erected
by Nero (r. 54–68) and the Colosseo built by Vespasianus (r. 69–79). Its position alone
therefore gave the arch a certain importance. But the arch itself was a monument that
exuded a sense of power and importance all on its own. For example, no cost was spared
in bringing together a wild display of precious coloured marble imported from throughout the empire to adorn its façades. So precious were these marbles that many of them
were stripped away by plunderers and subsequent reconstructions.

The marble reliefs that still remain have many different stories to tell about how
Constantine wanted to be seen by his public. One of these is the story of Constantine as
a great conqueror. In fact, the most original part of the monument—a series of detailed
and vividly carved reliefs from Constantine's own day, placed on the middle register of
the west, south and north sides—largely tells the story of Constantine's 312 campaign
across the Alps to Rome via the cities of Milan and Verona. A similar lesson in *imperium*,
or an emperor's power to command, was present in the eight statues of barbarian prisoners embedded in the façade, reminding the Arch's public that Constantine had deci-
sively conquered the northern frontiers before his fateful conquest of Italy.

The arch transmits yet another important message about Constantine, as well: his
special commerce with the gods. The arch is contemporary with the most intense period
of Constantine's personal spiritual journey, a time when he was convinced that he was
favoured by the gods. But which God or gods? The arch answers this very question in several ways. For instance, when approached from its most natural viewpoint, from the Via

Triumphalis to the south, the arch perfectly frames the ancient colossal bronze statue of the god Sol behind it. This statue was erected in the time of Nero but was still standing in all of its glory in Constantine's day just in front of the Colosseo, and by looking through the main central arch of the Constantine Arch from a distance, images of emperor and god became visually superimposed upon one another. Constantine also added a bold if ambiguous inscription to both sides of the arch crediting *instinctu divinitatis* (divine inspiration) for his victory over Maxentius. Last but not least, the arch's many monumental relief sculptures return repeatedly to the themes of Constantine's piety and his close association with gods. Christ is missing from this repertoire, except perhaps in the ambiguous phrase just noted, while a predicable cast of pagan gods closely associated with him are emphatically on display on other panels, including Sol, Apollo, and Hercules. About the time that the arch went up, Constantine also started minting gold coins with his own image on the obverse side and Sol Invictus ("Invincible Sun") on the reverse. This was a way to deliver, in miniature and with more focus and currency, the very same message that he hoped to make with the arch.

Everything about Constantine's Arch was political, even the religious aspects of the monument. Yet some of its features were more explicitly political than others. The arch's inscription was worded in the fashion of a famous inscription at the tomb of the emperor of Augustus, for example, and the iconography of Constantine, young and unbearded, on various reliefs of the arch was reminiscent of Augustan imperial portraiture as well. This association with the founding emperor of Rome, not to mention one of Rome's most successful emperors ever, sought to make a point about Constantine's political achievements and future potential. This was an invitation to see Constantine as the young Octavian Augustus, newly victorious over his own Marc

Anthony at a battle comparable to the Battle of Actium, thus bringing the hope of peace and prosperity to Rome after decades of civil war. These Augustanizing elements were accompanied by numerous reliefs that sought to give Constantine a deeper imperial pedigree still. Spolia from the ages of Trajan, Hadrian, and Marcus Aurelius make up a large part of the decorative program of the arch, and much of this material consisted of sculptural reliefs illustrating emperors hard at work—on the battle field, negotiating treaties, performing civic rituals, hunting, and conducting government business. These Nerva-Antonine emperors were considered to have been some of Rome's best and so were good company for Constantine to keep.

Only the dullest eyes among Rome's senate and people may have been forgiven for failing to grasp the political rhetoric of the arch: an affirmation of Constantine's right to rule with the best of them, based on his suggested imperial pedigree. However, even the dullest would not have overlooked two of the arch's master strokes. First, a now headless Constantine is seated on the speaker's platform or Rostra in the Foro Romano, surrounded by an enclave of enthralled Romans, with depictions of hallowed civic build-ings and symbols of good rule in the background (fig. 24). This relief is of particular interest because it appears to simulate just the sort of relationship—not perfect but still friendly—that Constantine's predecessor, Maxentius, had enjoyed in Rome. To this extent, Constantine's message was that he was not the wild-eyed, foreign warlord that some might take him for but rather a cooperative figure who could be counted to fill his predecessor Maxentius's shoes responsibly. And in a second brilliant move, he went out to prove his worthiness by finishing a number of building projects that his predecessor had started, including the large Basilica Nova as well as the Arch of Maxentius itself, now completed and rededicated as his own Arco di Costantino. Constantine, a worthy succes-sor to the Roman-friendly Maxentius: that was the implicit message of the arch.

Constantine Reinvented at the Basilica dei SS. Quattro Coronati

Despite his truly amazing life story, along with his own best efforts at promoting that story, later generations found that the biography of Constantine could be improved upon. Stories circulated about him for centuries after his death, some attempting to cover-up and correct errors while others exploited his name for gain. It was an awkward fact that Constantine had ordered his own wife's death, for example, prompting some later admirers to skip over or explain away this grievous act in their otherwise sym-pathetic accounts of him. Constantine's wobbliness on important matters of Christian dogma needed a similar fix. Most notably, writers favourable to him learned not to dwell on the fact that the emperor had himself presided over an ecumenical council that decided in favour of the Nicaean dogma of the Trinity over Arianism, only to rehabilitate unrepentant clergy in later years and even receive his last rites at the holy hands of a prominent Arian bishop. The reinvented Constantine of these later centuries enhanced his Christian profile while blunting some of its more offensive details.

Rome's Basilica dei Santi Quattro Coronati preserves one of the most successful and fantastic Constantine-friendly legends of all time. One of Rome's oldest churches, SS. Quattro Coronati was destroyed in 1084 by Norman troops and then rebuilt by the early twelfth century. Within a century of its reconstruction, significant enlargements to the church had taken place, including the addition the Chapel of St. Sylvester. It is on the walls of this chapel that we see a depiction of the so-called Donation of Constantine, a testimony to the vitality of one of the most ambitious stories about Constantine ever circulated, with great implications for an understanding of the relationships between Church and State in medieval Europe.

The Donation had its origins in a fifth-century dossier of the life of Pope Sylvester, a contemporary of Constantine during the years when both the emperor's political power and his commitment to Christianity were visibly on the rise. Sylvester and Constantine certainly met in real life, and the two were jointly responsible for advancing the cause of Christianity in the Roman Empire. The fifth-century *Acta Sylvestri* takes this known history of collaboration between the two men and transforms it into a fantastic tale of high drama. The culmination of this drama has Constantine cured of the scourge of leprosy through the waters of baptism, administered by Sylvester himself. The thirteenth-century walls of the Chapel of St. Sylvester faithfully preserved the main episodes of the *Acta* in a series of four lively and colourful fresco panels. Never mind that there is no historical evidence that the real Constantine ever had leprosy, nor is it true that he was baptized in Rome by Pope Sylvester.

Nonetheless, two additional fresco panels complete this legend of Sylvester and Constantine. Healed and baptized, Constantine now rewards Sylvester for his help by handing him a tiara as a symbol of the rights and honour of imperial temporal power (fig. 22). The last panel then has Constantine leading the pope away in procession on horseback. Constantine is presumably bidding Sylvester goodbye in this scene, as Constantine leaves Rome for his new capital in Constantinople, while Sylvester dons the tiara which effectively added secular, imperial authority to the given spiritual authority of his office.

These were bold statements to make about the nature and scope of papal authority at the time when the Donation was finalized and circulated, ca. 800. Slowly, though, the concept took hold. Papal teaching promoted the Donation as early as 850, and despite occasional challenges from secular rulers and intellectuals in subsequent centuries, its validity held up throughout the West until about the year 1500. Consequently, any reasonably informed visitor of the Basilica dei Santi Quattro Coronati or other sites where the Donation was illustrated might well come away thinking that Constantine was baptized in Rome by the good Nicaean Bishop Sylvester and had, in some fashion, granted his western empire to the same pope. All other things being equal, this legendary narrative of his life rehabilitated Constantine's image in ways that he himself would never had imagined.

Essential Reading

Barnes, Timothy. *Constantine, Dynasty, Religion and Power in the Later Roman Empire.* Chichester: Wiley-Blackwell, 2013.

Eusebius, *Life of Constantine.* Translated by Averil Cameron and Stuart G. Hall. Oxford: Oxford University Press, 1999.

Holloway, R. Ross. *Constantine and Rome.* New Haven: Yale University Press, 2004.

Krautheimer, Richard. *Rome, Profile of a City, 312–1308.* Princeton: Princeton University Press, 1980.

Lenski, Noel, ed. *The Cambridge Companion to Constantine.* Cambridge: Cambridge University Press, 2011.

Marlowe, Elizabeth. "Framing the Sun: The Arch of Constantine and the Roman Cityscape." *The Art Bulletin* 88 (2006): 223–42.

Potter, David. *Constantine The Emperor.* Oxford: Oxford University Press, 2013.

Van Dam, Raymond. *The Roman Revolution of Constantine.* Cambridge: Cambridge University Press, 2007.

Other Places to Encounter Constantine in Rome

- Arco di Giano: probably erected by Constantine.
- Battistero lateranense: with a fresco cycle depicting the main scenes of Constantine's religious life, including legends.
- Musei Capitolini: preserves fragments of a colossal statue of Constantine, once located in Basilica di Massenzio.
- Obelisco lateranense (otherwise called the Obelisk of Thutmose III and Thutmose IV): the oldest and tallest obelisk of Rome, transferred from the Circo Massimo to the Lateran in the sixteenth century with a dedication to Constantine.
- Musei Vaticani, Constantine Room: with a fresco program of the main scenes of Constantine's religious life, including legends, planned by Raphael and painted by his students.
- Basilica di S. Pietro, narthex (north): Equestrian Statue of Constantine by Gian Lorenzo Bernini, dated to 1670.

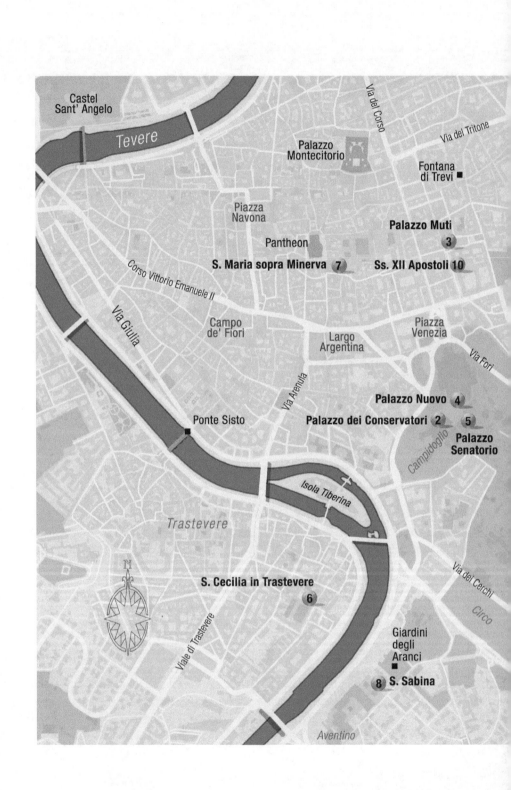

MAP OF ROME FOR CHAPTERS 10–12

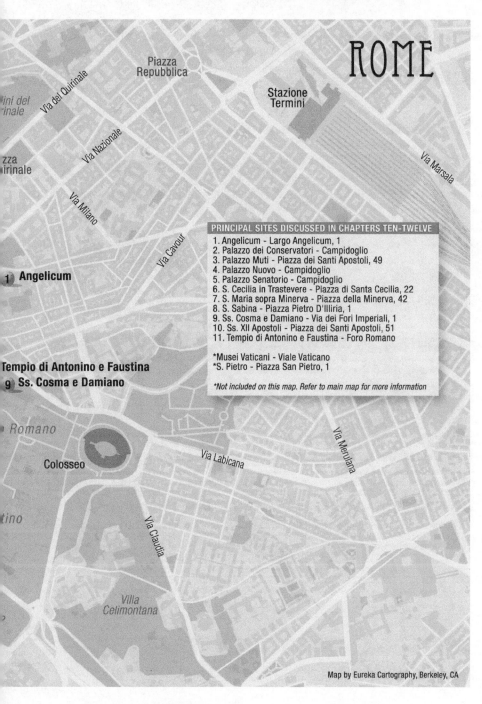

ROME

Piazza Repubblica

Stazione Termini

Via del Quirinale

ini del rinale

Via Nazionale

zza irinale

Via Milano

Via Cavour

Via Marsala

1 Angelicum

PRINCIPAL SITES DISCUSSED IN CHAPTERS TEN-TWELVE

1. Angelicum - Largo Angelicum, 1
2. Palazzo dei Conservatori - Campidoglio
3. Palazzo Muti - Piazza dei Santi Apostoli, 49
4. Palazzo Nuovo - Campidoglio
5. Palazzo Senatorio - Campidoglio
6. S. Cecilia in Trastevere - Piazza di Santa Cecilia, 22
7. S. Maria sopra Minerva - Piazza della Minerva, 42
8. S. Sabina - Piazza Pietro D'Illiria, 1
9. Ss. Cosma e Damiano - Via dei Fori Imperiali, 1
10. Ss. XII Apostoli - Piazza dei Santi Apostoli, 51
11. Tempio di Antonino e Faustina - Foro Romano

*Musei Vaticani - Viale Vaticano
*S. Pietro - Piazza San Pietro, 1

*Not included on this map. Refer to main map for more information

Tempio di Antonino e Faustina
9 Ss. Cosma e Damiano

Romano

Colosseo

Via Labicana

Via Merulana

tino

Via Claudia

Villa Celimontana

Map by Eureka Cartography, Berkeley, CA

Fig. 25: Piazza del Campidoglio, aerial view, Rome. Photo Credit: Alinari / Art Resource, NY.

Chapter Ten

POPE PAUL III (1468–1549, r. 1534–49 CE), MICHELANGELO BUONARROTI (1475–1564 CE), AND THE CAMPIDOGLIO

ROBERT S. DUPREE

Rome's Historic Hill Among Hills

The Capitoline (*Campidoglio*) is a hill for the ages. In ancient times it served as the holiest place in the Roman world, from which auguries were best performed, where two of Rome's most important temples stood—those of Juno and Jupiter—and where Rome's armies thanked the gods in triumph after returning from major military victories abroad. The fall of Rome in the fifth century CE set in motion a period of serious decline that reduced the Campidoglio to an abandoned knoll for a time. But as symbolically important and strategically located as the Campidoglio is, it did not remain barren for long. Indeed, the construction of a series of civic and religious structures followed in the twelfth through fifteenth centuries. Then came a definitive reworking of this important area in the mid-sixteenth century under the guidance of Pope Paul III Farnese (r. 1534–49) and his architect Michelangelo Buonarroti (1475–1564). Three buildings, an inspiring piazza, and the elegant *cordonata* (staircase) ascending from street level to the Campidoglio emerged from this collaboration. Construction of the Palazzo Senatorio, Palazzo dei Conservatori, and Palazzo Nuovo was well underway while Paul and Michelangelo were still alive and was completed after their deaths. The cordonata and piazza were likely completed more quickly, as was a special feature of the new Campidoglio project: the placement of a famous Roman equestrian statue at the piazza's very centre (see fig. 26). When Paul ordered this bronze equestrian statue to be removed from the Basilica di S. Giovanni in Laterano in Rome and placed atop the Campidoglio, there were a number opposed to his decision, including his architect Michelangelo. Nevertheless, the move was carried out, and at the end of 1537, Michelangelo himself was asked to design a pedestal for it. The ultimate consequence was the creation of a new architectural ensemble that was to reshape the city of Rome and become one of the most impressive achievements of Renaissance design.

Michelangelo's plan elicited some groundbreaking commentary and iconographic studies half a century ago. In his influential chapter on the subject, James S. Ackerman notes that "it is difficult to explain the choice of the [equestrian statue of] Marcus Aurelius, not because the meaning of the transfer is unclear, but because it had so many meanings." He goes on to summarize some of them: "Paul III must have stolen the statue because it bristled with symbolic significance, recalling at once the power of the Roman Empire and of Christianity, republican liberties, and the romantic hero popular in the Italian literature of the time" (164–65). Part of that significance may have included an earlier notion that it depicted the emperor Constantine, Rome's last pagan emperor and its first Christian one.

The Good Pope Paul III

One interpretation of the statue has been overlooked, however, by all those who have so brilliantly expounded the program of the Campidoglio. The reason for this oversight is suggested indirectly by Ackerman himself: "The inscription designed for the statue by Michelangelo identifies the rider as Antoninus Pius; though the correct identification had been made in the fifteenth century, it still was not accepted generally, and mattered only to antiquarians" (164–5). The real problem is that our own certainty concerning

Fig. 26: Statue of Antoninus Pius or Marcus Aurelius, Piazza del Campidoglio, Rome.
Photo courtesy of Peter Hatlie.

the identity of the figure as Marcus Aurelius (r. 161–80) causes us to ignore the significance of Paul's and Michelangelo's inscription on the pedestal.

The character of the pope provides several hints. He was a native of the city, a member of the prestigious Farnese family, and the first Roman to be elected pope in 103 years. He had known six popes before him and managed to remain in their favour. As a cardinal he had ample opportunity to develop his considerable diplomatic gifts. He was not elected pope until his sixty-seventh year, and his experience in consultation and diplomacy was without parallel among contemporary churchmen. As Ludwig Pastor puts it, "in the most varying posts ... he behaved so admirably that he was loved by high and low. The Romans especially delighted in his brilliant state; there was therefore general rejoicing at his election as Pope" (24–25). Paul's papacy was a momentous one. During his reign the Protestant sects began to multiply rapidly, and the diplomatic and spiritual atmosphere of Europe changed drastically. Paul was the first pope to respond vigorously to the new era that was beginning. It was he who excommunicated Henry VIII (in 1533), arranged a ten-year truce between Charles V and Francis I (in 1538), approved the foundation of the Jesuit Order (in 1540), unveiled Michelangelo's *Last Judgment* (in 1541), and called the Council of Trent (in 1545–63). He initiated new plans for the city which were to transform it after the great sack of 1527. He was a man who bridged two eras, a Renaissance humanist who brought about major reforms in the spiritual life of the Church and ushered in the Counter-Reformation. Pastor notes that his coronation was a manifestation of the great hopes vested in him: "There was a magnificent torchlight procession, in which the civic magistrates and great nobles took part. ... In its ranks were observable three triumphal cars, the decorations of which symbolized the beginning of a new and more spiritual era; the figure of Rome was supported by those of the church and Faith" (25). Paul fulfilled the expectations, civic and international, of his early reign as a peacemaker and a leader in the attempt to reunify Europe. By coming to the papacy at an advanced age and exercising all the caution that his diplomatic training had taught him, he managed to maintain his own independence of opinion and neutrality in dealing with the Sacred College while still promoting free discussion with his religious and political peers over a range of subjects.

Though the identity of the equestrian figure he placed on the capitol was indeed of purely antiquarian interest, Paul was not ignorant of such concerns. As a youth he had as his tutor the famous Pomponio Leto (1428–98), a major authority on Roman monuments and topography. Leto was the main force during the generation that succeeded Flavio Biondo and Poggio Bracciolini in the study of Rome's antiquities. An admirer of Leto, the outstanding amateur archaeologist Bernardo Rucellai, proposed Antoninus Pius (r. 138–61) as the figure on the horse, though Bartolomeo Platina (1421–81), cofounder with Leto of the Roman Academy, had earlier identified the statue as Marcus Aurelius by using numismatic evidence for his conclusions. Thus Paul and Michelangelo had good authority for designating either of the Antonine emperors as the figure on the horse. But given that the statue had sufficiently strong historical and civic associations to be chosen for the centrepiece of the Capitol, would Antoninus Pius be any more significant in that role than Marcus Aurelius?

Good Emperor Antoninus Pius as a Model for Paul III

When Michelangelo began to restore the equestrian statue, he was certainly aware of the symbolic implications of the pope's choice to set this particular image on this particular hill. The abandonment of the Foro Romano in ruins as the centre of Rome and the re-establishment of civic rule housed on the Campidoglio had occurred during the medieval period. We may well wonder what might be implied by Michelangelo's apparent acceptance of the statue as a portrait of Antoninus Pius, as the inscription on his pediment indicates, rather than of Marcus. As they were both part of that succession of emperors known as the "Antonines," does it really matter that later sixteenth-century and all subsequent scholars refer to the statue as Marcus Aurelius? I believe that it does, and a glance at the achievements and personality of the older emperor reveals why.

Among the surviving histories of the emperors in which Renaissance humanists could have found accounts of Antoninus Pius were Dio Cassius's *Roman History* and the *Historia Augusta*. Dio's account was missing from the manuscript; an epitomizer had to fill in the gaps from other sources. One paragraph is of particular interest:

> Antoninus is admitted by all to have been noble and good, neither oppressive to the Christians nor severe to any of his other subjects; instead, he showed the Christians great respect and added to the honour in which Hadrian had been wont to hold them. For Eusebius Pamphili cites in his *Ecclesiastical History* a letter of Hadrian in which the emperor is seen to threaten terrible vengeance upon those who harm in any way or accuse the Christians and swears in the name of Hercules that punishment shall be meted out to them. Antoninus is said to have been of an enquiring turn of mind and not to have held aloof from careful investigation of even small and commonplace matters; for this the scoffers called him Cummin-splitter. (471–73)

In the *Historia Augusta* biographies, the emperor is also praised:

> In personal appearance he was strikingly handsome, in natural talent brilliant, in temperament kindly; he was aristocratic in countenance and calm in nature, a singularly gifted speaker and an elegant scholar, conspicuously thrifty, a conscientious landholder, gentle, generous, and mindful of other's rights. He possessed all these qualities, moreover, in the proper mean and without ostentation, and, in fine, was praiseworthy in every way and, in the minds of all good men, well deserving of comparison with Numa Pompilius. (103)

Other historians, such as Eutropius, Suidas, and Orosius, make many of the same points about his worthiness as a bearer of the title *pius*, bestowed upon him by the Senate. Antoninus's reputation was enhanced by the order and prosperity of the provinces during his reign, his sensible and just treatment of all citizens, and his generosity, both public and private. In the *Historia* it is reported that "he gave largess to the people, and, in addition, a donation to the soldiers, and founded an order of destitute girls, called Faustinianae in honor of Faustina. Of the public works that were constructed by him the following remain to-day. ... Besides all this, he helped many communities to erect new buildings and to restore the old; and he even gave pecuniary aid to Roman magistrates and senators to assist them in the performance of their duties" (*His. Aug.* 119). Finally, the account ends with the same sentiment expressed by the epitomizer of Dio: "Almost alone of all emperors he lived entirely unstained by the blood of either citizen or foe so far as was in his power and he was justly compared to Numa, whose good fortune and piety and tranquility and religious rites he ever maintained" (*His. Aug.* 131).

Niccolò Machiavelli (1469–1527), in book 1, chapter 10 of his *Discourses on Livy* (1531), writes of the "five good emperors." The last four of this group belonged to the Antonines, a succession of emperors in which each was only a distant biological descendant of his precursor. The means of bypassing the rule of hereditary descent that characterizes most monarchies more or less originated in Julius Caesar's official designation of his grandnephew Octavian as his adopted son. Roman law recognized a bond so established as the legal equivalent of direct biological kinship. Machiavelli's point is that the evidence of the Roman emperors from Nerva to Marcus Aurelius shows that arranging for succession by adoption (that is, choice of a successor based on perceived abilities) was far superior to succession to the throne by heredity, which so often results in disorder, sedition, and cruelty:

> Let a prince therefore look to that period which extends from Nerva to Marcus, and contrast it with that which went before and that which came after, and then let him say in which of them he would wish to have been born or to have reigned. For during these times in which good men governed, he will see the prince secure in the midst of happy subjects, and the whole world filled with peace and justice. He will find the senate maintaining its authority, the magistrates enjoying their honors, rich citizens their wealth, rank and merit held in respect, ease and content everywhere prevailing, rancour, licence corruption and ambition everywhere quenched, and that golden age restored in which every one might hold and support what opinions he pleased. He will see, in short, the world triumphing, the sovereign honoured and revered, the people animated with love, and rejoicing in their security. (35)

Hadrian's attempts to arrange for his succession were complicated by numerous factors, beginning with the death of his first emperor-designate, Lucius Aelius (101–38, r. 138). Antoninus Pius, his subsequent adoptee, was obliged because of childlessness and his own advanced age to designate a successor before accession and adopted, in turn, both Hadrian's adoptive grandson Lucius Verus (130–69, r. 161–9) and the emperor's biological nephew, Marcus Aurelius, to ensure continuity of rule. After Hadrian, Antoninus Pius ruled until his own death in 161, when the adopted duo took command as co-emperors. Subsequently, Lucius, the younger by nine years, passed away prematurely in 169, and Marcus Aurelius ruled alone, dying in 180.

Like Antoninus, a kind person of incorruptible character, genuinely committed to his duties as ruler and little concerned with wealth, fame, or self-promotion, his immediate successor stood for the best qualities imaginable in a person of the highest public authority. The adjective "pius" attached to his name and eventually to his adoptive son's is broader in meaning than our word "pious." It implies, in addition to an obedience to the will of the gods, a caring attitude towards others, a willingness to respect them for their virtues while pardoning their failings, and an ability to rule moderately and with compassion. His statuary depiction as an unarmed warrior mounted on a horse offering a gesture of peace and goodwill seemed an apt symbol for the worthiest form of rule. Although most of these qualities were attributed to the Antonines in general, Antoninus Pius, who was known to have protected Christians, may have been the definitive model. There are parallels between the personalities of Antoninus Pius and Paul: their common diplomatic skills, command of respect from contemporaries, generosity in public and private works. The character of the emperor had obvious public implications for the pope's policies.

Fig. 27: Design for the Piazza del Campidoglio, engraving by Étienne Dupérac, 1568, British Museum, London. Photo Credit: Erich Lessing/ Art Resource, NY.

To be sure, Marcus Aurelius is also depicted in the histories as a model ruler, but his reign was marred by almost continual warfare. If Paul wished to suggest that his reign was to be the beginning of a new golden age for the city of Rome and the renewed piety of the Church, an era of peace conjoining the Holy Roman emperor with the papacy, Antoninus Pius was as apt a figure as he could find for a public and permanent display of those ideals. By placing him at the centre of his native city, he was suggesting that a return to the Rome of Numa Pompilius was not altogether impossible, that Europe could find the refuge from disorder and heresy in his reign that it could not enjoy during the time of his immediate predecessors.

The Campidoglio as Link between Past and Present

Two inscriptions, placed on the wall at the entrance to the Palazzo dei Conservatori on the Campidoglio, point to the original foundation of Rome and its dedication to Jove on the one hand and its new consecration to Christ on the other. This double identity, Paolo Portoghesi points out, is extended to the spatial organization of the architectural ensemble in relation to the whole city:

> As in a pilgrimage, the visitor ascends to a platform which provides a view of the city from which an edifying moral has already been extracted. The new Capitol is the reverse of the old (literally the reverse, since its access has been inverted), but at the same time it represents a continuity of the old building, lying open towards the city and having as its plane of reference the dome of S. Pietro. If we look towards the background, beyond the bulk of the castle-palazzo dei Senatori we see stretching before us a dead, funereal majesty: in the forum and Palatino ruins, nature and history have become inextricably

interwoven. In contrast, the spectacle from the other side is brimful with life. The majesty of the past lives once more in the Capitoline monuments which stand as a demonstration of continuity, where public authority and its alliance with the church are celebrated together. (206–7)

This linking of past and present is given even more cogency when the statue is identified as Antoninus Pius, for the one temple in the Foro Romano that remained visible all through the medieval and Renaissance periods was that of Antoninus and Faustina, originally erected in memory of the emperor's deceased spouse and re-dedicated to the couple by Marcus Aurelius after his adoptive father's death. In the 1569 engraving by Dupérac (see fig. 27), it is visible in the distance beyond the Palazzo Senatorio on the left, in the Foro below. Its monumental dedicatory inscription, while not quite decipherable from the Campidoglio, is easily legible from below. The statue as a representation of Antoninus Pius makes sense on this level of visual perspective and politico-historical allusion for someone standing on the hill, connecting with the inscription on Michelangelo's central pediment. Here, the Campidoglio is united with the forum by means of a narrow vista on either side of the Palazzo Senatorio, Palatino on the right, temple on the left. The temple itself was converted into a church in the eleventh century, and so the building in the Foro that bears Antoninus's name illustrates in an overt fashion the very union of old and new that Portoghesi discusses.

The equestrian statue suggests a procession, with the statues of the Dioscuri as an advance guard and the sculptures placed above the balustrades as witnesses. The direction of this procession, down the monumental staircase and formerly along a narrowing piazza that funnelled into a slender street, marks part of the ceremonial "taking possession" of the city of Rome by the newly-elected pope. It began at the Basilica di S. Giovanni in Laterano, the cathedral church of the city and the original site of the equestrian statue, then proceeded through the Foro Romano up to the Campidoglio, and then finally moved into the city proper and onward towards S. Pietro. The imperial triumph—which in classical times began at the Circo Massimo and culminated at the top of the Campidoglio, where the usual sacrifice was offered before the Tempio di Giove Ottimo Massimo—did practically the same thing, albeit stopping at the Campidoglio. Antoninus Pius, as the ideal civic leader, prefigures Paul as he moves from the ancient to the new, from the pagan to the Christian, from the secular to the sacred centre of the city.

The Palazzo Senatorio is a medieval building completed in the fourteenth century and facing away from the Foro. In effect, it turns its back on the pagan Roman past and points towards the Vatican in an obvious reorientation. However, the past is also deeply buried beneath the hill itself, evident here and there in shards and buried remnants of ancient shrines. During the medieval period it had benefitted from the construction of buildings associated with the governance of the commune. By now the lower plain of the Foro had long been overgrown by enough vegetation to support a bovine population and a cattle market, hence the name "cow pasture," as it was then popularly known. The medieval orientation of the Campidoglio remained unchanged by the later improvements, and the statue of Antoninus Pius was placed facing away from the Foro. Are we to interpret this position, accentuated by the surrounding buildings and the forward movement of the steed on which the emperor rides, as indicative of the new directions taken by a succession of rulers in the past from Augustus to Antoninus and finally to Constantine? Is it simply tracing the path of history as pagan emblems of worship yield to their Christian successors? The Palazzo Senatorio was built over the ancient Tabularium, which once housed the records of Rome, and the Palazzo dei Conservatori over the ruins of the ancient Tempio di Giove Ottimo Massimo. Michelangelo embellished their façades with a double staircase, fountain, and statues for the former and colossal Corinthian pilasters and Ionic columns and entablatures for the latter. These embellishments evoke the grandeur of the sacred building it replaced without denying its role of providing offices and a tribunal for the guilds that had been active in the Foro area cattle market since medieval times.

Michelangelo's Campidoglio after Michelangelo

Michelangelo's plans for the transformation of the piazza of the Campidoglio, begun in 1538, could not be executed all at once. Indeed, it was not near completion until late in the seventeenth century and the pattern of the paving was not even executed until the mid-twentieth century. Speaking of the area as it developed in the course of the next hundred years, Richard Krautheimer notes:

> The Forum Romanum was yet another reminder of Roman antiquity, in indecorous shape at the time and yet highly visible, with the columns of a few temples rising high and famous all over Europe.... Located at the edge of town right behind the Capitoline Hill, it was no longer the wasteland it once had been; it had become a link, as it were, between the built-up town and the *disabitato*. Ever since the mid-sixteenth century impressive structures had been rising along its rim: to the south, on the slope of the Palatino, the Villa of the Farnese, the Orti Farnesiani, and at the foot of the hill, the church of S. Maria Liberatrice, to the north a whole series of churches—S. Nicola de' Falegnami, Cortona's SS. Luca e Martina, S. Adriano, S. Lorenzo in Miranda, SS. Cosma e Damiano, S. Francesca Romana—all except the first two ensconced in Roman ruins and all remodelled in the first half of the seventeenth century. (109–10)

In the second half of that century it was to be further transformed by Pope Alexander VII (r. 1655–67). Well over a century after the decision to shift the equestrian statue, this pontiff moved the cattle market elsewhere and cultivated an unruly expanse of land, turning it into a public green with a tree-lined promenade down its centre, around which the city would continue to be reorganized. As Krautheimer points out, it was only the beginning of a papal program to extend the dominion of the Campidoglio beyond the ancient city walls:

> The renewal of Rome was to extend beyond the city proper; the vast enveloping area of the *disabitato* and its offshoots into the countryside, the highways, were to be integrated with the built-up core and like this core architecturally articulated by the long, sceno-graphic vistas of tree-lined avenues, green *teatri*, as it were. The zone of gardens and fields extending to the Aurelian walls and the highways beyond, like the built-up area, was an integral part of Alexander's Rome, as he envisioned it. (113)

The oval pavement pattern, which art historians have interpreted as alluding at once to the twelve tables of the law, the twelve apostles, astrological signs, and the cosmic order, is so shaped because of the trapezoidal nature of the space and the moundlike elevation of the pavement towards its centre, with the smaller end at the top of the entrance stairs, a kind of massive egg waiting to be hatched by ruler and architect and disclose the next stages of human history. It suggests a power within that will emerge, grow, organize, and change all around it, needing only to have its concealing shell removed. Such is the spectacle presented by the reordered space that ultimately emerged out of the centuries-old mud covering the ancient hill.

A Theatre of Human Time

In *The Architecture of Michelangelo*, Ackerman observes that this twelve-part division also suggests both the shape of a shield and the pavement of a theatre. Since the Campidoglio served mostly as a ceremonial site at which the ritual of power was performed, this theatrical setting suggests yet another complex figure of organization. The remaking of Rome as a city surrounded by yet dominating a vast, staged scene extending all the way to the enclosing third-century Aurelian defence system and beyond, alludes unmistakably to the imperial past. At the same time, its orientation as well as the codes embedded within Paul's and Michelangelo's visual references reflect unmistakably upon their own time and their aspirations for the future.

In a word, the past and future are restaged on the Campidoglio of Michelangelo and his patron Pope Paul III, although neither man lived to see the full completion of his original plans for this space. The architectural imitation of the styles of Greco-Roman antiquity as found here necessarily suggest as much. Ancient ruins, in Rome or elsewhere, are only spectacles of destruction when left in their decrepit states. To build in a classical style not only asserts continuity with the past (or a reaction to a decline in architectural quality suffered during the intervening ages); it also draws attention to the future, suggesting the paths towards renewal and perhaps even inventions that will improve upon what came before. We can see things neither Antoninus nor Marcus could have imagined: the triumph of Christianity that the man mounted on his forward-moving horse witnesses in full view across the city, looking to S. Pietro. Behind him, the mingling of churches and his temple, still visible above the silted-up grounds of the Foro Romano behind the "scena" of the Palazzo Senatorio, is a reminder of the constant presence of the past and its achievements. The public aspect of the city from the stage of the Campidoglio is a kind of theatrical set upon which past, present, and future deeds are acted out. But even though we view and learn how to cope with the present from the spectacle of what came before us, the past is also a spectator. In this sense the statues atop Michelangelo's buildings are not just emblems of bygone days; they are witnesses of what is to come.

Antoninus Pius, seated on horseback, is viewed from the rooftops of the surrounding edifices by an audience consisting of the ghostly but statuesque images of ancient figures, as though he were the sole actor on a grand stage they survey from above. We, the newly-arrived spectators, after being greeted by the first group of statues facing us as they stand on the balustrade at the top of the cordonata by which one mounts to the piazza, look up to him from ground level as the model of righteous rule. Some historians consider the reign of Antoninus Pius as the high point in the history of the Roman Empire. Whether the Renaissance humanists considered his achievement in that light or not, the disorders that were to mark the decline of the empire over the centuries began in the reign of a very worthy successor, Marcus Aurelius. His son, Commodus (r. 161–92), succeeded him in a reign that proved most unfortunate, confirming Machiavelli's point that adoption is superior to primogeniture as a means of promoting righteous and effective rule. Did Marcus somehow fail to learn from the practices of the other "good emperors" how to maintain in perpetuity the principles they practiced? Hadrian and Antoninus Pius seemed more fortunate in their adopted successors.

If Paul had wished to emphasize his stoic piety and intellectual interests, this last Antonine emperor would have been an excellent symbol for his reign; but in looking to the future, the pope must have hoped to suggest much more. According to H. M. D. Parker, Marcus Aurelius's rule was marked by almost incessant warfare, the near bankruptcy of the state, and a disastrous successor in his profligate son, "but apart from these momentous factors in the history of Rome stands out the personal tragedy of Marcus himself, the sacrifice of a life intended by nature for the pursuit of learning to the demands of an active public service" (14). As a symbol of the future, then, Marcus might have appeared rather ominous, compared with his more fortunate precursor. Ultimately, Paul's vision of a future Rome, as architecturally executed by Michelangelo, implies that allusions to the achievements of the past are useful for convincing viewers not only that the grandeur of the past has been reborn in the present but indeed that such greatness has been surpassed.

Essential Reading

Ackerman, James. *The Architecture of Michelangelo.* Harmondsworth and Baltimore: Penguin, 1971.

Argan, Giulio Carlo and Bruno Contardi. *Michelangelo Architect.* Translated by Marion L. Grayson. Milan: Electa Architecture, 2004.

de Tolnay, Charles. *Michelangelo: Sculptor, Painter, Architect.* Princeton, NJ: Princeton University Press, 1975.

Coleman, Nathaniel. "The Individual and the City: Abstract and Concrete." In *The Individual and Utopia: A Multidisciplinary Study of Humanity and Perfection*, edited by Clint Jones and Cameron Ellis, 45–66. London and New York: Routledge, 2016.

Dio Cassius. *Roman History*, Vol. VIII. Translated by Earnest Cary and Herbert B. Foster. Cambridge, MA: Harvard University Press, 1925.

Historia Augusta, Vol. I. Translated by David Magie. Cambridge, MA: Harvard University Press, 1921.

Krautheimer, Richard. *The Rome of Alexander VII, 1655–1667.* Princeton: Princeton University Press, 1985.

Pastor, Ludwig. *The History of the Popes, From the Close of the Middle Ages*, vol. XI. Edited by R. F. Kerr. London: Kegan Paul, Trench, Trübner, 1912.

Portoghesi, Paolo. *Rome of the Renaissance.* Translated by Pearl Sanders. New York: Phaidon, 1972.

Smithers, Tamara. "'SPQR/CAPITOLIVM RESTITVIT': The *Renovatio* of the Campidoglio and Michelangelo's Use of the Giant Order." In *Perspectives on Public Space in Rome, from Antiquity to the Present Day*, edited by Gregory Smith and Jan Gadeyne, 157–86. London and New York: Routledge, 2016.

Other Sites to Encounter Pope Paul III* in Rome

– Palazzo Venezia: large parts the fifteenth-sixteenth century reconstruction of this complex were ordered by Paul.

– Via del Corso: parts of the sixteenth century reconstruction of this road were ordered by Paul.

– Palazzo Farnese: Paul initiates project of construction before he becomes pope, i.e. as Cardinal Alessandro Farnese

– Chiesa di Santo Spirito in Sassia: Paul continues work Sixtus IV to reconstruct the interior of this church.

– Castel Sant'Angelo: Significant parts of interior owe to Paul commissions, including the Loggia di Paolo III and the Sala Paolina.

– Basilica di S. Pietro: The Monumento di Paolo III, located near the papal cathedra in the apse and made by Giuglielmo Della Porta, commemorates Paul.

* For Michelangelo, see chapter 19 in this volume.

Fig. 28: Portrait of St. Thomas Aquinas, fresco by Fra Angelico, 1447–51, Niccoline Chapel, Musei Vaticani, Rome. Photo Credit: World History Archive / Alamy Stock Photo.

Chapter Eleven

ST. THOMAS AQUINAS (1225–74 CE) AT SANTA SABINA, THE ANGELICUM, AND THE BASILICA DI SANTA MARIA SOPRA MINERVA

FR. JAMES LEHRBERGER, O. CIST.

The Angelic Doctor

Even when he is measured by the yardstick for Christian saints, St. Thomas Aquinas stands tall. What other doctor of the Church disparaged his writings as nothing more than straw? Whom else has the Roman Catholic Church canonized as a saint just fifty years after suggesting that he was a heretic? How many other saints drove off, with a burning torch, a prostitute deliberately sent to seduce them? Many of Aquinas's confreres recognized his saintly genius in his time, and the whole of the Church acknowledges it in our time. To come to understand his particular expression of the holy life, it is essential to begin with the fact that for most of his life Aquinas dedicated himself to teaching, writing, and engaging in controversies over religious and philosophical issues. Even though many of his most memorable moments in life took place at the University of Paris, he lived much of his life in Italy, notably in Rome as a resident of the Dominican Order's magnificent Basilica of Santa Sabina. Despite his early canonization, Aquinas's thought has received an uneven reception from his death through to today. One crucial reason for his enduring importance to theologians and philosophers, however, is his solution to the problem of faith and reason. For this and other of his many remarkable insights he is called the "Angelic Doctor," an honorific title that today is reflected in the unofficial name of one of Rome's eleven pontifical universities, the Angelicum (Pontificia Università S. Tommaso D'Aquino).

Naples, Paris, Cologne: The Young Aquinas

Aquinas was born in 1225 into a family of minor nobility in Roccasecca, a town south of Rome. At the age of five he was sent to the nearby Abbey of Monte Cassino for his primary education. Ten years later he began higher studies at the newly founded University of Naples. During his five years there from 1239 to 1244, he studied the liberal arts and natural philosophy, especially the newly translated writings of Aristotle. These studies provided the grounding he needed in later years for his thinking on ethics, natural philosophy, rational psychology, metaphysics, and theology. Moreover, at the University of Naples he became acquainted with and inspired by the friars of Dominic Guzman's (1170–1221) newly founded Order of Preachers, usually referred to as the Dominicans.

Much to the displeasure of his family, the nineteen-year-old Aquinas heeded the call to become a friar, and in 1244 he left the university to don the Dominican habit. Almost immediately, however, members of his family kidnapped him and held him under virtual house arrest in the family castle in Roccasecca for a year. So intent were they on discouraging his Dominican vocation that during his forced confinement they sent a beautiful prostitute, suitably undressed for the occasion, to seduce him. But instead of succumbing to her blandishments, he picked up a burning torch, made the sign of the cross over her with it, and thereby drove her away. Still, Aquinas was never one to let a misfortune go to waste. He used that year of imprisonment to read, study, and memorize the entire Bible. The many thousand biblical quotations and references which later would suffuse his writings owe much to that confinement.

Realizing that they could not dissuade the young Aquinas from his vocation, his family set him free in 1245. Rejoining the Dominicans, he spent the next three years at the University of Paris completing his study of the liberal arts and philosophical sciences under the tutelage of St. Albertus Magnus (ca. 1200–1280), the widely acclaimed "universal doctor" of his day. Then from 1248 until 1252 he studied theology at the University of Cologne with Albertus, whom he had accompanied from Paris. His fellow students at Cologne soon tagged him "the dumb ox" because he was a big, heavy-set man (an "ox") who spoke only when he had something good to say ("dumb"). Albertus, recognizing Aquinas's genius and sanctity, predicted that one day the "bellowing" of this dumb ox would be heard throughout the world. During his Cologne years he was ordained a priest. He also taught his first courses there, on the prophets Isaiah and Jeremiah.

Aquinas in Paris

In 1252 Aquinas's Dominican superiors sent him back to Paris to complete his graduate studies in theology. His main task was to write a commentary on Peter Lombard's *Book of Sentences*, a project that entailed addressing problems raised by Lombard's text. This work was a thirteenth-century equivalent of today's doctoral dissertation which, following the prevailing Scholastic methodology, needed to draw distinctions, to raise questions as well as convincingly answer them, and to cogently address possible objections to his proposed solutions. Aquinas continued to employ this quintessentially Scholastic procedure of commentary-questions-objections-answers in his later works. As he was completing his graduate studies in Paris he also began to write for larger audiences. His *On Being and Essence* (1252–1256) dates from these years. In this small but dense volume—one of the most important treatments of metaphysics ever written—Aquinas draws his famous distinction between "essence" and the "act of existence." This early writing remains a staple for anyone studying Aquinas's thought.

With his formal studies now complete, Aquinas's superiors nominated him for one of the two chairs in Theology held by the Dominicans at the University of Paris. Unfortunately, his appointment to the faculty set off a firestorm. The secular clergy had founded the University of Paris and from the beginning they had held all the chairs of Theology. With the arrival of the Dominicans and Franciscans, however, the secular priests had to hand over four of the twelve Theology chairs to these newcomers. Unhappy with their loss, the priest professors attacked the new religious orders. One of them wrote that these religious should go back to contemplating in their monasteries and leave the apostolic work of teaching to the diocesan clergy. Aquinas responded to this challenge on several fronts. He pointed out that Dominicans were not monks, that is, men completely devoted to contemplation and to living by the fruits of their labour, but rather they lived from the alms freely given to them by the faithful. He further noted that Dominicans indeed contemplated the word and works of God, but by teaching and preaching they handed on to others the fruits of their contemplation, and in so doing they exercised a spiritual work of mercy. Aquinas's answer won the approval of the Holy See and a few months later he assumed his professional duties as a "regent master" (professor). Aquinas held together both prayerful contemplation and the apostolic activity of teaching; he would not separate them, much less set them against each other.

From 1256 until 1259 Aquinas taught at Paris, fulfilling the three tasks of a regent master: teaching his classes, debating disputed points in philosophy and theology, and preaching to the university's students and faculty. The works he wrote during this period include the beginning of his first great theological synthesis, *The Summa Contra Gentiles* ("On the Truth of the Catholic Faith"). This four-volume work is divided into two parts: the first three volumes analyze those truths which both are professed by the Christian faith and are knowable to human reason through philosophical inquiry, such as the existence of one God and the immortality of the human soul. The fourth volume explores those truths which are known only by faith, for example the Trinity and the Incarnation. When his three-year appointment in Paris ended in 1259, he was sent to Italy, and from 1259 until 1264 Aquinas lived and worked primarily at the papal court in Orvieto. There he completed the *Summa Contra Gentiles*, compiled a running commentary on the four Gospels from the Church Fathers, and wrote magnificent eucharistic hymns such as the *Ave Verum Corpus* ("Hail True Body") still sung in churches today.

Aquinas's *Summa Theologiae* and Rome

Sent by his superiors in 1265 to the Dominican general house at Santa Sabina in Rome to establish a *studium* (house of studies) for young Dominicans, Aquinas had a free hand to organize the young friars' studies as he thought best. This assignment also gave him the opportunity to begin the work for which he is most famous, the *Summa Theologiae*.

Aquinas wrote the *Summa* to correct the faulty organization of theological studies that prevailed in his time. Beginning theology students were taught the individual books of the Bible and different Christian writings in no proper order. Such teaching imparted knowledge of particular aspects of the faith, but it failed to convey the sense of the Christian revelation as a whole. Aquinas saw the need to present a synthesis of the entirety of sacred teaching in a manner suitable to the instruction of "beginners." Above all, future Dominican initiates needed a bird's-eye view of the entire Christian gospel. These seminarians heretofore had been taught about virtues and sins without learning how they fit into the whole program of the Christian faith. The recovery of Aristotle—whose ethics, natural philosophy, metaphysics, and rigorous rationality he had first encountered in his studies at Naples and now integrated into his own thought—enabled him to develop and articulate a much broader science of Christian doctrine in the *Summa* than had ever been attempted by earlier theologians.

This great work's *First Part* begins with God One and Three, and then moves to his Creation, especially his creation and providential guidance of the human race. The *Sec-

ond Part considers human acts, the different factors which make them virtuous or sinful, and God's law and grace, which are the sources of their goodness. Its *Third Part* culminates in the account of Christ who at once is both God and human. This part continues with an uncompleted discussion of Christ's continued presence to the faithful in the Sacraments. Also left unwritten was his proposed account of Creation's return to God in the Last Judgment, heaven, and hell. Still, he had completed enough of the *Summa* that future readers could see the doctrines and morals of the Christian religion as a unified whole. Aquinas's *magnum opus* remains a work to be carefully read and studied by all who are eager to learn Christian thought. In fact, the *Summa Theologiae* may well be the finest account of Christian wisdom ever written.

International Fame, Controversy, and Death

After working steadily in Rome from 1265 until 1268, Aquinas's Dominican superiors again sent him to Paris as a regent master. This return to his old chair was due to the controversy over faith and reason then raging at the Sorbonne. The very brilliance of Aristotle's accounts of logic, nature, metaphysics, and ethics posed a problem for Christian theologians. Aristotle had developed a rich account of the world that not only contradicted several central tenets of the Christian faith but also implicitly denied the very possibility of divine revelation. The "Averroists" or "radical Aristotelians" who dominated the faculty of liberal arts by this time were so attached to the teachings of this ancient Greek philosopher and his most able medieval interpreter to date—the Islamic Andalusian scholar Averroes (1126–98)—that they came to be accused of several controversial claims. Notable among these were the perceived beliefs that the world was uncreated and necessarily eternal, that God had no knowledge of or providential guidance over human events, and that the human soul was neither personal nor immortal. According to their critics, some of their students began to doubt or even deny their Christian faith; after all, why should anyone accept the irrational superstitions taught by the scriptures rather than the objective truths discovered by Aristotle? In reaction to these events, the Franciscan followers of St. Augustine in the Sorbonne Theology faculty, who traditionally favoured the idealistic Plato over what they viewed as a largely materialistic Aristotle, started to look with a jaundiced eye on the whole Aristotelian enterprise. They began to assert that the brackish "water" of philosophical speculations, as they put it, should not be allowed to corrupt the "good wine" of God's word.

Arriving in Paris early in 1269, Aquinas immediately threw himself into the fray. He saw the recovery of Aristotle as an opportunity—even a gift—from God. Convinced that Aristotle provided tools which enabled the Christian faith to be synthesized and harmoniously developed, he wrote illuminating commentaries on several of Aristotle's most important works. Although Aristotle was a pagan, he had discovered truths that Christians could use to understand, explain, and defend their faith. Moreover, those parts of Aristotle's teachings which contradicted the faith could be shown to be merely his personal opinions rather than actual knowledge. Thus, Aquinas argued against the Aristotelian Averroists from reason as well as from revelation for the existence of a personal creating God, for the individuality and immortality of the human soul, and for the freedom of the human will. Nonetheless, his stance on these and other bitterly controverted questions earned him the enmity of both the Franciscans in the theology faculty and the secular Aristotelians in the liberal arts faculty.

With the completion of his second Paris regency in 1272, Aquinas undertook the task which proved to be his final one. His Dominican superiors charged him with organizing a major house of studies, a *studium generale*, in Naples. This house of studies would be associated with the University of Naples where he first had matriculated as an undergraduate in 1239. He established this house and taught there in 1272 and 1273, during which time he also began writing the *Third Part* of the *Summa Theologiae*. On December 6, 1273, however, Aquinas experienced a vision which led him to cease work on the *Summa*. Receiving in this vision a glimpse of God, he saw that all his writings so paled before the divine reality that he declared: "compared with the things I have been shown, all I have written seems to me straw." Three months later, on his way to a Church council, Aquinas fell ill and was taken to the Cistercian monastery of Fossanova, located about an hour south of Rome, where he died. It was March 7, 1274; he was forty-nine years old.

Aquinas's Legacy

Even in death, Aquinas found no respite. Three years to the day after his death, on March 7, 1277, the Augustinian-inspired bishop of Paris condemned 219 propositions which he deemed tainted with Averroistic principles. He claimed that, though these philosophical propositions contradicted the faith, they were being taught as true at Paris; a few days later the bishop of Oxford echoed the Parisian condemnation. Since Aquinas had held several of these propositions, his reputation came under renewed attack. Members of the Franciscan Order supported the posthumous condemnation while most Dominicans defended his teaching as thoroughly orthodox. Debate over the issue continued until he was canonized a saint in 1323, and the Condemnation of 1277 was held to be inapplicable to him.

By that time, however, the damage to his legacy had been done. For fifty years not only had Aquinas's thought been held under a cloud of suspicion, but the intellectual impetus he spearheaded had evaporated. During this half-century, philosophers and theologians went off in other directions, and the kind of wisdom-seeking theology that he had championed faded away almost everywhere except in the Dominican Order. New trends in philosophical and religious thinking emerged and these helped prepare the way for the subsequent secularization of philosophical thought in the West. Concretely, the Condemnation of 1277 set in motion a chain of events which included a return to the hair-splitting character of late medieval theology, the Renaissance humanists' reaction against the sterility of post-Thomistic theology, the development of non-teleological natural science, and the anti-supernatural thrust of the Enlightenment. By the turn of the nineteenth century, the Western intellectual tradition, which in some ways had reached its high-water mark in Aquinas, was almost entirely secularized in a way that ignored or even opposed Christian philosophical inquiry and insights.

Still, Aquinas's thinking and influence survived in some places. Despite the late medieval eclipse of Aquinas's thought, a partial recovery of it began during the Renais-

Fig. 29: *Triumph of St. Thomas Aquinas over the Heretics*, fresco by Filippo Lippi,
Cappella Carafa, Basilica di S. Maria Sopra Minerva, Chapel, Rome.

Photo Credit: Mondadori Portfolio
/ Art Resource, NY.

sance, and, with peaks and valleys, has continued to this day. During the Renaissance a particular version of Thomism reappeared and it had some influence throughout the sixteenth century. Disciples of Aquinas, especially those associated with the University of Salamanca in Spain such as Francis de Victoria (1492–1546) and Francis Suarez (1548–1617), helped lay the groundwork for the development of international law. The Spanish Dominicans Bartholomew de las Casas (ca. 1484–1566) and the aforementioned De Victoria, inspired by the teachings of Aquinas, defended the humanity of the indigenous Americans against the Europeans who wished to enslave and exploit them. Further, Aquinas's theology proved vital to the Council of Trent (1545–65).

This revival of Aquinas's thought ground to a halt in the seventeenth century, however, when certain conservative Thomistic theologians opposed the discoveries of Copernicus and Galileo. The embarrassment to the Church caused by the Galileo affair landed Aquinas once more on the back-burner. The steady advance of scientific materialism throughout the eighteenth and nineteenth centuries, however, led Catholic thinkers to look for an orthodox and rational account of the world which could meet the philosophical challenges posed by the now firmly entrenched proponents of materialistic explanations of reality. They found an resource in Aquinas's thought. During the second half of the nineteenth-century,

Fig. 30: *Elephant and Obelisk*, sculpture by Gian Lorenzo Bernini, 1667,
Piazza della Minerva, Rome. Photo courtesy of Peter Hatlie.

interest in Aquinas's thinking began to gather steam, culminating in Pope Leo XIII's 1879 encyclical *Aeterni Patris* calling for the revival of Thomistic study and thought. Pope Leo's clarion call was heard, and throughout the twentieth century a genuine and intense renewal of interest in Aquinas's writings emerged within Catholic (and some non-Catholic) intellectual circles. Still, a wide range of divergent and sometimes unsympathetic interpretations of his thought developed as well. As a consequence of these conflicting forces, Aquinas's thought once again went into partial eclipse over the course of the late twentieth century. At present, Thomism is making a modest but real comeback, especially and unexpectedly in Anglo-American circles. Leading voices in the Thomistic revival of the past century include Étienne Gilson (1884–1978), Jacques Maritain (1882–1973), Bernard Lonergan (1904–84), and Alasdair MacIntyre (1929–).

Aquinas on Faith and Reason

Why is it that, despite waxing and waning over the centuries, interest in Aquinas's thought has never fully disappeared and recoveries always have followed its eclipses? His understanding of the relation between the Christian faith and human reason primarily accounts for this fact. Aquinas's understanding of their connection is a striking alternative to other views on this issue. Many continue to assert, as did the Sorbonne philosophical elites of old, that the only correct understanding of reality is that which philosophical and scientific reason discovers, while faith-rooted accounts traffic in irrational nonsense. Others, in ways reminiscent of some medieval theologians of the Sorbonne, reverse the relation: faith alone reveals God's plan while reason is nothing more than a problem-solving ability competant only insomuch as it allows us to create the technology to build snazzier computers, cure cancer, and forge bigger nuclear bombs. However, Aquinas rejects both dogmatic rationalism and religious fundamentalism. He maintains that both reason's ability to understand first principles and divine revelation are complementary gifts from God. The two must never be confused with each other, any more than they should be separated from one another. In fact, he teaches that they mutually strengthen one another: because of the Christian faith, human reason becomes "more rational"; because of sound thinking, the faith becomes more credible.

Aquinas at the Basilica di S. Maria Sopra Minerva and the Angelicum

While Aquinas is rightly associated with Paris, his connection with Rome is even stronger. In fact, his enduring influence owes more to Rome than to any other place. As noted above, Aquinas began writing the *Summa Theologiae* at Santa Sabina's in Rome. Shortly after he left Italy for his second Paris regency, the Dominicans started moving the Santa Sabina house of studies to their convent in the very heart of Rome, to the Basilica di S. Maria Sopra Minerva, located right near the Pantheon. Though originally built as a shrine to the Roman goddess Minerva, it eventually became a Christian site and in 1265 Pope Clement IV (r. 1265–68) turned it over to the Dominican Order. From 1288 until the newly constituted Italian state closed it in 1873, the S. Maria Sopra Minerva complex housed the Dominican studium in Rome and, for a while, the Inquisition. The mission of this house of studies was to preserve and advance the teachings of Aquinas. Indeed, in 1577 it received the name "The College of St. Thomas Aquinas."

Construction of the complex's basilica began in 1280. Originally designed as a Gothic church (the only one in Rome), subsequent reconfigurations unfortunately obscured its Gothic structure. Though the church houses several valuable works of art, its jewel is the Cappella Carafa dedicated to Aquinas and constructed on the basilica's right transept. The Florentine artist Fra Filippo Lippi (1406–99) adorned its walls and vault with exquisite paintings, three of which portray Aquinas. *The Triumph St. Thomas* (see fig. 29) pictures the angelic doctor overthrowing various heretics through the liberal arts, philosophy, and theology (personified as women). Filippo Lippi adapts an annunciation scene to his theme in *Aquinas presents Cardinal Carafa to the Virgin*. In the *Miracle of the Book*, Christ on the cross says to the praying Aquinas, "you have written well of me, Thomas." In the church's piazza, Bernini's elephant, carrying an obelisk on its back, greets the visitor with the inscribed words "a strong mind is needed to support real knowledge." Bernini's *Elephant and Obelisk* (see fig. 30) and its inscription, which were completed while the Dominicans still housed their studium at this site, well prepare the visitor entering the church to contemplate the Thomistic treasures it contains.

Though driven from the S. Maria Sopra Minerva complex in 1873, the College of Aquinas continued in temporary locations for sixty years until the 1920s, when it found a home in its present location on the Quirinal Hill overlooking the ancient Foro Romano.

It is now officially named "The Pontifical University of St. Thomas Aquinas," though it is called the "Angelicum." Due in large part to the efforts of the faculty of this school through the centuries, the heritage of Aquinas's thought remains alive and robust. The buildings of the university long predate its twentieth-century foundation. A Dominican convent stood on the site since the thirteenth century, and the Church of Dominic and Sixtus was erected on the foundations of an older church in the sixteenth century. Statues of Dominic and Pope Sixtus II (r. 257–58) by Carlo Maderno (1556–1629) and Marcantonio Canini (1622–69) decorate the exterior of this church. Within the church there are several memorials to Dominic and prominent Dominicans, including the *Apotheosis of St. Dominic* by Domenico Maria Canuti (1625–84) in the ceiling of the nave and a burial monument to Hyacinthe-Marie Cormier, O. P., Master of the Dominican Order during the years 1904–16 and beatified by Pope John Paul II (r. 1978–2005) in 1994.

Conclusion

The life of Aquinas shows that adversity can be the mother of wisdom. When imprisoned by his family over his decision to become a Dominican, he undertook a profound study of the scriptures. Opposition to members of religious orders engaging in education led him to offer a stirring defence of the Dominican way of life. Failures within medieval religious education spurred him to write the *Summa Theologiae*. Problems arising from the respective claims of philosophy and revelation generated in his mind a solution which made ample room for both. The continuing relevance of his thought through the centuries is witness to Aquinas's perennial wisdom.

Essential Reading

Aquinas, Thomas. *The Summa Theologica of Thomas Aquinas*. Edited and translated by Fathers of the English Dominican Province. 3 vols. New York: Benziger, 1947.

——, *Summa Contra Gentiles*. Translated by Vernon J. Bourke. 4 vols. Notre Dame, IN: University of Notre Dame Press, 1975.

——, *Selected Writing*. Edited by Ralph McInerny. New York: Penguin, 1998.

——, *Introduction to Thomas Aquinas*. Edited by Anton Pegis. New York: Modern Library, 1965.

Chesterton, G. K. *Saint Thomas Aquinas: The Dumb Ox*. New York: Doubleday, 1956.

Gilson, Étienne. *The Christian Philosophy of Thomas Aquinas*. New York: Random House, 1956.

Lonergan, Bernard J. F. *Verbum: Word and Idea in Aquinas*. Notre Dame, IN: University of Notre Dame Press, 1967.

MacIntyre, Alasdair. *Three Rival Versions of Moral Inquiry*. Notre Dame, IN: University of Notre Dame Press, 1990.

Maritain, Jacques. *Art and Scholasticis, and the Frontiers of Poetry*. Translated by Joseph William Evans. New York: Charles Scribners Sons, 1962.

Pieper, Joseph. *Guide to Thomas Aquinas*. San Francisco: Ignatius, 1996.

Torrell, Jean-Pierre. *Saint Thomas Aquinas*. Translated by Robert Royal. 2 vols. Washington, D.C.: Catholic University of America Press, 1996–2003.

Other Places to Encounter Aquinas in and near Rome

- Musei Vaticani, Stanze di Raffaello, Stanza della Segnatura: Aquinas is pictured in the *Disputa* fresco

- Niccoline Chapel of the Musei Vaticani with its mid-fifteenth-century frescoes by Fra Angelico, one of them (in the arch) depicting Aquinas (see fig. 28).

- Pontifical Academy of St. Thomas Aquinas: located in the Villa Pia or Casino Pio IV in Vatican City and tasked with studying and disseminating Aquinas's thought.

- Convento di San Domenico in Orvieto (north of Rome), where a fourteenth-century fresco commemorates Aquinas's sojourn there in the years 1261–65.

Fig. 31: Memorial Tomb to Maria Clementina Sobieski, by Pietro Bracchi, 1742,
Basilica di S. Pietro, Rome. Photo courtesy of Peter Hatlie.

Chapter Twelve

MARIA CLEMENTINA SOBIESKA (1702–35 CE) AT THE BASILICA DI S. PIETRO, PALAZZO MUTI, AND THE BASILICA DEI XII SANTI APOSTOLI

ROMAN WARDEN

Polish Heiress, Pretender Queen of England, Roman Princess

She never founded a republic, led an army, wrote a treatise, or frescoed a chapel. But in the history of Rome, no one's story is more romantic and more poignant than that of Maria Clementina Sobieska. *Hamlet's* Polonius would classify its genre as romantic-historical-comical-tragical-swashbucklerical-picaresque. A savvy Hollywood producer might see in it the plot for a blockbuster film that would appeal to most every demographic. Clementina's odyssey to Rome featured the *dramatis personae* of a fairy tale: an honourable king, a beautiful princess imprisoned in a castle, and a brave and loyal knight sent to her rescue. Her journey to Rome alone is an adventure worth retelling. But it is in Rome that the story is most human and most affecting, and it is appropriate that the tale of a Pole, a Briton, and an Irishman should conclude in Rome—the setting for so many dramas featuring an international cast, both then and now.

Seemingly England was her destiny. Even in the cradle and later by her playfellows, Clementina had been jocularly called "Queen of England." By the time she was seventeen years old, this prognostication technically came true. Clementina was the grand-daughter of King John III Sobieski of Poland (r. 1674–96), one of Europe's most notewor-thy kings following his victory over an invading Ottoman Turkish army at the Battle of Vienna (1683), for which he was hailed the saviour of Western Christendom. Her father was James Louis Sobieski (1667–1737), who as a mere adolescent also fought at Vienna; her mother was Hedwig Elizabeth of Neuberg (1672–1722), one of Europe's wealthiest countesses. Both of Clementina's parents were well integrated into the age-old network of European royal family politics long before their daughter was born. The family's Eng-lish alliances, for example, included the sponsorship of Henrietta Maria, queen consort of England and wife to King Charles I (r. 1625–49), who was also godmother of Clemen-tina's father, James. This English alliance grew stronger (if more complex) in 1719, when Clementina herself was married to James Francis Edward Stuart, Prince of Wales, son of the deposed English king James II (r. 1665–88), and pretender to the English throne from 1701 until his death in 1766. In theory, if not in fact, she would have been queen of Eng-land by virtue of marrying James, the "Jacobite" (from *Jacobus*, Latin for James) pretender to the throne of England. As it turned out, Clementina would become a "queen of Eng-land" who never saw England, living the first half of her brief life in her homeland of the Commonwealth of Poland and Lithuania and the last half in Rome. Her husband James never was crowned, dying in Rome with the nickname of "Old Pretender." Clementina died in Rome at age thirty-two and is now buried in the Basilica di S. Pietro (see fig. 31).

A Challenging Marriage Plan

The first of many difficult challenges in Clementina's life began with her family's decision to offer her in marriage to James the Old Pretender. James had been living in exile since his failed attempts to take back his father's throne from his half-sister Anne (r. 1702–14) in 1708 and then again from his second cousin George I (r. 1714–27) in "The Fifteen" uprising of 1715. After these failures, James settled in Rome as an exile, and from there he and his advisors proposed marriage to Clementina. Upon hearing of the couple's betrothal, Britain's King George I grew concerned about this new potential advantage for his rival for the British throne and ordered his ally Charles VI (r. 1711–40), Holy Roman emperor and king of Austria, to prevent the marriage. George had reason to worry: there was still much support for the Stuarts in Britain, in particular among Scottish Highlanders, Irish Catholics, and some English Tories, who, when a toast was offered to the king at dinners, would surreptitiously raise their wine glass over their water glass before drinking, a sign of allegiance to "the king over the water." But that king, James, was passed over for the throne in 1714, as were the next forty in the line of succession, all Catholics, in favour of George, the closest Protestant claimant, from the kingdom of Hanover. With his claim to the throne tenuous and many in Britain still loyal to the Jacobite cause, the unpopular George was all the more worried when James became engaged to a daughter of the house of Sobieski. As Poland was an elective monarchy, James Louis Sobieski had not succeeded his father John III as king, but he was still from one of Europe's most important families, related to royalty throughout the continent, and Poland was still a powerful kingdom.

James charged an Irish Jacobite adventurer, Charles Wogan (ca. 1698–1752), also known as Chevalier Wogan or Captain Wogan, with finding him a Catholic princess, and Wogan eventually settled upon Clementina as the ideal choice. After bringing together James and Clementina Sobieska, Wogan later wrote about the adventure, first in English in 1722, just three years after the wedding, and again in 1745 for a French audience more interested in entertainment than politics. It is on the basis of these two accounts, the first restrained and documentary and the second romantic, that we can construct the difficulties that Clementina faced in leaving her homeland and coming to Rome.

Romantic Road to Rome

Wogan was from an old Catholic family of Kildare (Ireland) that had remained loyal to the Stuarts during the English Civil Wars. He had first demonstrated his own valour in "The Fifteen" (1715) revolt against King George I, when he had fought for James, been taken prisoner, and then, before a likely death sentence could be carried out, had escaped from London's Newgate Prison. From there he made his way to France and first made contact with James's advisors about a marriage plan with the Sobieski family. James's Scottish followers convinced him, however, that it would harm his reputation in Britain to rely so much on the Irish Catholic Wogan, and so instead Sir John Hay of Cromlix (1691–1740), the Jacobite Duke of Inverness (Scotland) and a rising star in James's inner circle, took up the task. By 1718 Hay was sent to escort Clementina, accompanied by her mother, from her father's court in Silesia to Rome under the pretext that they were pilgrims on the way to the Holy House in Loreto (Italy). James's court in exile failed to keep secret the engagement and word soon reached the ears of King George's ministers and spies in Europe. Hay could not get the mother to recognize their danger; she insisted on stopping along the way to spend a week with her brother, the bishop of Augsburg, and then "found that she just had to have her jewelry mended and reset by the craftsmen of that city" (Wogan, *Memoirs* 45). The emperor's orders reached Innsbruck just before they did and in September of 1718, the princesses, mother and daughter, found themselves prisoners in the care of General Heister, Innsbruck's governor.

In such a predicament, James had only one option: "to employ a man so gifted in matters of escapes" (*Memoirs* 49), as Wogan says about himself in his pamphlet, reminding the reader of his earlier Newgate Prison adventure. The Irishman Wogan forgot about the earlier Irish snub and accepted the commission without delay:

> Chevalier Wogan was a dutiful subject, for whom danger and even death counted as nothing when it came to carrying out the orders or avenging the honor of his Prince; thus he did not hesitate an instant as to the decision he had to take. He saw clearly, however, that if he failed in his attempt, he could only expect to be put to death on a scaffold in Germany; or, what he envisaged with greater horror, be sent back to King George of England. (*Memoirs* 47)

And so Wogan left on his secret mission, known then only to James and to Pope Clement XI (r. 1700–21), who sent him on his way with a collection of spurious passports.

After avoiding several close-calls on the road—spies, informers and even an arrest warrant—Wogan arrived in Innsbruck disguised as a French merchant and found a way to enter the house where the princesses were being held. They enthusiastically agreed to an escape attempt, provided that Wogan first obtain the approval of Clementina's father back in Poland. Initially, James Sobieski wanted nothing to do with "a mad and foolish project .... The season for such Quixotic escapades had long passed" (*Memoirs* 51). Yet Wogan's devotion to his pretender king so impressed Sobieski that he relented, putting his wife and daughter completely under the Irishman's command. Wogan proved worthy of this trust. Clementina would escape her house arrest and flee Innsbruck for Italy. By Wogan's account, she "laughed happily all the way" (*Memoirs* 99) as she was freed from her imprisonment on April 27, 1719 by Wogan and his collaborators, including Major Richard Gaydon, Captain Luke O'Toole, and Captain John Missett, fellow Irishmen and Stuart loyalists fighting in exile for France. Clementina brought with her a large package containing, among other items, an engagement gift from James the Pretender with the jewels of the House of Stuart, as well as her own jewels. Within a matter of weeks, after negotiating a variety of mishaps and dangers during their journey over the Brenner Pass connecting Austria and Italy, the party arrived in Venetian territory and sang a *Te Deum* in thanks for their safe arrival.

A Stuart Royal Household in Rome

On May 9, 1719 came the wedding between James the Old Pretender and Clementina in Verona. However, since James was at that time in Spain as part of yet another failed Jacobite attempt to invade Britain, the marriage was by proxy. Soon afterward Clementina arrived in Rome, accompanied by Wogan, and was greeted with adulation by both pope and people. Their actual wedding occurred on September 1, 1719, once James returned. They soon moved into a palace provided them by Clement XI facing the Piazza dei Santi Apostoli, with its historic Basilica dei Santi XII Apostoli ("Church of the Twelve Holy Apostles"). The latter soon became the Stuarts's local parish, a few dozen yards from the Stuart court in exile: Palazzo Muti, renamed Palazzo del Re ("The King's Palace") and today known as Palazzo Balestra. A year later, the couple gave birth to a son who would become the stuff of song and legend, Charles Edward Stuart (1720–88), better known as Bonnie Prince Charlie. On that day the College of Cardinals came to kiss his little hands; the fountains ran with wine and fireworks illuminated the Roman sky. Five years later would come a second son, Henry Benedict Stuart (1725–1807), the future Cardinal Duke of York, baptized within hours of his birth by Pope Benedict XIII (r. 1724–30).

For years to come, James and Clementina were lionized by the Romans who were thrilled to have a Catholic royal family living among them in the papal city. The Stuarts were, for example, granted three boxes at the opera rather than the usual one for monarchs, in view of the fact that they were the king and queen of three kingdoms: England, Ireland, and Scotland. So too were they given a summer residence in the Castelli Romani, now the municipal building in Albano. Their sons were adored and Clementina in particular was beloved. Wogan writes of the aura of adoration that surrounded her in her earlier years as pretender queen:

> And [in Rome] she became the Admiration of all People, for the Beauty of her Person, her
> Sweetness of Temper, and Vivacity of Wit; but above all for her Virtue and Conduct, in all
> which she was so conspicuous, that even her greatest Enemies who have since travelled
> that Way, and made the strictest Enquiry into her Character, have not been able to object
> any Thing to her Merit, but are forced to allow her justly possessed of all the great and
> good Qualities that can be thought necessary to adorn a Court. (*Female Fortitude* 40)

This aura of hope and admiration that surrounded Clementina and James could not, however, stand up to some of the more bitter realities facing them. For one, papal largesse could only go so far and, with so many Jacobite exiles dependent upon them, James decided that there was not money to establish a separate household for Clementina, as was typical for queens. This was the first occasion of marital strife and more were to follow.

Far greater animosity between James and Clementina arose over the education of Prince Charles. James was so devout a Catholic that, after the deaths of his two Protestant half-sisters, Queens Mary II (r. 1689–94) and Anne (r. 1702–7), he still refused to deny his faith, even though the British crown was his for the taking had he been willing to convert. He was that rare creature—a king willing to sacrifice an earthly crown for a heavenly one—though he dearly sought after both. But he scrupulously avoided the error of his father who was widely perceived as a Catholic bigot, and instead proclaimed a policy of religious toleration for Anglican, Catholic, Presbyterian, and dissenter alike. He sponsored Protestant chaplains at the Palazzo del Re for his Protestant followers. Furthermore, the Cimitero Acattolico outside the Aurelian walls (where John Keats's bones lie) began after James requested that Clement set aside a space for the burial of Protestant Jacobite exiles. And so, though he had appointed an Irish Catholic priest to teach Charles his catechism, he named the Protestant James Murray, earl of Dunbar

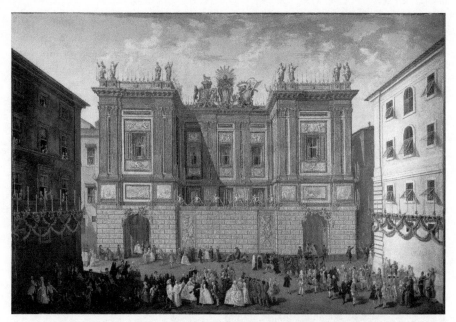

Fig. 32: *Prince James the Old Pretender Receiving his son Henry in front of Palazzo del Re*,
oil painting by Paolo Monaldi, Scottish National Portrait Gallery, Edinburgh.
Photo Credit: National Galleries of Scotland, Dist. RMN-Grand Palais / Art Resource, NY.

(1690–1770), as governor of the young prince in order that the boy be comfortable with and so prepared to rule a kingdom primarily Protestant. The intensely pious Clementina was sure that this would entail proselytism and endanger her child's eternal soul. This dispute was part of a larger conflict between two factions of Jacobites: Murray and his brother-in-law Hay, Duke of Inverness, were widely despised by other Jacobites, both Catholic and Protestant. Clementina found them insulting, and most shared her judgment. Yet James remained loyal to them, likely because of their prominence and because they had been loyal to him. That loyalty even spawned an ugly rumour that James was having an affair with Hay's wife Marjorie, something the Hanoverians made much of. It was, however, a falsehood, as he was a royal rarity in another way: a king who remained true to his wedding vows. As part of the factional dispute, Clementina's aide Eleanor Missett, who had travelled with her on the perilous journey from Innsbruck to Italy, had quickly been dismissed from her position as governess to the infant Charles, and Wogan had been encouraged to leave Rome to accept a commission in the Spanish army. The appointment of Murray was the last straw for Clementina; she abandoned the Palazzo del Re in November 1725 for a Benedictine convent attached to the Basilica di Santa Cecilia in Trastevere, where she would stay for the next nineteen months.

Clementina of the Convent, Court, and the Basilica di S. Pietro

Things went from bad to worse for Clementina in the later years of her short life. Maybe she would have fared better if circumstances had been different; if one of the Jacobite

Fig. 33: Memorial to Maria Clementia Sobieska,
by Filippo della Valle, 1775, Cappella dell'Immacolata,
Basilica dei Santi XII Apostoli, Rome.
Photo Credit: Alinari Archives, Florence.

revolts in Britain had not been undermined by bad weather, bad planning, or bad luck, and she with her energy had been able to act the role of queen. But as it was, her existence at court was largely purposeless. Even more damaging was the fact that she, at first a high-spirited teenage girl whose laughter and zest for her great adventure had won forever the hearts of her Irish companions, was left alone, her few friends dismissed from Rome. And so she sulked. James, a morally decent man with a strong sense of duty who had real affection for her, nonetheless was oblivious to how her unhappiness had legitimate causes, maybe because he himself was overwhelmed by difficulties. The Hanoverians mocked him as "old Mr. Melancholy," and though he threw himself into each new attempt to return to Britain, which he thought himself morally obliged to do on behalf of his followers and descendants, failure after failure sapped his spirit. Reserved by temperament and then worn down by exile, he failed to provide the attention an emotional young wife needed. Clementina eventually returned to the Palazzo del Re but their relationship remained strained, all the more so because in the convent she embraced a harsh regime of asceticism. She lived a holy life—giving of her wealth to the poor, serving them in hospitals, forgoing the social life of Rome for its churches and masses, her time at the palace largely given to solitary prayer. And yet it is dangerous to live the vocation of a nun without a mother superior. From the undirected intensity of her praying and fasting, the once beautiful and sprightly queen grew haggard and weak. On January 18, 1735 CE, only thirty-two years old, she died.

Pope Clement XII decreed that Queen Maria Clementina Sobieska should be given a state funeral with full royal honours. Thirty-two cardinals first paid tribute at the Basilica dei XII Santi Apostoli, where she lay in state on a huge bier beneath a magnificent canopy commissioned for the occasion, dressed in her queen's robes, in gold, velvet and ermine, with a sceptre in her hand. They then accompanied her to S. Pietro, the funeral procession passing the throngs of Romans who had come to regard her as a saint. After a requiem mass, her royal robes were removed and she was buried in the habit of a Dominican nun in the basilica's crypt. Eventually her husband and sons would be buried there also. The family is forever linked by the memorials that face each in the basilica. Just before the doors exiting the basilica, on one's left, is the neo-classical *Monument to the Royal Stuarts* by Antonio Canova (1757–1822). This is a monument to the last three men of the Royal House of Stuart, paid for in part by one of the last Hanoverians, King George IV (r. 1820–30), who in the next century could afford to indulge in the romantic myth of those who were once his family's greatest enemies. By this time, James had long since died—on New Year's Day in 1766—accompanied by only seven minor servants, not the hundreds of Jacobites who once thronged the Palazzo del Re. By this time, too, his son Bonnie Prince Charlie's promise gave way to disappointment, alcoholism, and aimlessness before his death in 1788. The only viable heir to Jacobite political aspirations at the opening of the nineteenth century was James and Clementina's younger son, Henry, who had however become a Catholic cardinal and thereby renounced all political claims and ambitions. Upon his death in 1807, he too was buried in the crypt of S. Pietro and later commemorated in the *Monument to the Royal Stuarts* located in the main church above.

Opposite the Canova *Monument* in S. Pietro is the memorial honouring Clementina by the Italian sculptor Pietro Bracchi (1700–1773) and commissioned by Pope Benedict XIV (r. 1740–58) soon after her death (see fig. 31). The monument depicts the white marble figure of Charity above a porphyry sarcophagus covered with flowing pink marble, holding in one hand a portrait of Clementina, in the other, her flaming heart. The Queen's actual heart, however, is not in S. Pietro but back at their parish church, Basilica dei XII Santi Apostoli, in a monument on the second pillar to the right (see fig. 33). This one too commemorates her heart: one of the *putti* mourning her too-early death holds it up towards heaven. The inscription reads, in translation, "Here rests the precordia of Clementina, for the heart which heavenly love did not allow to survive." Her husband, who despite all his reserve and inattentiveness did love her and grieved her death, would pray in front of it most every day for the rest of his life.

Wogan's Romantic Adventures and Take on the Stuart-Sobieska Affair

The person who had brought James the Old Pretender and Clementina together in marriage in the first place in 1719, and then later wrote lively, romantic accounts about her in 1722 and again in 1745, would pray to her, too. First, though, he continued to live like the hero of a medieval romance, the last knight of Europe before his compatriot Edmund Burke lamented at the century's close that "the age of chivalry is dead." In yet another struggle against the odds, he did battle with the Moors at the Spanish fortress of Santa Cruz outside Oran in 1723, leading a detachment of 1300 Spaniards against a besieging army of 20,000 men. Though he was seriously wounded, his troops helped defeat the Bey's army and break the siege, for which he was rewarded with a governorship: the province of La Mancha in central Spain. It was the province destined for the man whom

Clementina's father derided for wanting to perform "quixotic escapades." As the governor of La Mancha, Wogan had time to cultivate his literary interests. He continued an epistolary friendship with the Anglo-Irish author Jonathan Swift (1667–1745), whom he honoured as "the mentor and the champion of the Irish nation." Swift notes that Wogan sent him "a history, a dedication, a poetical translation of the penitential psalms, Latin poems, and the like," as well as casks of Spanish wine. Finally, in 1745 Wogan wrote his *Mémoires*, which does not tell sad stories of the deaths of queens but is instead a comedy in which the journey ends in lovers meeting. Like his first account of the adventure in 1719, it concludes with a tribute to Clementina, now in the form of a prayer:

> O beautiful and happy soul, glory of the illustrious blood of Sobieski and Neuburgh, remember in the ecstasy of the presence of the living God, whom you have the happiness of seeing, your royal spouse and the beautiful Princes, your children, noble and only surviving descendants of Fergus the great Irish prince, founder of the Scottish monarchy; descendants also of the famous Egbert, West Saxon pupil of Charlemagne and founder of the monarchy of England; and of the illustrious houses of Normandy and Anjou in France, of York and Lancaster in England, of Tudor in Wales, of Stuart in Scotland, who all have given history so many heroes.

Wogan's prayer then ends with him asking that Clementina pray for him too.

We hear of Wogan once more. Later that year, more than three decades after he first fought for the House of Stuart in "The Fifteen," he joined Clementina's son Henry (as yet a layman) in Dunkirk in the hope of sailing to Britain to fight with the latter's brother Bonnie Prince Charlie in a Jacobite rebellion commonly called "the Forty-Five." But the French invasion fleet they hoped to accompany never left harbour, and in the end, after a promising landing in Scotland, Bonnie Prince Charlie's invasion of Britain in 1745 failed miserably. For all intents and purposes, the Stuart claim on Great Britain was finished forever, making Rome in effect the place that remembers them best.

Essential Reading

Aronson, Theo. *Kings Over the Water: The Saga of the Stuart Pretenders.* London: Thistle Publishing, 2015.

Camp, Judith. *The English Pilgrimage to Rome: A Dwelling for the Soul.* Leominster: Gracewing Publishing, 2000.

Corp, Edward. *The Stuarts in Italy, 1719–1766: A Royal Court in Permanent Exile.* Cambridge and New York: Cambridge University Press, 2011.

Harney, Martin P. *Medieval Ties between Italy and Ireland.* Boston: St. Paul Editions, 1963.

Siedina, Giovanna. *Latinitas in the Polish Crown and the Grand Duchy of Lithuania.* Florence: Firenze University Press, 2014.

Wogan, Charles. *Female Fortitude, Exemplify'd in an impartial Narrative of the Seizure, Escape, and Marriage of the Princess Clementina Sobiesky, As it was particularly set down by Mr. Charles Wogan (formerly one of the Preston prisoners), who was a chief Manager in the Whole Affair.* London, 1722. Reprint, Belfast: Gale Ecco Print Editions, 2008.

Wogan, Charles. *Memoirs of the Innsbruck Adventure of 1719.* Translated by Cathy Winch. Paris, 1745. Reprinted Belfast: Belfast Historical and Educational Society, 2008.

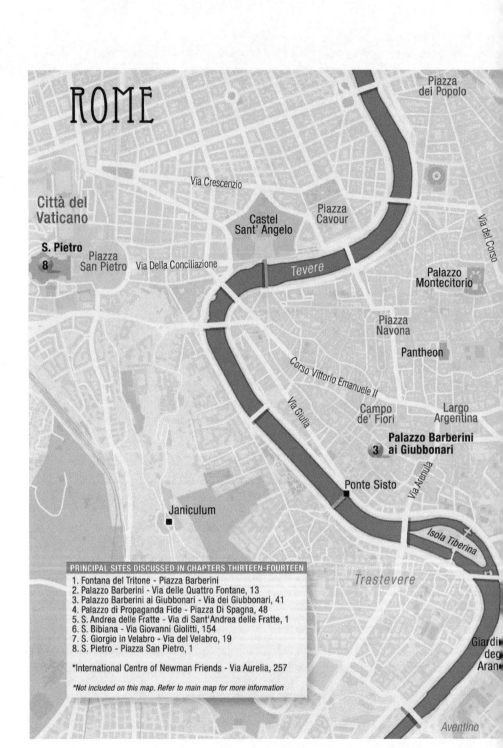

ROME

Piazza
dei Popolo

Via Crescenzio

Città del
Vaticano

Piazza
Cavour

Castel
Sant' Angelo

Via del Corso

S. Pietro
8   Piazza
San Pietro   Via Della Conciliazione

Tevere

Palazzo
Montecitorio

Piazza
Navona

Pantheon

Corso Vittorio Emanuele II

Via Giulia

Campo
de' Fiori

Largo
Argentina

Palazzo Barberini
3   ai Giubbonari

Ponte Sisto

Via Arenula

Janiculum

Isola Tiberina

Trastevere

PRINCIPAL SITES DISCUSSED IN CHAPTERS THIRTEEN-FOURTEEN
1. Fontana del Tritone - Piazza Barberini
2. Palazzo Barberini - Via delle Quattro Fontane, 13
3. Palazzo Barberini ai Giubbonari - Via dei Giubbonari, 41
4. Palazzo di Propaganda Fide - Piazza Di Spagna, 48
5. S. Andrea delle Fratte - Via di Sant'Andrea delle Fratte, 1
6. S. Bibiana - Via Giovanni Giolitti, 154
7. S. Giorgio in Velabro - Via del Velabro, 19
8. S. Pietro - Piazza San Pietro, 1

*International Centre of Newman Friends - Via Aurelia, 257

*Not included on this map. Refer to main map for more information

Giardi
deg
Aran

Aventino

MAP OF ROME FOR CHAPTERS 13–14

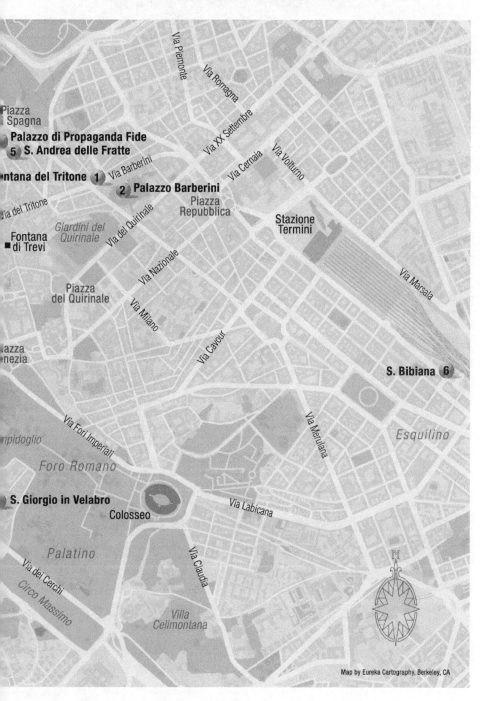

Piazza
Spagna

Palazzo di Propaganda Fide
5 S. Andrea delle Fratte

Via Piemonte

Via Romagna

Via XX Settembre

ntana del Tritone 1 *Via Barberini*

Via Cernaia

Via Volturno

2 **Palazzo Barberini**

Piazza
Repubblica

Via del Tritone

Stazione
Termini

Giardini del
Quirinale

Via del Quirinale

Fontana
di Trevi

Via Nazionale

Via Marsala

Piazza
del Quirinale

Via Milano

Via Cavour

azza
nezia

S. Bibiana 6

Via Fori Imperiali

Via Merulana

Esquilino

npidoglio

Foro Romano

S. Giorgio in Velabro

Via Labicana

Colosseo

Palatino

Via Claudia

Via dei Cerchi

Circo Massimo

Villa
Celimontana

N

Fig. 34: *Portrait of Pope Urban VIII*, oil painting by Gian Lorenzo Bernini, ca. 1625,
Galleria Nazional d'Arte Antica, Palazzo Barberini, Rome.
Photo Credit: DeA Picture Library / Art Resource, NY.

Chapter Thirteen

POPE URBAN VIII (1568–1644, r. 1623–44 CE) AT THE BASILICA DI S. PIETRO, FONTANA DEL TRITONE, AND PALAZZO BARBERINI

ELIZABETH LISOT-NELSON

Pope and Patron of the Arts

Power, ambition, and determination came together during the reign of Pope Urban VIII (r. 1623–44) to energize the office of the Roman papacy and reshape Rome itself. Among Urban's many initiatives, he increased the landholdings of the papal states even at the cost of impoverishing the Holy See with enormous debts due to lavish spending and wars. He gave new life to Catholic missions throughout the world in various ways but above all through his refounding of one of the Church's main evangelical bodies, the College for the Propagation of the Faith. He understood how to wield power as pope and politician, crushing his enemies when he deemed it necessary while also pursuing the pastoral and ecclesial responsibilities of his office with energy and dedication, including presiding over one ordinary Jubilee Year in 1624 and calling another eight extraordinary Jubilees through the course of his pontificate. In addition, through his patronage and oversight, Urban put his papacy and the city of Rome itself at the centre of a great revival of arts and letters. Among the bevy of brilliant sculptors, architects, and painters whom he patronized we find such great names as Carlo Maderno (1556–1629), Gian Lorenzo Bernini (1598–1680), Francesco Borromini (1599–1667), Caravaggio (1571–1610), and Pietro da Cortona (1596–1669). Intellectuals of all disciplines equally sought out and gained his support over the years, including Galileo Galilei (1564–1642), who stood in Urban's favour throughout most of his career, until the publication of his *Dialogue Concerning the Two Chief World Systems* (1632), for which he was condemned and put under house arrest. This episode with Galileo notwithstanding, Urban's influence on culture was prodigious. Arguably his most lasting accomplishment as pope, therefore, was the energy and impetus that he gave to art and architectural developments within the city of Rome. Hence, the baroque heritage of Rome owes this pope a great debt.

Ascent within the Roman Curia

Born Maffeo Barberini in the city of Florence in 1568, the future Urban VIII lost his father at an early age and was thereafter entrusted to the care of his uncle Francesco di Carlo Barberini in Rome. Urban's father had been a wealthy Florentine merchant while his uncle was a high-ranking official in the Roman Curia. Significant wealth and a useful network of contacts accompanied the young Urban, therefore; as he came of age, he rapidly ascended the social and ecclesiastical ladder of his day. By 1586, at age eighteen, he had already received initial religious orders, and his appointment to the offices of deacon, priest, bishop, and cardinal followed in a swift succession of promotions completed well before his fortieth birthday. His studies during this period include basic ecclesiastical education at Rome's Collegio Romano, a recently established centre of learning founded by the Jesuit saint Ignatius of Loyola (1491–1556), later generously supported by Pope Gregory XIII (r. 1572–85). Urban then completed his education with a doctorate in canon and civil law from the University of Pisa.

The future Urban's studies and ecclesiastical appointments drew him periodically away from the city of Rome during the 1580s and once again in 1601–4, when he served as Pope Clement VIII's (r. 1592–1625) legate to the court of the French King Henry IV (r. 1589–1610). But his contacts and influence in Rome both during these temporary absences and afterwards remained solid. In 1600, Urban took the palace he had inherited from his uncle on the Via dei Giubbonari (near Campo de' Fiori) and both expanded and renovated it in lavish style to create the so-called Casa Grande Barberini, which served thereafter as a platform both for conspicuous personal display and for reinforcing his social network with Rome's lay and religious aristocracy. His appointment to be the archbishop of Nazareth kept him in Rome for many years to come, too, given that this largely honorary see lay in the Holy Land which at the time was under the control of the Muslim forces of the Levant. In 1606 he became a cardinal and was given San Pietro in Montorio as his titular church (thought to mark the place of St. Peter's crucifixion), a prestigious appointment that increased his influence and reputation even more. From there it was only a matter of time; some fifteen years of service under Popes Paul V (r. 1605–21) and Gregory XV (r. 1621–23) culminated with his own election to pope in August 1623. In addition to his ecclesial offices, Urban was a man of letters, publishing several volumes of poetry in both Latin and Italian under the title *Maphei Cardinalis Barberini poemata*.

The *Baldacchino* at the Basilica di S. Pietro

Shortly after his election in 1623, Urban VIII commissioned Bernini to begin work on the *Baldacchino*, a canopy rising at the very heart of the Basilica di S. Pietro under Michelangelo's magnificent dome. Built over the tomb of St. Peter, upon whom Jesus said he would "build my Church" (Matt. 16:18), the *Baldacchino* remains to this day the central focus of the enormous edifice. Bernini was aided in the design and construction by the uncredited Maderno and Borromini. The bronze structure, rising to a height of 93 feet 6 inches (or twenty eight metres) including its marble base, appears more a work of architecture than sculpture, or rather it purposely conflates these two disciplines into one. It is constructed using four twisting Solomonic columns, so named because from the twelfth century onward a popular but erroneous legend held that the Roman emperor Constantine (312–37) brought them to Rome from the Jewish Temple in Jerusalem; however, they most likely date to the Middle Ages. Bernini incorporated these columns into the *Baldacchino* using their unique form to demonstrate how the Christian Church echoed its Judaic foundations. The appropriation of this supposed ancient typology, combined with visual references to the Barberini coat of arms through its repetitive bee motifs and to Urban VIII's own passion for poetry through its depicture

Fig. 35:
Fontana del Tritone,
Gian Lorenzo Bernini,
1642–43, Piazza
Barberini, Rome.
Photo courtesy of
Peter Hatlie.

of laurel leaves, secured the pope and his family a place at the apogee of papal patronage. As the gilt bronze laurel vines wrap around the spiral columns swarming with cherubs and its golden Barberini bees, an intense vitality pulls the viewer's eye upward in a rush of dynamic vertigo. A bit of alchemical magic transforms the cast bronze columns into the semblance of wood, while the metallic hanging valances appear to be made of leather or cloth. The optical tricks continue as angels at the top of the canopy give the impression that they effortlessly hold the construction together with golden garlands while a pair of fat *putti* play with the papal keys and tiara. The entire work is crowned with an orb on which rests a cross. From below, one can look up and see the interior of the valance emboldened with the Holy Spirit as a golden dove, from which gilded beams of light stream forth. The bird hovers over the altar, which in turn is placed above the tomb, fulfilling Christ's prediction that upon Peter he would build his Church.

The artifice in both design and conception places the *Baldacchino* among the most magnificent large-scale sculptures in the world. And by placing Bernini in charge of the project—the first of this artist's many large-scale sculptures, architectural sculptures, and fountains conceived of for public viewing in Rome—Urban tethered his reign to this rising artistic prodigy, dazzling the curia and wealthy collectors of Rome in his day. "You were made for Rome and Rome for you," Urban is reported to have told Bernini, along with this more prophetic comment about the artist: "An exceptional man, with a sublime genius, born of divine providence for the glory of Rome to bring light to the ages." With the *Baldacchino*'s erection began the energetic artistic patronage that whipped Rome into a baroque frenzy, forever keeping the Barberini name buzzing on the lips of viewers, then and now.

Fontana del Tritone, Piazza Barberini

Bernini's *Fontana della Barcaccia* ("Fountain of the Ugly Boat") near Rome's Piazza di Spagna was under construction at about the same time that he began work on his *Baldacchino* and was already finished by the time the latter was completed in 1634. Urban's commission of the *Barcaccia*, which was finished ca. 1630, marked the beginning of a remarkable series of public fountain commissions to come, some under Urban himself and others under his successors. The one most closely identified with Urban is the *Fontana del Tritone* ("Triton Fountain"), completed by Bernini in 1642–43 (see fig. 35) within a short walk of both the Piazza di Spagna and the pope's recently purchased and reconstructed Palazzo Barberini.

The *Tritone* functions as an attractive centrepiece for the public square, Piazza Barberini, and when installed was appreciated as a philanthropic gift by the pope to the locals. Functionally speaking, it brought fresh water flowing from the *aqua felice* aqueduct, built by Sixtus IV (1471–84) and restored by Urban, into this neighbourhood. And it did so with beauty and humanistic style, featuring the sea-god Triton as mentioned in a well-known passage from Ovid's *Metamorphoses* at the centre of the fountain. Son of Poseidon, part man and part scaly sea-creature, the Triton is depicted by Bernini as a young, muscular creature in a kneeling position, his spine erect and his head tilted back as he sips water gushing from a shell raised above him. He is positioned high in the air at the centre of an even larger two-winged open shell that in turn is perched on the tails of four classically rendered dolphins. As water spurts from the small conch, it spills first into the larger shell-pool below it, and then again into a broad and deeper pool located further down at street level, from which the ready dolphins drink. Made of travertine, the work is visually appealing from the front as well as from behind. In particular, the effect of water cascading and caressing down the muscular back of the merman Triton is impressive. Given its faithfulness to Ovid's depiction of the Triton and its association with triumph and salvation, this was a master stroke of genius by Bernini for his patron and that patron's public. The Ovid passage represented, *Met.* I:324–47, reads as follows:

> Triton, sea-hued, his shoulders barnacled
> With sea-shells, bade him blow his echoing conch
> To bid the rivers, waves and floods retire.

He raised his horn, his hollow spiraled whorl,
The horn that, sounded in mid ocean, fills
The shores of dawn and sunset round the world:
And when it touched the god's wet-bearded lips
And took his breath and sounded the retreat,
All the wide waters of the land and sea
Heard it, and all, hearing its voice, obeyed.

Palazzo Barberini and Pietro da Cortona's
The Triumph of Divine Providence

Shortly after ascending to the pontifical throne, Pope Urban VIII began to plan one of the most sumptuous palaces in Rome for his family. Palazzo Barberini, 1627–33, now a museum called Galleria Nazionale d'Arte Antica, was designed by several architects, the first and foremost being Carlo Maderno (1556–1629), who had earlier worked for Pope Paul V Borghese (r. 1605–21) on the construction of the Basilica di S. Pietro. Maderno's design for the palazzo greatly enlarged an existing structure, once owned by the Sforza family, in order to provide spacious accommodations for both of the pope's nephews: Cardinal Francesco Barberini (1597–1679), who would reside on one side of the new palazzo, and Francesco's brother, Taddeo Barberini (1603–47), whom the pope appointed as commander of the papal army and who would come to live on the other side with his wife. It was an ingenious move for Urban to hire the well-known Maderno as the architect of his family palace, the man who had expanded the nave of S. Pietro and erected its façade. However, Maderno died only a few years into the project. This left the pope in a dilemma. Maderno's assistant was his own nephew, Francesco Borromini, another brilliant architect whose difficult temperament created much conflict with his patrons. Borromini was already responsible for designing the *trompe l'oeil* windows on the third story of the façade of the palazzo, but he was passed over for Urban's favourite artist, Bernini, in the end. Bernini's experience with architecture to date was limited to his work on the façade of Santa Bibiana (1624–26), a monument still intact near Rome's Termini railway station. Nonetheless he was made chief architect of this massive project by 1629, working on and off with Borromini as his colleague until its completion until 1633. Between them Bernini and Borromini created some extraordinary architectural features within the palazzo, notably the two intricate and dizzying staircases that provided access to each of its two separate dwellings and typify the boldness and ambition of the best of baroque architecture in this age.

Despite the impressive architectural achievement of the palazzo itself, the *pièce de résistance* of this luxurious residence remains a fresco painting by Pietro da Cortona (1596–1669), a masterpiece of the leading baroque painter of his time. Located in the palazzo's grand salon, da Cortona's *The Triumph of Divine Providence and the Fulfilment of Her Ends under the Papacy of Pope Urban VIII* (1632–39) is a work of huge proportions and serious themes that is often credited with setting a new standard for the artist's contemporary baroque fresco painters (see fig. 36). It is based upon a five-hundred page poem penned by a close friend of Urban, Francesco Bracciolini (1566–1645), who wrote it to honour Urban's papal election to the pontificate in 1623. Da Cortona must

Fig. 36: *Triumph of Divine Providence*, fresco by Pietro da Cortona, 1632–39, Galleria Nazionale d'Arte Antica, Palazzo Barberini, Rome, Grand Salon, Rome. Photo Credit: Scala / Art Resource, NY.

have attended closely to the poem or worked with Bracciolini and perhaps with Urban himself when creating the artistic design as there is a strong relationship between text and image. The iconographic program is complex with many layers of meaning, and due to the sheer size of the fresco it takes time to digest all of the imagery. The energy of the artwork helped establish the popularity of illusionistic ceilings in the baroque period, which continued with *The Triumph of the Holy Name of Jesus* fresco (1676–79) painted by Giovanni Battista Gaulli (1639–1709) in the Chiesa del Gesù in Rome, and culminated with the *quadratura* painting of *The Apotheosis of Saint Ignatius and Jesuit Missions to the Four Continents* (1688–94) by Andrea Pozzo (1642–1709) in the Chiesa di Sant'Ignazio. While these two later works are overtly religious and inspirational, da Cortona's *Triumph* incorporates theology, history, and mythology to convey a propagandistic program that pushed both egotistic and artistic boundaries. It was also a hugely expensive work, earning the artist almost four thousand *scudi*, nearly ten times the sum that some of his contemporaries were earning for similar commissions at the time.

While working on the project, da Cortona and another artist, Andrea Sacchi (1599–1661), held a series of public debates at the Roman Accademia di San Luca (the art academy where Cortona had been elected director in 1634) concerning the appropriate quantity of bodies to be included in a composition. Sacchi's position was that fewer figures produced a more unified and clear schema, while Cortona argued that the use of numerous characters allowed for multifaceted ideas to be constructed and communicated. Sacchi, too, painted a ceiling in the Palazzo Barberini. *The Allegory of Divine Wisdom* (1629–33) is located just outside a private chapel in the wing occupied by Taddeo Barberini and his family. Limited to sixteen figures, Sacchi's fresco is simple in comparison to Cortona's. It depicts an enthroned female personification of Wisdom, accompanied by attendants. As she looks over her shoulder at the sun (Maffeo's personal symbol), she points with a sceptre toward the earth. The meaning is perspicuous: the Barberini pope was destined to rule. While the *Divine Wisdom* fresco exemplifies Sacchi's theory of art, da Cortona's ceiling is a visual manifesto of his thesis that more figures create a powerful interaction of polyvalent meanings. In 1642, Girolamo Tezi published a description of Cortona's Barberini masterpiece in *Aedes Barberinae ad Quirinalem*, a lavish and detailed treatise written in an epistolary format and modelled on letters of the ancient Roman author Pliny the Younger. Although highly interpretative in nature, Tezi's work nevertheless aids the modern viewer in understanding the *Triumph* and in gauging its considerable impact on contemporary baroque-age viewers. Scacchi's work is less regarded in Tezi's publication, a judgment shared by later art criticism on these two works.

Da Cortona's fresco composition gives the illusion that the ceiling is open to the sky with a faux marble architectural cornice supporting sculpture, figures, and creatures. In the centre is the personification of Providence herself, clothed in gold and raising her hand toward a large laurel garland, the latter referencing Urban's poetic accomplishments along with encircling three bees that, for their part, reference the Barberini family coat of arms. To Providence's side, in the lighted clouds are seated personifications of Purity, Justice, Mercy, Truth, and Beauty. Beneath them is Father Time (or *Chronos*) devouring his children, as well as the Three Fates (or *Moirai*) to his right, holding in their hands the thread of life. Another female figure in gold, representing Immortality, flies toward the bees with her star-studded Crown of Immortality. The garland is held aloft by the three Theological Virtues: Faith in white, Charity in red, and Hope in green. Above the bees are the two papal keys, one signifying temporal authority and the other divine. They are embraced by *Ecclesia*, the Church, who looks over her shoulder towards a side vignette dominated by the personification of Peace in a gold dress with blue cloak, accompanied by a female Prudence in white and red. At the summit of the garland is a personification of Roma herself, ready to crown Urban with the papal tiara. The central theme conveys the idea that Divine Providence has gifted Rome and the Christian world with the enlightened rule of this extraordinary pope.

As an emphatic reminder of this point, radiating out from the centre in each direction are allegorical scenes describing the auspicious consequences of Urban's papacy. The four gilt-bronze octagonal medallions correspond to a creature in each corner. These represent moments in Roman history that foreshadow the wisdom of the Urban's pontificate: the Justice of the Roman consul Titus Manlius Torquatus (ca. 350 BCE) above a hippogriff, a symbol of intelligence; the Prudence of the general Fabius Maximus (ca. 280–30 BCE) above two she-bears, symbols of sagacity; the Temperance of the general Scipio Africanus the Younger (185–29 BCE) above the unicorn, symbol of purity; and the Heroism of Mucius Scaevola (fl. ca. 500 BCE) above the lion, symbol of fortitude. The four outer sections on the short and long sides of the ceiling, beyond the faux marble cornice, contain allegorical and mythological references. In the space above the windows, to the left, is Hercules, who swings his club at the attacking Harpies symbolizing the victory of virtue over vice. The mythic hero is pointed to by the figure of Roman Judicial Power, holding wooden rods (*fasces*) and an axe, accompanied by Abundance, bearing a cornucopia of gifts. This scene represents the idea that with the banishment of evil by the pope's virtuous rule, both righteousness and prosperity will proliferate and Rome will become great again.

The optimistic propaganda continues on the long side of the *Triumph*, where to the left of the window is a scene representing the good governance of the Barberini overcoming sin. To the far left, a semi-nude female figure reclines on a bed with her arm raised; a voyeur above her peeks at her exposed body from behind a red cloth. She is Lust, also draped in red. Above her fly two putti representing chaste and erotic love, who fight with each other. To the right of the prone female of Lust, towards the centre background, another woman, Vanity, combs her hair as she sits in a garden with a group of ladies, referencing the lure of the temporal world. To the far right, falling down in a stupor, is portly Papa Silenus, the mythological satyr who taught Bacchus to cultivate grapes and drink to excess. He holds out a goblet being filled to the brim with wine. The baby god Bacchus rests on the lap of a topless bacchante to the right. This scene of drunken debauchery connects with the representations of Lust on the left and Vanity towards the centre. Above them all are two triumphant figures, Religion and Science with their helpers. The figure on the right with head covered is Religion, who clutches a smoking tripod with a base shaped as a ram, symbol of sacrifice. She glances down at the bacchanalia while holding fast to her tripod, suggesting the remedy for gluttonous inebriation is to cling to faith. On the left, flying out from behind a cloud, is the personification of Purity, cloaked in white. She carries a lily in one hand and reaches out toward the cherub of chaste love, offering continence as the cure for lust. Seated at the height of the cloud is Science; adorned in pink and gold, she kneels with arms out-spread, her head raised to the heavens, specifically towards the figure of Providence. She overshadows the figure of Vanity. In one hand Science holds an open book, in the other a pot with flames producing abundant light. Directly behind is the winged figure of Divine Aid, her assistant.

Death and Legacy

Da Cortona's masterwork on behalf of his patron and pope was completed fairly late in Urban's life, indeed at about the same time as another commission honouring him came to light touching on similar themes: the *Tomb of Urban VIII* (1628–37) by his cherished artist Bernini. Located in a prominent position on the main level of the Basilica di S. Pietro, just to the right hand of Bernini's later great work, *Cathedra Petri* ("Chair of St. Peter") (1657–66) in the church's central apse, the tomb cleverly depicts the winged figure of Death rising from a sarcophagus to write the pontifex's name on the open pages of a black marble book. Seated on a throne and offering a blessing with his right hand, the bronze statue of Urban presides high above two personifications fashioned of white marble, Justice and Charity, residing below.

This was Urban's last word on his own papal tenure, so to speak, and confirms some if not all of the talking points that da Cortona explored in his famous *Triumph* fresco in Palazzo Barberini. His tomb could not and need not reinforce all of his many initiatives and achievements but likely limited itself intentionally to the pope's pastoral concerns. Who could argue with a pontificate dedicated to justice and charity in a space such as S. Pietro, after all? Returning to the near contemporary *Triumph*, it is worth noting how this work projects Urban's legacy into several other domains of service and achieve-ment, but perhaps most notably in the direction of culture. Science occupies a promi-nent place in the Barberini fresco, for example, inasmuch as it is placed higher than the personification of Religion in the work. But why so? In search of an explanation, we must look to the meaning of science for the ancients and the Church. The Latin word *scientia* meant knowledge, particularly rational knowledge, to the people of Urban's age. Cor-responding to the Greek word *episteme*, it was regarded as a type of rational knowledge arrived at through mathematical and philosophical proofs. For the Church, such knowl-edge always needed to be reconciled with another type of knowledge arrived at through the study and interpretation of inerrant and inspired scripture. According to the seven-teenth-century Christian worldview, the mysteries of the universe, though examined by the human intellect, could only be fully comprehended by the mind of God. Therefore the two sources of knowledge, science and religion, are understood to be handmaidens to each other, yet always under the control of divine providence. This is the message that is conveyed in da Cortona's *Triumph*, when the outstretched hands of the figure of Science raise a book and the burning flame of enlightenment up to Providence. Urban's intellec-tual interests and perhaps even his patronage of the arts are put into relief through this reflection on the role of learning within religion and religion within learning. Urban had seen contemporaries such as Galileo disrupt this balance between scientific and sacred realms, and he was prepared to intervene and correct such imbalances when necessary.

The lasting value of his pontificate may or may not be his aggressive defence of this prevailing worldview of the day. Unquestionably, however, his extraordinary contribution to the arts, architecture, and letters in early seventeenth-century Rome was the fruit of Urban's belief that culture had an important role to play in religion and his readiness to patronize it for the greater good of Rome, the Church, and his own name.

Essential Reading

Avery, Charles. *Bernini: Genius of the Baroque*. New York: Thames & Hudson, 2010.

Bacchi, Andrea. *Bernini and the Birth of Baroque Portrait Sculpture*. Oxford: Oxford University Press, 2008.

Bellori, Giovanni Pietro. *The Lives of the Modern Painters, Sculptors and Architects*. Translated by Alice Sedgwick Wohl. Cambridge: Cambridge University Press, 2005.

Bianco, Anna Lo. *Pietro da Cortona's Ceiling*. Rome: Gebart, 2013.

Kirwin, William Chandler. *Powers Matchless: The Pontificate of Urban VIII, the Baldachin, and Gian Lorenzo Bernini*. New York: Peter Lang Publishing, 1997.

Merz, Jorg Martin. *Pietro da Cortona and Roman Baroque Architecture*. New Haven: Yale University Press, 2008.

Morrissey, Jake. *The Genius in the Design: Bernini, Borromini, and the Rivalry That Transformed Rome*. New York: Harper, 2005.

Ovid. *Metamorphoses*. Translated by A. D. Melville. Oxford: Oxford University Press, 1986.

Rietbergen, Peter. *Power and Religion in Baroque Rome: Barberini Cultural Policies*. Leiden: Brill, 2006.

Teti, Girolamo. *Aedes Barberinae ad Quirinalem*. Rome: Excudebat Mascardus, 1642.

Wittkower, Rudolf. *Art and Architecture in Italy 1600–1750, Vol. 2: High Baroque*. New Haven: Yale University Press, 1999.

Other Works and Places to Encounter Urban VIII's Patronage in and near Rome

- Chiesa di Santa Bibiana: frescoes by Pietro Cortona, statue of *S. Bibiana* and façade by Bernini, located near Termini station.
- Palazzo Barberini: a marble bust and painted *Portrait of Pope Urban VIII* (see fig. 34), both by Bernini.
- Palazzo di Propaganda Fide: main façade by Bernini.
- S. Maria in Aracoeli: *Memorial for Carlo Barberini* by Bernini.
- Musei Capitolini: *Memorial Statue of Pope Urban VIII* by Bernini.
- Basilica di S. Pietro crossing: *Balconies in the Pillars*, and *St. Longinus* by Bernini.
- Papal Palace of Castel Gandolfo by Carlo Maderno.

Fig. 37: Portrait of John Henry Newman, oil on canvas by Sir John Everett Millais, 1881.
Photo credit: National Portrait Gallery, London.

Chapter Fourteen

JOHN HENRY NEWMAN (1801–90 CE) AT THE PALAZZO DI PROPAGANDA FIDE, BASILICA DI SANT'ANDREA DELLE FRATTE, AND THE CHIESA DI S. GIORGIO IN VELABRO

BERNADETTE WATERMAN WARD

Heart Speaks to Heart

Far beyond his home in nineteenth-century England, John Henry Newman's influence is still felt in educational and religious circles. Rome transformed him. He is perhaps best known as a high-profile convert from the Church of England to Roman Catholicism in the mid-1800s, when such conversions were unusual and controversial. After his conversion he founded a university and a school, wrote lasting philosophical works, and gained a continuing reputation as a saintly, enlightened servant of the Church.

Newman was assigned to establish a Catholic university in Ireland, today's University College Dublin. As its founding rector he wrote *The Idea of a University* (1852), a classic in educational theory. He championed the voice of the layman in the Catholic Church by writing "On Consulting the Faithful in Matters of Doctrine" (1859), and famously defended individual freedom of conscience in a pamphlet on papal infallibility (1875). Pope Leo XIII (r. 1878–1903) made him a cardinal in 1879. His epistemological theories later influenced the philosophy of Popes John Paul II (r. 1978–2005) and Benedict XVI (r. 2005–13). The latter pope recognized Newman as a candidate for sainthood by a beatification ceremony in Britain in 2010. Newman's reputation for holiness came from his kindness: tending the sick during a cholera epidemic, writing countless letters to the suffering and lost, and, as an aged cardinal, tottering on foot to the Cadbury candy factory in Birmingham, England to ask the owners that Catholic workers might say their own prayers instead of attending mandatory Protestant prayer services at the factory. Impressed by the great man's concern for unskilled workers, the owners agreed. Newman's motto was *cor ad cor loquitur*: heart speaks to heart.

Passionate in his Christianity, Newman always wanted to know on what authority to accept belief. This imperative ultimately determined his conversion from the Anglican to the Roman Catholic faith. In the four centuries since the reign of Henry VIII (1491–1547), the state had controlled English religion. In 1833, while he was both a prominent Anglican priest and on the academic staff of Oriel College (Oxford University), Newman helped instigate the "Oxford Movement" to insist that the Anglican Church stand on the authority of the apostles rather than of the king. After closely examining early Church history and doctrine over the years, Newman came to the conclusion that the Church of England's lack of a genuine apostolic foundation made it irremediably flawed. He turned to the Roman Catholic Church and its well-established apostolic traditions. Attacked for leaving the Anglicans, he defended his conversion so honestly and powerfully in his *Apo-*

logia pro vita sua (1864) that official British anti-Catholicism began to wither. In 1871, for instance, Oxford ceased to require that undergraduates subscribe to the Articles of Religion, which had been crafted in opposition to Catholicism.

Newman visited Rome four times. He first visited in 1832 at a time in his life when he was still officially an Anglican priest but had come to oppose the unity of the English Church and State. In 1846–47, a year after his controversial conversion to Catholicism, he trained for Catholic priesthood in Rome and chose to enter the Congregation of the Oratory, a longstanding religious fellowship of Rome founded by St. Philip Neri (1515–95). In 1856 he travelled there briefly on business for the English Oratorians. Then, in 1879, when Newman was nearly eighty years old, Pope Leo XIII made him a cardinal of the Church and assigned him his own titular church in Rome, requiring another sojourn in the city.

Young Cynic Turns Calvinist (1801–17)

Newman's lifespan coincides with the height of British power in every way. Economically, England's industrial revolution preceded America's. Culturally, English Romanticism reoriented minds around the world and Victorian novels were read everywhere. Politically, the British Empire enveloped the globe. The English Church held dogma loosely, but its zealous missionaries planted churches in colonies worldwide. In America, Anglican influence was strong, especially in its opposition to Catholicism, which even dissenting Protestant bodies preserved.

Born into a firmly Anglican family, Newman showed early talents in music, math, and especially logic. He enjoyed the intense rationalism of historians like Edward Gibbon and philosophers like David Hume but also indulged strong Romantic tastes: the poetry of Wordsworth and Southey and the swashbuckling novels of Walter Scott. Jane Austen's sharp observations impressed him but she disappointed him with "no romance— none at all!" Austen exercised her wit on his familiar social world: an orderly and well-regulated class system where state-sponsored clergymen filled a genteel role in civic order and jostled for parishes with good incomes. Many Victorian novelists depicted such parsons as familiar figures and, in real parishes, the clergy, hired by local gentry, often avoided controversy by downplaying the supernatural or even basic Christian doctrine. Wild Methodists might go out in the fields to have visions and preach conversions or to hold Sunday schools, but respectable people were undemonstrative about religion. Moreover, among the intellectual classes to which Newman belonged, a principle of practical human historical judgment was becoming fashionable: look for the lowest motive in any historical account, and automatically disbelieve anything else, especially anything supernatural. This cynicism attracted young Newman, though he had been brought up to respect the Bible. During a phase of questioning religion, the argumentative fifteen-year-old became deathly ill in a boarding school epidemic. Fearing contagion, everyone left except one master who nursed Newman with (among other things) large doses of strict Calvinism. Newman rose from his sickbed a fiery evangelical. He harassed his father about work on Sundays and hustled his brother to prayer meetings. Eager to dedicate his life to foreign missions, he became sure that God wanted him to remain unmarried, ready for deployment when his call should come.

Oxford Don and Church Vicar

Soon afterwards, while the coachman was waiting, his somewhat impulsive father decided that Newman would attend Oxford instead of Cambridge. Once there, Newman fell in love with Oxford's atmosphere and history. He even found intellectual excitement there, although in those days Oxford was a school mostly for gentlemen who liked to drink and hunt. Newman was a serious student and became even more serious after the death of his father burdened him with family finances. Because he seemed an excellent prospect for an academic career, Newman's tutors pressured their young intellectual phenomenon to take his exams for the bachelor's degree a year too early. He barely passed. Ashamed, he intensified his studies and competed for a fellowship at the master's level in Oriel, the most rigorous of the colleges of Oxford. This time he won.

At twenty-two he was set up for life. Oxford required its staff to be unmarried clergy. Voluntarily celibate, he was guaranteed a permanent, well-paying, prestigious post. He could support his brother's education and create a comfortable home for his mother and sisters. As he resided at the university, happily preparing for ordination, he shed his evangelical rough edges. The Oxford academic culture encouraged disparagement of the uncomfortably supernatural aspects of Christian tradition. Newman began to express the sentimental view that religion did not need the "too scientific" language of creeds. Yet his personal spirituality was intense and he quietly clung to Christian dogmas. Like an acceptable young Oxford don, he busied himself with ancient rhetoric and history.

After his ordination in 1825, Newman accepted a parish in a poor Oxford district, St. Clement's. He discovered that his parishioners did not feel well served by either the emotional but rigid Calvinism he had adopted early, or his later, coolly intellectual evasion of the "doctrinal principle." Newman threw himself into popular good works. He heated the church, started a Sunday school, and made sick calls. Academic acumen and eloquence gained him invitations to preach university sermons, boosting his career considerably. Then two blows changed him: he collapsed while conducting an exam, and was sent home for a long recovery. Then, in his presence, his dearest younger sister died of a violent fever she suffered for less than a day. Shaken, he rethought the way he was drifting with the fashionable academic tide. On reflection, his parish work showed him that he had put a distance of social snobbery between himself and his religious calling. His sermons subsequently became sober and searching as he explored academic theology in a more scholarly way than he had in his teens. He read the ancient Church Fathers and accepted the theory of apostolic succession: that bishops taught their successors Christian tradition, guided by God. He concluded that ancient heretics had rebelled against the apostolic faith, confusing the faithful by using biblical texts as weapons against tradition. Eventually, the depth and scholarly power of his preaching garnered him an appointment as vicar to the University Church of St. Mary, Oxford's main church. Students flocked to his services.

Newman then accepted a commission for a book in a series on Church history. He wrote on the councils that articulated Christian creeds, starting with the Council of Nicaea (325) and its response to the claims of a priest named Arius (256–336). Arius had challenged the equality of Jesus—in time, space, substance, and power—with His utterly divine Father. Among other things, Newman's *The Arians of the Fourth Century*

(1833) faced him with serious questions about state interference in religious affairs. Although the Roman emperor Constantine (312–37) called and presided over Nicaea, both he and his successors politicized its declarations in subsequent decades by tolerating Arian beliefs. Thus the state prevented Church authorities from disciplining clergy who denied the traditional doctrines. Yet ordinary lay Christians stood firmly up for the Nicaean creed, Newman discovered, and through this insight he came respect lay Christians' unarticularted tradition, faithful even under government disapproval. Newman's research for *The Arians* changed his personal point of view on Church history but the editor rejected it because of its lopsided treatment of just one of the many councils. Newman published it separately.

Journey to Italy in Turmoil (1833–34)

Newman thought that university tutors should form their students not only intellectually but spiritually. His superiors at Oriel disagreed, and by late 1832 took away his students, though Newman still received his fellowship income. With time and money to spare, Newman embarked on a trip to Italy with his like-minded friend Hurrell Froude (1803–36), another reformist Anglican priest and scholar. Froude's trip to warm southern Europe was meant as a remedy for his failing health; Newman accompanied him to help. Yet throughout the trip Newman was drawn into thinking deeply about his vocation. As their ship awaited clearance from quarantine, for example, he wrote his most famous hymn, "The Pillar of the Cloud":

> Lead, Kindly Light, amid the encircling gloom,
> Lead Thou me on!
> the night is dark, and I am far from home—
> Lead Thou me on!
> Keep Thou my feet; I do not ask to see
> The distant scene—one step enough for me.
>
> I was not ever thus, nor prayed that Thou
> Shouldst lead me on.
> I loved to choose and see my path, but now—
> Lead Thou me on!
> I loved the garish day, and spite of fears,
> Pride ruled my will; remember not past years.
>
> So long Thy power hath blessed me, sure it still
> Will lead me on,
> O'er moor and fen, o'er crag and torrent, till
> The night is gone;
> And with the morn those angel faces smile
> Which I have loved long since, and lost awhile.

This hymn conveys Newman's strong sense of humility before God, a theme that carries over into his later years at well. But he was still writing other works to support the strong anti-Catholic views that he brought to Rome with him as part of the usual Church of England prejudices of the day: the pope was Antichrist; statues and holy pictures were idolatry; and Catholic ceremonies were superstition. Only very good music could tempt him to witness Catholic worship. *Loss and Gain* (1848), a novel he wrote after his conversion, reconstructs his attitudes at that time. The character Charles, who speaks at the end, is a version of young Newman:

> the churches are so unfinished, so untidy. Rome is a city of ruins! The Christian temples are built on ruins, and they themselves are generally dilapidated or decayed; thus they are ruins of ruins ... he often wondered what took so many foreigners, that is, Protestants, to Rome; it was so dreary, so melancholy a place; a number of old crumbling, shapeless brick masses, the ground unlevelled, the straight causeways fenced by high monotonous walls, the points of attraction straggling over broad solitudes, faded palaces, trees universally pollarded, streets ankle deep in filth or eyes and mouth deep in a cloud of whirling dust and straws, the climate most capricious, the evening air most perilous. Naples was an earthly paradise; but Rome was a city of faith. To seek the shrines that it contained was a veritable penance, as was fitting. He understood Catholics going there; he was perplexed at Protestants. 'There is a spell about the *limina Apostolorum*,' said Charles; 'St. Peter and St. Paul are not there for nothing.'

But Newman was impressed nonetheless. Details of the Roman prison of Peter and Paul, the Carcere Mamertino, emerge in Newman's later novel *Calllista* (1855), set in the third century. In the same novel, he describes a painting like one he saw in a catacomb, with Mary lifting her arms advocating for the faithful before God. His letters show how Rome captivated Newman as the seat of the apostles; as the place where Ignatius and other ancient fathers were martyred; as the cradle of European Christianity. Yet in his letters he called the Roman Catholic Church "insane," and he found it "cruel" that these important sites were surrounded by tokens of Roman Catholicism.

The Oxford Movement and A New Chapter in Life (1833–45)

Back at Oxford, Newman and others instigated a movement to reform the Church of England. They campaigned to halt government interference and align doctrines and disciplines more closely with those of the early Church. He was chagrined that the English Church did not require consistency in its doctrinal positions. Bureaucrats even assigned Anglican bishops to serve doctrinally dissenting Protestants abroad. Parliament could establish or suppress bishoprics. Newman's "Oxford Movement" promoted a theology about the importance of sacraments and respect for apostolic tradition in a series of pamphlets called *Tracts of the Times* (1833–41). Before long, public controversy gathered around the Newman and other "Tractarians" of the movement. Anglican apologists accused them of being too "Roman" and undermining the state Church. In 1841 Newman's bishop finally ordered him to stop the tracts. And even though he was the most famous preacher in England of the time, he obeyed.

His fellow Anglican clergy had rejected his reformist campaign. His bishop's disapproval drove Newman into a period of questioning and asceticism. Now in his early forties, he retreated into some converted stables with a few disciples for two years where they translated ancient Church documents and wrote saints' lives. The most serious Anglican objection against Roman Catholicism was that the Catholic Church invented new dogmas. Newman conducted an honest search to see if this was the case, culminating in his *The Development of Christian Doctrine* (1845). This research convinced him that Catholicism had not invented new teachings but merely clarified and defined dogmas already implicit in the earliest Christian writings and liturgical practices. Now convinced that he had been wrong, Newman retracted in print the anti-Catholic work he had been publishing for most of his career (1845).

Consistency demanded that if he could no longer protest against Roman Catholicism he would have to become Catholic. That would mean alienating his surviving family, being unable to legally practice a learned profession or hold political office in England, and losing his post at Oxford. He wrote a prayer on this situation in his *Meditations and Devotions*:

> O my God, I confess that Thou canst enlighten my darkness. I confess that Thou alone canst. I wish my darkness to be enlightened. I do not know whether Thou wilt: but that Thou canst and that I wish, are sufficient reasons for me to ask, what Thou at least hast not forbidden my asking. I hereby promise that by Your grace which I am asking, I will embrace whatever I at length feel certain is the truth, if ever I come to be certain. And by Your grace I will guard against all self-deceit which may lead me to take what nature would have, rather than what reason approves.

The Convert in Rome (1845–54)

In October 1845, Newman entered the Roman Catholic Church, abandoning his hopes for the Oxford Movement. Close friends and family rejected him. He lost his job and his residence at the college. The popular press portrayed him as a Catholic spy planted at Oxford to corrupt the young. Still feeling called to preach, he left for Rome to study for the Catholic priesthood.

This time, Rome was positive and enriching for him. Religious art that had earlier seemed idolatrous to him now spoke to him of the earliest Christian worship. Archaeological artifacts that he had once approached suspiciously now emerged with immense significance. For instance, he saw a picture of Mary in a chapel within the catacombs and wrote of it in a letter of December 8, 1846:

> Fancy a chapel under ground, deep and of the 2d or 3rd century highly painted. This strikes me as a most remarkable fact, that church decoration should be a part of Christianity, that is should be practiced in the midst of persecution and in the heart of the earth. The chapel I speak of has an apse, and an altar .... Also I am told that in another catacomb there is a picture of St. Peter and St. Paul holding up the Blessed Virgin's hand in prayer, as Hur and Joshua the hands of Moses.

When Newman encountered ancient inscriptions asking martyrs to pray for the living, he marvelled at the fact that, "one can pray at their graves as the early Christians did." Now his powerful, first-hand encounter with early Church locations impressed him differently than on his first visit to Rome:

> I went to see things, admiring them indeed, but chiefly to be able to say I had seen them as a matter of duty. And I was cut off from the churches, and almost from religion altogether. It is miserable to travel and to hear bells to which you may not respond, and to see processions and functions from which you feel it a duty to turn away. I did so as a duty then, and I have my reward now.

Newman had never experienced religious life with the richness that he did in these Roman years.

Fig. 38: *Madonna
of the Miracles*, oil
painting by Natale
Carta (1790–1884),
Basilica di
Sant'Andrea delle
Fratte, Rome.
Photo courtesy
of Peter Hatlie.

The new convert was much prized by the Roman hierarchy. He was taken to meet
Pope Gregory XVI (r. 1831–46) and housed near the Spanish steps in the missions headquarters of the church, the Propaganda Fide building. The rooms he was assigned, along
with a convert friend who was also studying to be a priest, occupied the end of a cor-
ridor and overlooked the Basilica di Sant'Andrea delle Fratte. At that church in January 1842, a Jewish atheist, Alphonse Ratisbonne (1814–84), had experienced a vision
of Mary and converted. Later that year Natale Carta (1790–1888) painted Mary under
Ratisbonne's instructions. The new image in the chapel had a miraculous reputation
(see fig. 38). Newman now rejoiced in the idea of special divine graces coming from
visits to see sacred art, and he wrote to a friend (*Letter to J. Walker*, October 14, 1846),
"altars so privileged and crucifixes and pictures abound. I think we are badly off in England in this respect and wish things were improved." Newman no longer had qualms
about shrines or the ceremonies held in them. He visited shrine after shrine, altar after
altar, venerating images and relics.

The image in Sant'Andrea remains where it was in Newman's time, its frame crowded with tokens from devotees who claim miracles were granted them after pilgrimages there. This chapel was important not only to Newman but to a twentieth-century Catholic priest, Maximilian Kolbe (1894–1941), the "saint of Auschwitz," who celebrated his first mass before its altar.

Newman made pilgrimages with extraordinary devotion, though he found the streets so dirty "that it is a real penance to walk in them." Rain transformed the "immense quantity of dung" horses left on the cobblestones into "a thick liquid." (In the 1850s, on his third visit to Rome, Newman walked barefoot from the Piazza di Spagna to S. Pietro, despite the filth.) Newman was ordained in the Chapel of the Magi at *Propaganda Fide* in May 1847. He first celebrated Mass upstairs, near his rooms, on an altar housing relics of St. Hyacynthus.

Newman now cherished all evidence of the continuity of Christianity—from cells of ascetics, like Ignatius Loyola (1491–1556), even to heavily baroque, dubiously religious displays of showy gifts to the church. Yet he himself came not in baroque pride but in humility, to learn. He was a famous expert in Christian doctrine and history. He had taught at Oxford for years. He had led a major religious movement that shook the state Church in the most powerful country in the world. Yet he patiently attended seminary lectures amongst an international, unevenly educated class half his age. Newman voluntarily followed the same rules as raw seminarians from missionary countries. He enumerated, "Indians, Africans, Babylonians, Scots, and Americans" as well as "Egyptians and Albanians" among his fellow students. By December 1846, he ended his coursework to consider which religious order to join. After soul-searching, he proposed founding a branch of St. Philip Neri's Oratorians in England. Pope Pius IX (r. 1846–78) approved, and so Newman rewrote the very culturally-Italian Oratorian Rule for England and recruited novices to establish the Birmingham Oratory. Newman's Oratorians served heroically in a cholera epidemic and built a church while Newman wrote his two novels, *Loss and Gain: The Story of a Convert* in 1848 and *Callista: A Tale of the Third Century* in 1855. Then he published some satirical lectures about anti-Catholicism titled *Lectures on the Present Position of Catholics in England* (1851). A defrocked priest, Giacinto Achilli (ca. 1803–60) sued Newman for libel in connection with one of those lectures. Newman's biting satire mocked Achilli's sensationalistic accusations against Catholicism in Achilli's lectures in Britain following his flight from Italy. Achilli blocked witnesses of his Italian misdeeds in court, so Newman lost the case. Yet public outrage at the manipulated trial proceedings limited Newman's penalty to a mere fine of £100 and a requirement that he remove the allegedly libellous text from the published *Lectures*.

Controversy, Consolidation, and Literary Fame (1852–78)

Meanwhile, trouble emerged from the Catholic side too, after Newman obeyed a papal call to start the Catholic University of Ireland, officially founded in May 1854 with Newman as its first rector. His magnificent founding *Lectures*, later compiled into the book *The Idea of a University*, followed in November of the same year. But soon after the university's foundation, Irish bishops started to oppose it, maintaining that the university might embolden laymen's independence. Newman's public stance on the very issue of the Church's relation to its lay members emboldened his opponents. His article, "On Consulting the Faithful in Matters of Doctrine" (1859), for example, argued on historical grounds that popular piety can preserve the true tradition of the Church against heresy, even when bishops go astray. Rumours that Newman was rebellious travelled back to Rome, reaching a tense Italian hierarchy just as Pope Pius IX (r. 1846–78) was facing the looming loss of the papal states of central Italy . So in 1859 Newman retreated—with practically everybody questioning his honesty—to the Birmingham Oratory in order to found a little secondary school. The university was given to the Jesuits, eventually including Newman's 1866 convert, the poet Gerard Manley Hopkins (1844–89), who was a professor of classics there in the 1880s.

By 1864, as the elderly Newman administered his school in Birmingham, the Christian Socialist clergyman, novelist, journalist and university professor of history, Charles Kingsley (1819–75), accused Newman of asserting that Catholic priests need not be truthful. Newman asked him, in print, to either retract or prove his statement. Kingsley dodged. They disputed in the newspapers for weeks. Finally, Kingsley attacked Newman's personal honesty in a pamphlet, "*What, then, does Dr. Newman mean?*" Newman took that as a challenge to explain the meaning of his life and religious opinions. Six weeks of blazing work produced his *Apologia pro vita sua* (1864), a best-selling autobiography that effectively silenced Kingsley's accusations. Read by Catholics and Protestants alike, the book did much to undercut anti-Catholic prejudice among the educated classes of England.

Popularity followed, but Newman was busy meditating on death and old age, culminating with a long verse-drama, *The Dream of Gerontius* (1865). Surprisingly, this poem about purgatory was a hit: General Charles George "Pasha" Gordon (1833–85), the British Governor of Sudan in Khartoum, famously had it in his pocket when he was killed. The composer Edward Elgar set the poem to music in his oratorio *The Dream of Gerontius* (Op. 38) in the year 1900. Newman followed this poem with a quite difficult philosophical essay about how people can rightfully believe what they do not understand: the *Grammar of Assent* (1870). He introduced the term "illative sense" to name the faculty by which a person moves, rationally but without fully articulating reasons, from evidence to assent. Twentieth-century phenomenologists developed similar ideas, and Newman's ideas influenced later philosophers like Bernard Lonergan. Newman continued his campaign against merely subjective judgment and in favour of respect for authority, in an open *Letter to the Duke of Norfolk* (1875) about papal infallibility. He rebuked the duke: "Certainly, if I am obliged to bring religion into after-dinner toasts, (which indeed does not seem quite the thing) I shall drink—to the Pope, if you please,—still, to Conscience first, and to the Pope afterwards." Newman believed in papal infallibility as defined by First Vatican Council (1869–70) but had hoped that the Vatican would not go so far as to declare the doctrine essential to the Catholic faith (*de fide*). He knew that the popular press would probably ignore the definition's limitation of infallibility to matters of faith and morals, and would also ignore the specific conditions required for an infallible declaration of doctrine. The declaration did offer anti-Catholics abundant opportunity for such criticisms; still, Newman did not criticize the dogma once it was declared.

The Cardinal (1878)

In old age, Newman became a widely beloved spokesman for Catholicism in England. The University of Oxford, which had banished him more than thirty years before, gave him an honorary fellowship in 1878. The next year he was vindicated in his theological opinions by Pope Leo XIII (r. 1878–1903) who put to rest the controversies surrounding Newman under the previous pope and proceeded to name him a cardinal. Now no Catholic bishop in England would assail his orthodoxy.

On his fourth and last visit to Rome, to receive this office, he was given titular authority over one Rome's oldest medieval churches, S. Giorgio in Velabro (see fig. 39). Located in the valley connecting the Foro Romano with the Roman meat market (*forum boarium*) and Tiber River, the Chiesa di S. Giorgio is near the circular Roman Tempio di Ercole Vincitore (second century BCE), the Roman Arch of Janus (fourth century CE), and the medieval Basilica di Santa Maria in Cosmedin (eighth century CE). When it was built in the seventh century CE, it was dedicated to St. Sebastian (ob. ca. 288). The church was reded-

Fig. 39:
Façade of the
Chiesa di S.
Giorgio in Velabro.
Photo courtesy of
Peter Hatlie.

icated when a relic of St. George, another soldier-martyr, arrived in the eighth century. Fittingly for Newman, an Englishman, St. George was also the patron saint of England.

After becoming a cardinal, Newman soon left Rome and lived another eleven fairly quiet years in England. In Birmingham, he continued his charity and his work at the Oratory school, and answered, as he did all his adult life, hundreds of letters from people in religious difficulties. His wisdom and reputation for sanctity lived on after him. Newman's ideas on the role of the laity and his proto-phenomenological discussions of the nature of faith and knowledge became tremendously important to many theologians, among them Edith Stein (1891–1942) and two philosophers who became popes: John Paul II (r. 1978–2005) and Benedict XVI (r. 2005–13). Newman was a prominent influence upon Second Vatican Council II (1962–65). In 2001, Deacon Jack Sullivan of Boston attributed to the intercession of Newman a miraculous healing of the crushed spinal cord that had left him unable to walk. Careful examination of Deacon Sullivan's medical records confirmed the miracle, so Benedict XVI declared Newman Blessed on a visit to England in September 2010.

Essential Reading

Crosby, John. *The Personalism of Newman.* Washington, D.C.: Catholic University of America Press, 2014.

Hoegemann, B. M. " Newman and Rome." In *Newman in his Time*, edited by Philippe Lefebvre and Colin Mason, 61–81. Oxford: Family Publications, 2007.

Ker, Ian. *Newman: A Biography*. Oxford and New York: Oxford University Press, 1989.

Newman, John Henry. All of his written works are available at "The National Institute for Newman Studies." http://newmanreader.org/.

Sullivan, Jack. "The Story of a Miracle." In *The Newman-Scotus Reader*, edited by Edward Ondrako, 483–92. New Bedford, MA: Academy of the Immaculate, 2015.

Sylva, Jo Ann Cammarata. *How Italy and Her People Shaped Cardinal Newman: Italian Influences on an English Mind*. Pine Beach, NJ: Newman House Press, 2010.

Tillman, Mary Katherine. *Newman: Man of Letters*. Milwaukee, WI: Marquette University Press, 2015.

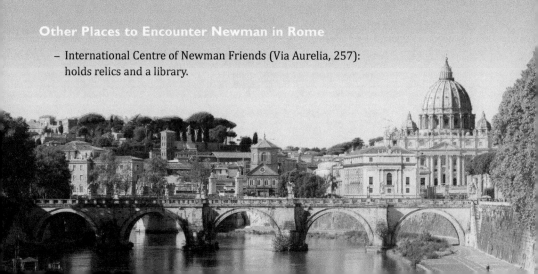

Other Places to Encounter Newman in Rome

- International Centre of Newman Friends (Via Aurelia, 257): holds relics and a library.

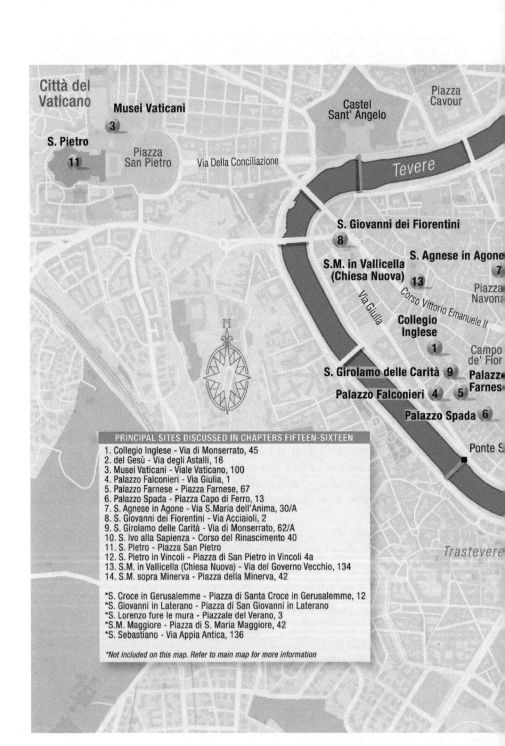

Città del
Vaticano

Musei Vaticani

3

S. Pietro

11

Piazza
San Pietro

Via Della Conciliazione

Castel
Sant' Angelo

Piazza
Cavour

Tevere

S. Giovanni dei Fiorentini

8

**S.M. in Vallicella
(Chiesa Nuova)** **13**

S. Agnese in Agone

7

Via Giulia

Corso Vittorio Emanuele II

Piazza
Navona

**Collegio
Inglese**

1

Campo
de' Fior

S. Girolamo delle Carità **9**

Palazzo Falconieri **4**

5

**Palazz
Farnes**

Palazzo Spada **6**

Ponte S

Trastevere

PRINCIPAL SITES DISCUSSED IN CHAPTERS FIFTEEN-SIXTEEN

1. Collegio Inglese - Via di Monserrato, 45
2. del Gesù - Via degli Astalli, 16
3. Musei Vaticani - Viale Vaticano, 100
4. Palazzo Falconieri - Via Giulia, 1
5. Palazzo Farnese - Piazza Farnese, 67
6. Palazzo Spada - Piazza Capo di Ferro, 13
7. S. Agnese in Agone - Via S.Maria dell'Anima, 30/A
8. S. Giovanni dei Fiorentini - Via Acciaioli, 2
9. S. Girolamo delle Carità - Via di Monserrato, 62/A
10. S. Ivo alla Sapienza - Corso del Rinascimento 40
11. S. Pietro - Piazza San Pietro
12. S. Pietro in Vincoli - Piazza di San Pietro in Vincoli 4a
13. S.M. in Vallicella (Chiesa Nuova) - Via del Governo Vecchio, 134
14. S.M. sopra Minerva - Piazza della Minerva, 42

*S. Croce in Gerusalemme - Piazza di Santa Croce in Gerusalemme, 12
*S. Giovanni in Laterano - Piazza di San Giovanni in Laterano
*S. Lorenzo fure le mura - Piazzale del Verano, 3
*S.M. Maggiore - Piazza di S. Maria Maggiore, 42
*S. Sebastiano - Via Appia Antica, 136

*Not included on this map. Refer to main map for more information

MAP OF ROME FOR CHAPTERS 15–16

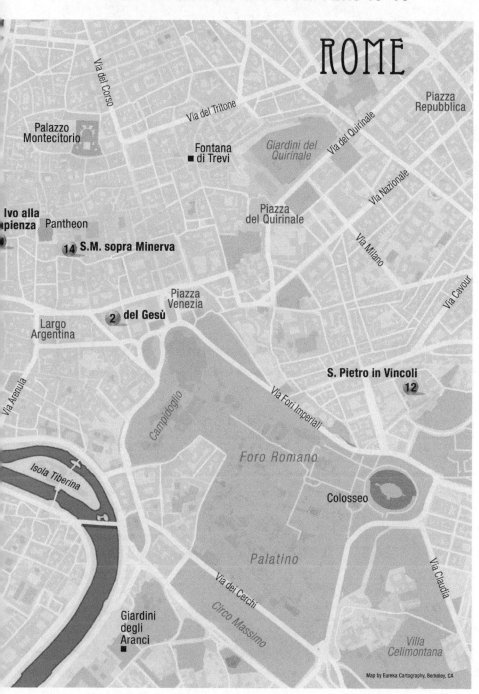

ROME

Via del Corso

Via del Tritone

Piazza Repubblica

Palazzo Montecitorio

Giardini del Quirinale

Via del Quirinale

Fontana di Trevi

Via Nazionale

Ivo alla Sapienza

Pantheon

Piazza del Quirinale

Via Milano

14 S.M. sopra Minerva

Piazza Venezia

2 del Gesù

Largo Argentina

Via Arenula

S. Pietro in Vincoli

12

Campidoglio

Via Fori Imperiali

Via Cavour

Foro Romano

Isola Tiberina

Colosseo

Palatino

Via Claudia

Via dei Cerchi

Circo Massimo

Giardini degli Aranci

Villa Celimontana

Map by Eureka Cartography, Berkeley, CA

Fig. 40: *St. Philip Neri in Ecstacy*, painting by Guido Reni, 1614,
S. Maria in Vallicella / Chiesa Nuova, Rome. Photo courtesy of Peter Hatlie.

Chapter Fifteen

PHILIP NERI (1515–95 CE) AT THE CATACOMBE DI S. SEBASTIANO, THE CHIESA DI SAN GIROLAMO DELLA CARITÀ, THE BASILICA DI SAN GIOVANNI DEI FIORENTINI, AND THE CHIESA NUOVA

GREGORY ROPER

The Fool for Love

Compared to all of the other historical figures represented in this book, St. Philip Neri (1515–95) did very little. He did not re-establish and expand an empire, convert it to Christianity, or establish a new capital city, as Constantine did. He did not produce ever-lasting artistic works that people still admire as did Michelangelo and Raphael. Nor did he found a religious order as St. Dominic did. The group he established, called the *Oratory* (or *Congregation of the Oratory*), is the loosest, least organized group of priests one can possibly imagine, with the fewest rules possible. Neri did so "very little" in life, in fact, that he ended up awakening hundreds of people to a deeper experience of faith and even changing the landscape of the capital city of Catholicism, Rome. By the time he died, people said he had done more to reform a corrupt, chaotic, troubled city than anyone else. And he did it not with important writings, political moves, organizational structures, or powerful armies. He did it instead with his own cheerful personality, one person at a time.

In light of his above accomplishments, Neri is known as the Second Apostle to Rome (St. Peter being the first), and is still beloved by Romans—so much so that every year on his feast day, May 26, the mayor of Rome presents a gold chalice to his community at the Santa Maria in Vallicella (Chiesa Nuova). Everyone who encountered Neri spoke of how warm, affable, inviting, and unfailingly cheerful he was, how you could not be around him without feeling this joy. He carried around with him at all times a book of devotions and a book of jokes by a Florentine comic writer, and he was as apt to use the latter on people as the former. He greeted people—especially young men, the kind who think they are tough and cool and sophisticated—with a simple phrase: "How shall we do good today?" or "Gentlemen, when shall we begin to do good?" With this disarming opening, he drew people out, asking about their lives, their struggles, and their aspirations. Few could resist him; many found their lives irrevocably changed. Soon cardinals, theologians, leading women of Rome—as well as street sweepers and plumbers—were changing their lives, all because of their encounters with this man. He knew three popes personally as their confessor, and lived in Rome through the pontificates of five others.

What they really called him was *Pippo Buono*, a name he had received in childhood for being such a sweet child, and the name stuck. It translates to something like "Good Little Phil" or "Good Ol' Phil," but somehow both of these translations miss the connota-tions in English that it has in Italian: the affection, kindness, and sweetness that he conveyed to those around him. Even at the end of his life, when it was clear to all that Neri would become a great saint, he would not play the part but instead continued to make fun of himself and clown around. He was *Pippo Buono* even in his exchanges with the very formal cardinals and bishops who dominated cultural life in Counter-Reformation Rome of the middle and late sixteenth century.

Early Life in Florence and Move to Rome

Neri was born and raised in Florence, the son of a rather down-on-his-luck notary named Francesco and a mother, Lucrezia, who passed away when he was only five years old. He had some schooling with the Dominicans at the priory of S. Marco, which years before had been led by the stern, reforming prior, Girolomo Savonarola (1452–98), and this experience undoubtedly left its mark on him. Savonarola was a hugely influential figure within late-fifteenth-century religion, society, and politics. Appalled at the moral corruption of Florence, he led a conservative revolution in religion and politics, encouraged the destruction of secularly-minded Renaissance humanistic writings and paintings, challenged and then fell afoul of both local power brokers and the notoriously corrupt Pope Alexander VI (r. 1492–1502), and ruled the city for a short time (1494–98). Ultimately, he was excommunicated from the church, removed from office, imprisoned, tortured, and burned at the stake in the middle of Florence's Piazza Signoria. The young Neri always loved the Dominicans and revered Savonarola, keeping a bust of the man in his rooms all his life. When all was said and done, however, he chose a very different route than Savonarola in his dealings with people.

Upon turning age eighteen, Neri was dispatched by his father to his uncle Bartolomeo Romolo, who lived south of Rome near the city of Cassino, and who was well disposed to teach his young relative enough about the business world that he may one day take over. Neri's indifference was evident rather quickly: Pippo had no interest in business. He preferred to slip off to pray with the Benedictines at their mother house on nearby Monte Cassino or saddle a donkey and ride to a seaside locale near Gaeta, called La Montagna Spaccata. The latter, where huge cliffs descend to the sea and are split by a cleft that runs hundreds of feet down the centre of the rock, was a place primed to play on the imagination and soul of a sensitive, devout youth. Local legend says that these rocks split at the very moment of Jesus's crucifixion in Jerusalem, when the ground shook and the curtain of the temple was torn in two. Neri spent hours there praying. At one point, he had some sort of mystical experience there and decided, despite his affection for his uncle Bartolomeo, to give up the life of business and walk to Rome. Nineteen at the time, he arrived in 1533–34 and took up rooms in the attic of a Florentine businessman, Galeotto del Caccia, in the Piazza Sant' Eustachio just behind the Pantheon. By day he served as a tutor to Galeotto's two sons Michele and Ipolitto, lived simply and dedicated himself to study, first at the University of Rome and later with the Augustinians. His real calling, though, was the religious life. This latter pursuit distracted him so much that he could not pay attention in class, and he soon dropped all of his schooling.

Rome was just six years removed from the brutal sack of 1527 by mutinous troops working for the Holy Roman Emperor Charles V (r. 1519–56), and only sixteen years from the Halloween day in 1517 when Martin Luther had nailed his ninety-five theses to a church door in Wittenberg. Rome the city was a mess, and the Roman Catholic Church was divided, confused, and weakened after a succession of worldly, corrupt popes over the previous century. The then-current pope, Paul III (r. 1534–49) was a culturally refined man from the Farnese dynasty, and he had built the splendid Palazzo Farnese just around the corner from where Neri would eventually settle and create his movement. This palazzo, with its rhythmic, harmonious Renaissance lines, was Farnese's statement, his confidence that Rome could be rebuilt after the sack on this clean, orderly inheritance of classical forms. One can see this new confidence in how it rises from its rough-hewn first floor into regular repetitions of columns and windows. Farnese had been worldly and sensual in his youth, though he later took his duties as pope seriously and was even responsible for convening the reforming Council of Trent in 1545.

The Patron Saint of Hanging Out and a "Pentecost" in the Catacombs

Neri spent much of the next eighteen years (1534–52) dedicating himself to a religious way of life and to humanitarian causes. He volunteered at the hospitals of Rome, places with horrific conditions, bathing and helping the patients. He also lingered in the streets and piazzas of Rome with the idea of evangelizing the wealthy local youth, an especially restless, spoiled, and sometimes dissolute social group who began flow back into Rome after the disasters of 1527. By all accounts, Neri was a singular phenomenon in the city: he had a special talent for engaging all of these young people. He would come upon a group of men talking, chatting, planning the day's fun, and simply ask them, "Gentlemen, how shall we do good today?" And somehow, they weren't turned off; they didn't shoo him away as a do-gooder who wanted to ruin their fun. He brought these men to the hospitals, to vespers at the Basilica di S. Maria Sopra Minerva, the Dominicans' church just east of the Pantheon, Rome's "only Gothic church," full of arches and niches for prayer, where St. Catherine and Giotto once were in residence. He had these young men care for the homeless—and somehow they didn't mind, because he made it all fun. Soon everyone knew him and wanted to be around him. There is a story from a bit later when a group of Neri's young men were walking down the street with him, laughing on their way somewhere, and they saw a homeless man lying in a doorway. "Pick him up," Neri ordered one of the group following him. Now imagine young men in their flashy Renaissance dress, being asked even to touch the ragged bundle of filthy fabrics cowering in a doorway. The young men were horrified. "Take him to the hospital, and take care of him the rest of the day." The young dandy did, and they all accompanied him. It is a testament to Neri's attraction that he could ask young men to do astounding things and they would comply.

It was during this time that Neri came to know Ignatius of Loyola (1491–1556), who had just recently brought his new group, the Society of Jesus (or Jesuits) to Rome from Paris. It's difficult to imagine two more different people. Ignatius, the former soldier, was serious, even stern, an organizer and maker of organizations, a man with a military mission to reform the Church and spread its message world-wide. Neri was the jokester, the solitary hermit living in the attic of a man's house who wandered the streets engaging the youth. But by all accounts, they liked each other quickly, and grew to a deep respect for one another. Neri sent so many young men to join the Jesuits that Ignatius called him "the bell of the order"—always standing outside, but ringing people into church. Ignatius' church, the Gesù, now a wonder of baroque glory, with a ceiling that overwhelms, is just a short walk from the Pantheon area where Neri spent his time.

During this first period after his arrival in Rome, Neri also began to walk out the Via Appia to the Basilica di San Sebastiano fuori le mura and spend time in the catacombs. At the time no one did this. Located outside of the walls of Rome to the south, the Appia was basically unsupervised by city authorities and could be dangerous owing to hustlers and thieves residing there. As for the catacombs, there were none of the well-organized visits to lighted passageways that exist today in the local catacombs of S. Sebastiano, S. Callisto, and S. Domitilla. In the sixteenth century, you entered as if going down to an unexplored cave, a torch your only light source, and the visit was dark, tricky, and dangerous. Neri, however, was filled with a desire to be close to the early Church and would at times spend all night in the catacombs praying, before returning at dawn and walking home to teach Michele and Ippolito for another day.

It was in the catacombs in 1544, now age twenty-five, that Neri had the most important experience of his life, what has been called his "Pentecost." Apparently one night he was praying in the catacombs and a ball of fire entered his mouth and travelled to his heart. He cried out, "Enough, Lord, enough! I cannot take it anymore." From that moment on, he was often seen trembling and had a lump over his heart like a tumor. It is difficult, from our own standards of scientific inquiry and empirical attitudes, to credit these kinds of stories, but without them we do not have the complete portrait of the person. We know that Neri did not tell others about this experience, and in fact he felt that it added to his burdens. He was, after this, skeptical of anyone who claimed visions and mystical experiences, saying that anyone who desired them did not have any idea what he was asking for. And he was ruthless in exposing those who claimed them falsely, as he was asked to do several times. Finally, we do have some empirical evidence of this occurrence: he was, from this time forward throughout his life, constantly warm. People whom he would embrace would comment about it, and he would leave his windows open in the winter, wear only the lightest cassock, and leave it unbuttoned, even on cold winter days. After his death an autopsy was performed to check for the tumor. The doctors found that two ribs had been broken and pushed out from the inside, and that he had an enlarged heart which would not have fit within his chest cavity had not these two ribs been broken.

S. Girolamo, Mass, and Confession

Neri's official vocation to the religious life finally came in 1551 under the guidance and persuasion of his longtime confessor, Persiano Rosa. Although he felt unworthy of priestly status, he took the collar nonetheless and soon moved into the loose community of secular priests to which Rosa belonged at the Chiesa di S. Girolamo della Carità. This church suited Neri in a great many ways. First, like S. Sebastiano and other catacombs, it was associated with the early Church: apparently St. Jerome (347–420) himself had stayed there when it was just a "house church" owned by one of the wealthy Roman

Fig. 41: Interior of the Antamoro Chapel, S. Girolamo della Carità, Rome.
Photo courtesy of Peter Hatlie.

women who were early converts and benefactors. Second, it was located near one of the busiest and most important neighbourhoods of Rome, a neighbourhood which hosted not only the Via Giulia—a main pilgrimage route to S. Pietro—but also the commercial hub of Campo de' Fiori and Paul III's Palazzo Farnese. Neri loved this church because he was still be able to encounter the daily to-and-fro of people mixing and mingling in Rome. Finally, this loose congregation of priests, whose members were socially engaged and worked for a living just like their neighbours, seemed to suit him and provide the model for the group he would soon assemble.

Today, the Chiesa di S. Girolamo della Carità is a small church tucked in behind the Palazzo Farnese, not well known except by devotees of Philip, but it has two fine baroque side chapels (see fig. 41) decorated after his death, and a cross which, the stories go, once spoke to Philip when he was struggling with opposition. One needs special permission from the Opus Dei fathers to visit Philip's rooms above the church, but they are worth the visit, for as we shall see, his movement really began there. Once settled in the community of San Girolomo, Neri quickly made a reputation for himself. Not only was he brimming with energy, but he also became known for three things: the odd way he celebrated Mass, his devotion to the sacrament of confession, and the informal meetings in his rooms.

Neri was so moved by the Mass that his palpitations and tremblings would increase the more he moved through the liturgy. At the consecration, he often had to rest his elbows on the altar to keep himself from shaking too much, and he would raise and lower the host quickly because, he said, he was worried he would never be able to stop contemplating it if he did it slowly. He found the transformation of the wine into Christ's blood just as intense an experience, and would bite into the chalice to keep himself calm; today, in his rooms above the Chiesa Nuova, you can see the teeth marks in his personal chalice. At other times, however, the jokester in him would take over, and to distract himself away from his intense contemplation he resorted to all sorts of tricks—having the altar boys tug at his sleeves, or pausing to tell jokes from the altar. Once, in the middle of Mass, he stopped, motioned to the altar server, and had the startled boy give him a haircut, right there on the altar.

More significantly, he made frequent confession his mission. Persiano Rosa had pushed the notion of frequent, even daily, Mass attendance, and receiving communion at least once a week at a time when few received the sacrament more than once a year. Neri now did the same for confession. He became famous for the hours he spent in the confessional and for the unusual ways he responded to people during confession. All who went to him spoke about how perceptive he was, how he changed a mere recital of sins into a spiritual counselling session, how he was able to see into the problems and issues that people were bringing to him. When a man came and offered a kind of half-hearted recital of sins, Neri took off his glasses, handed them to the man, and said, "Try these. Now maybe you will be able to see yourself a little more clearly." Women came to him quite often; once a well-to-do young, confident woman came and asked him if wearing high heels was sinful. Neri allowed the heels, but "just be careful," he added, "that you do not fall." At times he would stand outside S. Girolamo in the morning and flag down passersby and others he knew, asking them to come in for a quick confession. Soon many were flocking to him for his spiritual guidance. Once at this time, a young man, encouraged to come to Neri by a friend, decided to test this process. He came to S. Girolamo and recited to Neri a long list of made-up sins, recounting a terrible life, to see how the priest would respond. "Now, we both know not a word of that was true," Neri said, seeing right through him. "Why don't you start again, and this time, tell me the truth." By the time the young smart-aleck was done, he was in tears, and a changed man.

Neri never lost this emphasis on his apostolate of confession, and to the end of his life was sought after by the great and powerful as well as the lowly and simple. His guidance, his creative penances, his spiritual insight, changed many a life in those few minutes in the confessional. But he soon realized that hearing confessions, especially of the young, was not enough; he had to give them something positive to fill their lives so they would not leave the confessional and simply go back to the same temptations. He thought the hours after lunch—the Italian *riposo*—were particularly dangerous times for these young men: time on their hands, a full stomach, perhaps cash in their pockets. There were plenty of temptations awaiting young men of sixteenth-century Rome.

The Early Meetings of the Oratory:
The Anti-Luther, the Anti-Savonarola

Neri began to gather his young followers together in his rooms during the riposo in meetings that came to be called the Oratory. The meetings were informal but followed a typical pattern: some spiritual reading, perhaps from scripture or the Fathers of the Church, followed by discourses and discussions, ending with some singing. All of this took place in Neri's small quarters above S. Girolamo, where the speaker would sit on a small, slightly raised platform so he could be seen and heard. Anyone could give the talks on the reading, even laymen, and Neri encouraged this, asking different young men to prepare discourses on various subjects, and expecting all to participate in the discussions. In this way he made them responsible for learning about their faith, studying it, and teaching others about it, in a way that would not be emphasized so strongly again until the reforms of the Second Vatican Council (1962–65) emphasized the role of the laity. Soon an evening Oratory developed as well, highlighted by thirty minutes of mental prayer, a recitation of the litanies, a short recital of the Passion of Christ, and more singing.

It was not long before these free and open, serious but always joyful meetings became the talk of the town, and young men flocked to be a part of the Oratory. Neri would have to sit on his bed to make room for the people crowded into his quarters. Again Neri's ability to bring together the wealthy dandies and the simplest of men was on display: students and Vatican clerics would come, but also a simple man named Giovanni, whose greatest ambition (which Neri helped him realize) was to be the sweeper of S. Pietro. Charles Borromeo (1538–84), the nephew of Pius IV (1559–65), cardinal at age eighteen, later the cardinal archbishop of Milan and one of the men most responsible for the ultimate success of the Counter-Reformation, started that journey in the meetings in the Oratory, and was always a devoted follower of Neri. Neri's love of singing soon brought the maestro of the S. Pietro chapel choir, Giovanni Animuccia (ca. 1500–1571) to the Oratory meetings. Later, the even greater composer Giovanni Pierluigi da Palestrina (ca. 1525–94) came, bringing some of the S. Pietro musicians with him.

But even the Oratory meetings were not enough, Neri realized. He had to reach more people and find ways to counter the attractions and temptations of life in Rome, especially at peak times of the festival and party season such as *Carnevale*, the period just before Lent. Thinking back to his youthful trips out the Appia, he came up with a perfect antidote to Carnevale: he transformed the early-Christian practice of making a pilgrimage to the seven main churches of Rome into a kind of picnic. The early Church had followed this tradition of moving from S. Pietro to S. Paolo fuori le mura, so as to begin with the two great saints of Rome; to S. Sebastiano and the other catacombs; then to S. Giovanni in Laterano; to Santa Croce in Gerusalemme to see the relics of the true cross; to San Lorenzo fuori le mura to honour this early martyr; and ending at S. Maria Maggiore. But Neri turned this solemn act into a day-long travelling picnic, starting with a Mass the night before and the pilgrimage walk the next day. What began with just a few of his followers soon attracted thousands, accompanied by Animuccia's musicians providing entertainment and spiritual uplift.

With this and other of his initiatives, Neri accomplished a remarkable thing: he at once became the anti-Luther and the anti-Savonarola of this time. Like Luther, he came and saw a corrupt Rome but he was not so appalled that he rejected it; instead, he saw weak, poor souls in need of help—cardinals as well as simple street sweepers. Like Luther, he loved the early Church and wanted to bring the Church of his day back in touch with it, but he chose to do that within the Church rather than to start a revolt against it. Like Luther, he saw important roles for the laypeople and valued their contributions, but he did not see this as necessitating a break with the clergy and the hierarchy. For Luther, sin was troubling, especially the notion that he would sin, be forgiven, and go right back and sin again. For sunny Neri, sin was troubling but not ultimately overpowering, and he worked inside and outside of the confessional to help men confess their sins, move on from them, and turn in Christian joy to a new life.

And thus while he revered Savonarola all his life, he followed exactly the opposite methods. Rather than rail and thunder and denounce young people's activities and attitudes, Neri tried to convey to them how a life of virtue was happier, more fulfilling, more joyful, and to give them activities and ways to spend their time to make this obvious. "Only let a little Divine love find an entrance into their hearts," he would say, "and then you may leave them to themselves."

The Holy Fool and Wise Counsellor

For Neri, the key was always humility, a kind of cheerful self-abasement that laughed at oneself. In his mature years, this principle became the key to his novel and sometimes controversial interpretation of Christian piety and love. Stories abound of his attempts to teach humility through mockery and self-mockery. He began wearing huge, pointed clown shoes in his walks around town. To shame a cardinal who seemed to pay more attention to his dog than his duties, Neri stole the pet, took it back to the Oratory with him, and occasionally paraded it in public on a silk pillow. Once, invited by a wealthy woman to dinner in order to show him off to her friends, Neri cheerfully showed up with the right half of his beard shaved, and deadpanned, acting as if nothing was wrong. Another time, a cardinal invited him to a swank dinner with multiple courses, and Neri sat down at the table with a small, wooden bowl he had brought full of nothing but lentils, which he proceeded to eat, refusing anything else, the entire evening.

According to another account of Neri's popular ministry, a simple man known as Alberto the Carpenter wanted to begin wearing a hair shirt, so moved was he to repent for his sins. Neri sensed that this was not good for him, that Alberto might start feeling prideful about his mortification, and told him no. But Alberto was a persistent man. After a long wait, Neri finally gave in, but told him he must wear it *outside* his coat—a ridiculous inversion of its very purpose. Until the end of his life, Alberto wore the hair shirt on the outside, telling everyone that Father Neri had told him to do so and thus earning him the nickname "Bertie the Hair Shirt." Neri took from Saint Bernard the idea that there are four steps in humility: "To despise the world, to despise no man, to despise oneself, and to despise being despised." It is likely this last step that keeps one from that sanctimony that Neri feared in Alberto, and which he saw as particularly dangerous. Thus the constant mocking of himself and of others.

People came to call the Oratory "the School of Christian Mirth." To Neri there was no reason not to be joyful, and he refused to have the people around him be anything but cheerful. When a group of Polish noblemen visiting Rome were sent by Clement VIII (r. 1592–1605) to see the "great saint," Neri made sure that upon their arrival one of his followers was reading to him from his book of jokes. He kept the reading going for some time, and then, turning to the Poles, said, "you see how I occupy my time in important matters." To be foolish means not to recognize reality, but the Holy Fool is one who sees through the appearances which dominate most of our lives and perceives the deeper reality the rest of us cannot (or refuse to) recognize. For Neri, only humility could bring one to this stage of holy foolishness, and he was cheerfully ruthless with himself and his followers in demanding this humility.

One final story from this period gives a glimpse into Neri's thinking on humility and methods of working with his followers. Cesare Baronius (1538–1607), one of the greatest intellectual talents of his day, came to Rome in 1557 and was immediately drawn to the Oratory. Neri gladly took him in and encouraged his intellectual pursuits but for-

Fig. 42:
Façade of the
Chiesa di S. Maria
in Vallicella /
Chiesa Nuova,
Rome. Photo
courtesy of
Peter Hatlie.

bade Baronius from studying his preferred subject, the theology of the Four Last Things (death, judgment, heaven, and hell). Baronius was persuaded to work within the relatively new field of Church history instead. In obedience to Neri, he went on to pursue historical studies, culminating with a series of presentations over several months before the Oratory. These lectures drew acclaim from all quarters. But then, in yet another twist to this story, Neri would not allow Baronius to publish his notes until he had delivered the entire series seven times over the course of twenty-seven years. When the *Annales Ecclesiasticae* finally appeared in 1588, Baronius knew the subject intimately, had fact-checked every statement, and as a result produced a work historians still find masterful. Interestingly, Neri never allowed Baronius to give up his other duties in the community. In fact, in the communal kitchen, Baronius scrawled on the wood "Baronius Coquus Perpetuus," as if to say, "[Here worked] Baronius, the perpetual cook."

From San Girolomo to San Giovanni dei Fiorentini and the Chiesa di Santa Maria in Vallicella (Chiesa Nuova)

By the 1570s Neri realized that the Oratory needed a permanent home. The original site of S. Girolamo was thus abandoned for another, the impressive Basilica di San Giovanni dei Fiorentini, in 1563. This church, on the banks of the Tiber, was the local home of the Florentine community, so close to Philip's heart. It is today an impressive church and houses the remains of the architect Francesco Borromini, the brilliant but troubled creator of some of Rome's most stunning architectural masterpieces, like Sant' Ivo and Sant'Agnese in Agone. But, just over ten years later, Neri cast his eye upon the crumbling Chiesa di S. Maria in Vallicella, located in a small valley along what is now the Corso Vittorio Emmanuele II and still in Neri's beloved corner of Rome. Pope Gregory XIII (r. 1572–85), another of Neri's close friends and penitents, granted him the church in 1575. Soon the decision was made to demolish it completely and start again. Funds began to flow in from many different benefactors, among them Borromeo and Gregory XIII himself. Ever since its dedication in 1577 the church has been known as the Chiesa Nuova, the New Church.

By 1578 all of the Oratorians had moved in, Neri, into rooms above the church where he could celebrate Mass, hear confessions, and continue his ministry. Ideally located, his new church helped attract even more people to the life he offered. More and more the princes of the church and simple people alike came to Neri's community, finding joy and healing in what was practiced there. Successive popes were supporters and sometimes confidants of Neri, including Sixtus V (r. 1585–90), Gregory XIV (r. 1590–01), and Clement VIII (r. 1592–1605). The near unanimous support that Neri enjoyed in these last years of his life, without compromising his own ideals, indicates how much he had accomplished during the many decades he had spent in ministering to Rome. A visit to the Chiesa Nuova today (see fig. 42) offers an experience of this now-baroque masterpiece, with its splendid altar and access to, among other things, his private rooms above the church and the Chapel of St. Philip Neri, where his relics are preserved.

Neri died in his rooms above the Chiesa Nuova on May 26, 1595. The account of his last day is quite moving and is read every year on this day in Oratorian houses around the world. Crowds immediately appeared to see and touch his body as it lay in state, and similar crowds appeared to give testimony in his canonization hearings: of healings, appearances on the day of his death, and testimonies to his personal sanctity, his way of life. In fact, the process was pushed so much by this popular veneration that Clement VIII decided it was important to slow down the process. By 1622 the process was over and on May 12 a canonization ceremony was held by Pope Gregory XV (r. 1621–23), for Isidore the farmer, Ignatius Loyola, Francis Xavier, and Teresa of Avila, along with Neri. The Romans immediately began to joke that the pope that day had canonized "Four Spaniards—and a saint."

Essential Reading

Bouyer, Louis. *Roman Socrates*. London: Geoffrey Chapman, 1958.

Gallonio, Antonio. *The Life of Saint Philip Neri*. Translated by Jerome Bertram. San Francisco: Ignatius Press, 2005.

Matthews, V. J. *Saint Philip Neri: Apostle of Rome and Founder of the Oratory*. Rockford, IL: Tan Books, 1984.

Maynard, Theodore. *Mystic in Motley: the Life of Saint Philip Neri*. Milwaukee, WI: Bruce Publishing, 1946.

Turks, Paul. *Philip Neri: The Fire of Joy*. Translated by Daniel Utrecht. New York: Alba House, 1995.

Other Places to Encounter Neri in and near Rome

- Collegio Inglese: where English priests have trained for hundreds of years. It is across the street from the Chiesa di S. Girolamo. During the time when Elizabeth I persecuted priests returning to England, Neri would bow to these men, usually Jesuits, before they left to return to the British Isles, singing *Salvete Flores Martyrum* to them in respect to their going to probable martyrdom.

- Palazzo Massimo alle Colonne: a Renaissance place, with a chapel on the second floor commemorating a miracle attributed to Neri in 1583.

Fig. 43: Portrait of Julius II, fresco by Raphael. Detail of the *Messa di Bolsena*, Stanza di Eliodoro, Stanze di Raffaello, Musei Vaticani, Rome. Photo Credit: Scala / Art Resource, NY.

Chapter Sixteen

POPE JULIUS II (1443–1513, r. 1503–13 CE) AT THE BASILICA DI SAN PIETRO, THE MUSEI VATICANI, AND BASILICA DI SAN PIETRO IN VINCOLI

DUSTIN GISH

Pope Julius II, Great Patron of Rome

Most travellers to the eternal city of Rome will visit the Vatican to see the Basilica di S. Pietro and the Musei Vaticani. These marvels of architecture and art attract over four million tourists every year. But while everyone can see the grandeur and glory of these High Renaissance masterpieces, it is easy to overlook the historical background of these and other great works that dominate the way we see Rome today. Five centuries ago, on the design of the great architect Donato Bramante (1444–1514), the foundation stone was laid for the monumental Basilica di S. Pietro that would eventually replace the decaying basilica that had stood over the burial site and altar of Peter for more than a thousand years. In the same year, Raphael (r. 1483–1520) received his commission to fresco some private rooms in the papal residence adjacent to the new basilica, which are today celebrated as the Stanze di Raffaello ("Raphael Rooms"). Meanwhile, the latter's rival, Michelangelo (1475–1564), started his work on the massive vault of the Cappella Sistina, the papal chapel linking residence and basilica. These masterworks of the High Renaissance, all commissioned in 1506, radically transformed the Vatican and Rome. To grasp the greatness of these extraordinary works of art and architecture, it is not enough to see them. One must also seek to grasp the moving force behind their creation, touching them at their source, as it were.

In fact, there is one common historical element linking all three of these works together, and many others in Rome as well: Pope Julius II. Also known as the "warrior-pope," Pope Julius II was born Giuliano della Rovere in 1443. He received a Franciscan education as a young man and was promoted to the offices of priest, bishop, and cardinal by his uncle Pope Sixtus IV (r. 1471–84), between the years 1471 and 1479, thereafter serving as pope from 1503 until his death in 1513. The Curia elected Julius during a papal conclave that lasted only a few hours, the fastest election in the history of the Catholic Church. His pontificate followed the twenty-six day reign of an aged and sick Pope Pius III (r. 1503), who himself had been elected in the aftermath of the controversial reign of the Spanish Cardinal Rodrigo Borgia as Pope Alexander VI (r. 1492–1503). Even more so than his predecessor, the unusual papal name selected by Giuliano della Rovere was evidently chosen to suggest a comparison with the Roman conqueror Julius Caesar (100–44 BCE) and signalled the new pope's own grand ambitions for Rome and the papacy.

Italian Disorder and the Emergence of a Warrior-Pope

The character and achievements of Julius's papacy inspired many of his contemporaries and disturbed others. Among his admirers was the Florentine intellectual Niccolò Machiavelli (1469–1527), who wrote his treatise *The Prince* in 1513, taking as his subject those events that had transformed the political landscape of Italy during the period from 1498 to 1513, or more specifically, during the pontificates of Alexander VI and Julius II. Machiavelli references the warrior-pope Julius frequently in *The Prince*, often praising his impetuous actions. The same cannot be said of famous contemporaries, like Desiderius Erasmus (1466–1536) and Martin Luther (1483–1546), who saw Julius as a deeply flawed character. Despite all that has been said in blame of him and his reign, however, history may unjustly have condemned Julius II without due consideration of the tumultuous times in which he lived.

At the time Julius became pope, Italy and the papacy were in an acute geopolitical crisis. In 1494, during the pontificate of Alexander, King Charles VIII of France (1483–98) invaded Italy and thereby altered forever the political landscape of the Italian peninsula by throwing into disarray the traditional balance of Italian powers between the Venetian republic, Duke of Milan, Florentine republic, king of Naples, and pope in Rome. Charles proved unable to hold his newly acquired state and left in his retreating wake a dangerous precedent. His son and heir, Louis XII of France (r. 1498–1515) invaded Italy again, in 1499 and 1500, this time with greater success. He managed to maintain the territory won in Italy by force of arms and reputation, notably claim to the kingdom of Naples. But from out of this profound disorder, his new outlook on the geopolitical order began to emerge.

If truth be told, Julius himself was responsible for some of the political disorder that he would one day inherit. As a younger man, in his capacity as Cardinal Giuliano della Rovere and archbishop of Avignon, he had waited impatiently for nearly a decade in self-imposed exile to strike a mortal blow against his sworn enemy, Pope Alexander VI and his son, Cesare Borgia (1475–1507). As leader of the opposition to Alexander's papacy, della Rovere encouraged—and for a time joined—the French invasion of Italy by Charles VIII in 1494. But his anticipated aim to bring an end to the papacy of Alexander failed because the wily Borgia pope ended up negotiating beneficial terms with the French king rather than opposing him. With the contingent of French troops that his father had acquired, Cesare Borgia proceeded to orchestrate the overthrow of the major *condottieri* families, Orsini and Colonna, who controlled Rome (and access to the Vatican), and then to compel the papal states in central Italy to submit to papal rule.

The power and authority of the Church was thus deeply entrenched in temporal affairs during the pontificate of Alexander. Cesare, among other things, carved out a stronghold for himself in the northern Italian region of Romagna, owing to his ability to retain command of his father's papal army and increase its size through mercenary recruits. Julius was, in effect, powerless to reverse this violent shift in papal fortunes until Alexander unexpectedly died in August 1503, and he himself was elected pope just three months later. Once in power, Julius first neutralized his rivals and then went on to take possession of, transform, and expand the great enterprise begun by his predecessors: a robust temporal principate for the papacy. In effect, his bold actions heralded a new era in papal governance and diplomacy. While Alexander and Cesare had succeeded in making themselves great by acquiring arms of their own, Julius increased the power of the armed Church that he had inherited. In a bravado move that startled his contemporaries, the impetuous pontiff forged an impressive alliance of powers and personally led out the papal army, fulfilling his vow to drive the French out of Italy. Wearing armour and a full beard (the first pope to do so since antiquity), Julius shocked the world as the only warrior-pope in the history of the Catholic Church.

Renaissance Popes and Roman Culture

As *de facto* rulers of Rome, the popes ostensibly had responsibility for the physical and spiritual needs of the city through their pastoral work and the salvation of souls. In this regard, the fourteenth and fifteenth centuries marked a low point in the history of papal relations with the Roman community. The removal of papal government to Avignon in 1309–77 was partly responsible for the sad state of Roman affairs, while factionalism inside the city's walls and regional wars beyond further destabilized Rome. By the mid-fifteenth century, Rome had decayed into a shade of its former self: an ancient city that once had swelled with a population of over a million and ruled the Mediterranean world, now home to a mere 30,000 souls. Its infrastructure was broken, its services were miserable, and its architectural development had halted.

The humanist Pope Nicholas V (r. 1447–55) was the first pope in centuries to take decisive steps to turn things around. Committed to high moral conduct in office, he also professed two great passions that he pursued avidly before and after his election: a love of books and a love of architecture. As to the first of these passions, after the fall of Constantinople to Ottoman Turks in 1453, Nicholas employed an army of scribes to track down and purchase or copy any extant manuscripts that had survived from the fall of the Byzantine Empire. A former cataloguist for the Dominican library in Florence, which was handsomely endowed by the Medici, Nicholas had embarked on a crusade to preserve classical antiquity. His passion bore fruit in the form of an unrivalled collection of Greek and Latin manuscripts which, in accordance with the pope's last wishes, became the foundation of the Biblioteca Vaticana. On his deathbed, the pope also urged the Curia to fulfill a promise that he had not had time to complete: to dedicate itself to the restoration of the architectural splendor and greatness of Rome for the sake of the Church. This was the first time in centuries that a pope in Rome had declared such an enterprise.

Nicholas's successor, Pope Sixtus IV, honoured the last wishes of his predecessor, and the papacy began to move Rome in the direction of cultural renewal and progress. An intellectual of the highest order before becoming pope, Sixtus sensed the opportunity and seized it. By 1475, he had completed and expanded his predecessor's foundation of the Biblioteca Vaticana, increasing the collection of holdings, doubling and perhaps tripling its size. His collection of Greek and Latin texts numbered 3,500 by the time of his death, by far the largest collection in the Western world at that time. Sixtus not only increased the number of volumes, he also provided suitable quarters to house the collection and appointed an accomplished humanist librarian as curator, Bartolmeo Sacchi (1421–81), nicknamed "Platina," who oversaw the collection and produced the first

Fig. 44: *Sixtus Appointing Bartolomeo Sacchi, called Platina, as Prefect of the Biblioteca Vaticana,*
fresco on canvas by Melozzo da Forli, 1477, Pinacoteca, Musei Vaticani, Rome.
Photo Credit: Scala / Art Resource, NY.

full inventory of the Vatican holdings. At the request of Sixtus, Melozzo da Forlì commemorated the inauguration of the new Sistine library and its librarian in a fresco (see
fig. 44). Platina appears, kneeling before the pope in the foreground, while the pope's
own nephew and cardinal, Giuliano della Rovere—the future pope Julius—stands prominently in the centre of the composition. The classical architecture in the background
depicts an idealized version of what the Musei Vaticani during Sixtus's time looked like.
The inscription at the base of the fresco highlights the construction of the library within
the context of Sixtus's broader accomplishments in Rome: "With the restoration of tem-

ples, houses, streets, fora, city walls, bridges, and aqueducts, Rome owes you an even greater debt: where once it languished in squalor, now the library has a setting truly befitting its fame."

It will be remembered that Julius II was the nephew of this very same Sixtus, and that Sixtus essentially laid the foundations for Julius's career as best he could by quickly making him a priest, bishop, and cardinal. Sixtus also put into motion Nicholas's grand ambition for Rome, which Julius would finally accomplish. The culture, civic spirit, and physical body of Rome had languished under the pontificate of Alexander, apart from a few investments in architecture that he made for the Jubilee celebration in the year 1500. With the accession of Julius II to the papal throne, however, the bold spirit of cultural and civic renewal returned. Julius aligned his own activities with that of his predecessors Nicholas V and Sixtus IV, with the difference that he was more ambitious than they were and commanded more resources to pursue his plans. Indeed, no pope before him had aspired to accomplish such bold and grand plans for Roman urban reform and cultural renewal.

Julius's Rebirth of Rome

On April 18, 1506, Pope Julius had himself lowered down into the ground to lay the foundational cornerstone of the new Basilica di S. Pietro. The creation of such majestic works of architecture would serve, as Pope Nicholas V had previously argued, as "perpetual memorials and eternal testimonies seemingly made by the hand of God himself," and as such would appeal to the eyes of the faithful and help to sustain the doctrines and authority of the Holy See. Julius had effectively begun the construction of "noble edifices combining decorum and beauty with grand proportions" that Nicholas had conceived and his own uncle Sixtus, in the Cappella Sistina and library, had expanded. Julius's decision to raze to the ground the old Basilica di S. Pietro and to erect in its place the most imposing temple since antiquity (surpassing even Brunelleschi's Florentine Duomo) demanded as much audacity as vision. No pope before him, not even the brash Sixtus or scheming Alexander, had aspired to such a bold innovation.

The architectural seeds first planted by Nicholas's dream and nurtured by Sixtus's example finally had taken root in Julius's Vatican, a fact celebrated in his own time. A marble inscription, dating from 1512 and attributed to Hieronymus Picus, set along the path of the papal procession near Castel Sant' Angelo, testified to Julius' architectural determination and to the transformation of the architectural vision that he had inherited:

JULIO.II PONT:OPT:MAX:QUOD FINIB: DITIONIS.SRE. PROLATIS ITALIQ: LIBERATA URBEM ROMAM OCCUPATE SIMILIOREM QUAM DEVISE PATEFACTIS DIMENSISQ :VIIS PRO MAESTATE IMPERII ORNAVIT

To Julius II, Pontifex Optimus Maximus who, after enlarging the boundaries of the Papal State and freeing Italy, adorned the city of Rome, which had formerly been like an occupied city rather than a well-arranged one, with fine streets which he measured and widened in accordance with the majesty of the empire

With rhetorical flourish, these lines of neo-Classical Latin invoked the example of ancient imperial Rome and heralded Julius's idea for a new Rome.

The Via Giulia and Tomb of Julius

Two of Julius's boldest statements about how he saw himself and how he envisioned the rebirth of Rome are readily accessible to visitors today. Outside the walls of Vatican City, in the area of Rome across the Tiber from the Vatican, is the Via Giulia, named for Julius (Italian *Giulio*) himself. The pope instructed Bramante, his favourite architect, to plan and construct this long, broad, and absolutely straight new boulevard to make an important statement: this was, among other things, the first effort since antiquity to make any radical alterations to the ancient city's urban landscape. Moreover, it would be done in grand style, in effect creating a "modern" neighbourhood within the core of the ancient and medieval city. He also intended to build a new bridge at the terminus of the Via Giulia, which would carry pilgrims back across the Tiber to the Vatican. By creating a modern pedestrian thoroughfare from Ponte Sisto to the new Ospedale di Santo Spirito in Sassia (the former built and the latter rebuilt by his uncle Sixtus for the Jubilee of 1475), Julius hoped to bypass and render superfluous a similar passage-way reworked by Alexander along the Tiber on the opposite bank in favour of the Via Giulia plan. According to Giorgio Vasari (1511–74), author of *Lives of the Most Excellent Painters, Sculptors, and Architects* and a good guide to Julius's thinking, the plan was to restructure the governance as well as urban design of Rome. To that end, he further instructed Bramante to begin constructing a great edifice along the new route of the Via Giulia to which administrative and governmental offices of the city would be moved.

Fig. 45: Portrait of Julius II, fresco by Raphael. Detail of the *Cacciata di Eliodoro dal Tempio*, Stanza di Eliodoro, Stanze di Raffaello, Musei Vaticani, Rome. Photo Credit: Scala / Art Resource, NY.

Today, the rusticated exterior foundations for that building, made from heavy travertine marble and which Romans refer to as Julius's benches (or "sofas"), are the only visible relics of Bramante's massive, yet unfinished, design for the Palazzo dei Tribunali.

Another ambitious if unfinished Julian commission can be found in the Basilica di San Pietro in Vincoli, his titular church as Cardinal Giuliano della Rovere. Here we see the cenotaph to Julius with Michelangelo's *Moses* at its centre. The colossal tomb that Michelangelo conceived for Julius—originally designed as a three-tiered, free-standing structure with more than forty statues, to be erected within the immense new Basilica di S. Pietro—aimed to secure the legacy of Julius for all those who visited Rome and the Vatican. After his death, however, his papal successors, the Medici popes, not only compelled Michelangelo to work on other commissions and insisted that the tomb project itself be severely diminished in scope, but also moved it across town to its much less prominent location in S. Pietro in Vincoli, near the Foro Romano. The magnitude and magnificence of Julius's commission is nonetheless still visible in Michelangelo's imposing figure of *Moses*, the only major statue to survive (in Rome). Carefully executed by Michelangelo, the *Moses* is a personification hewn in marble of the monumental vision of Julius himself—a sculpted effigy, worthy of the great pope and patron who commissioned it. Any number of the pope's ideations can be perceived in this commission, be it his role as saviour of the papacy from the grasp of its enemies or his role in conceiving of Rome as a new Jerusalem.

The Stanze di Raffaello

Returning to Vatican City and its former papal palace, now home to the Musei Vaticani, we encounter another stunning Julian commission: the Raphael Rooms (Le Stanze di Raffaello). Two of the four rooms which today are called the "rooms of Raphael"—the Stanza della Segnatura and the Stanza di Eliodoro—are the ones most closely associated with Julius as well as the most original work of Raphael himself. Frescoes by Raphael, crowded with images of philosophers, poets, Church Fathers, and learned saints, adorn the *Segnatura*, which was likely a place of study for Julius and otherwise highlights the humanist interests of the day. Hundreds of volumes from Julius's own private library of Greek and Latin manuscripts would have been housed in this grand room, two floors above his uncle Sixtus's Biblioteca Vaticana.

The frescoes by Raphael in the Eliodoro, which may as well be called the "room of liberation," are of particular interest for his own career path. The visual theme of this room is recovered liberty, triumphantly depicted in the major scenes executed by the artist. On the north wall is St. Peter's liberation from his prison chains by the luminous angel of the Lord, a subtle reference to the elevation of Julius as cardinal back in 1471. On the east wall we have the expulsion of the profaners from the temple by armed figures, one mounted on horseback, witnessed here by Pope Julius himself (see fig. 45). On the south wall is the release of Church doctrine from the shackles of doubt and heresy, with a portrait of Julius anachronistically affirming the transubstantiation and establishment of the Corpus Domini solemnity in ritual. Finally, on the Stanza's west wall one sees the repulsion of the barbarian threat to Rome from Attila and his Huns, a manifest reference to the French occupation of Italy that Julius vowed to end. In this last scene (see fig. 2 on p. 11, above), completed after Julius's death and the rise of the Leo X de' Medici (1513–27), the warrior-pope, mounted on his white horse in martial dignity and riding out to defend the Papal principate, would have been depicted as an active agent in the liberation of the city of Rome from the barbarian threat.

Taken together, Raphael's frescoes for Julius's Stanze can be read as a powerful example of the visual rhetoric of the age. But the images are more than a beautiful distillation of Renaissance humanism. Raphael's frescoes reflect not only the humanist ideal represented by the private library of Julius but are also ingenious representations of Julius's ambitions. The inspiration for Raphael's designs for Julius's papal apartments can be traced back to the influential oratory of the papal court. Literally, the visual rhetoric of Raphael echoes the sacred rhetoric of Julius's Rome, expressing the grand scope of the Julian enterprise.

The Public Rhetoric of Julius's Papacy

Julius did not hesitate to praise himself and encourage others to announce and praise his various projects to renew the arts and infrastructure of Rome. In 1507, for example, while presiding over the inauguration of construction on S. Pietro, he turned to Giles of Viterbo (1472–1532), prior general of the Augustinian Order, to place this project within the larger context of Julius's vision of his papacy. Giles used the occasion to create the rhetorical image of a Christian golden age, with Julius's new basilica rising up over the tomb of Christ's vicar on earth, part of a providential plan unfolding in their time under the felicitous auspices of the present pope. He went on to contrast the fallen empire of the pagan Roman emperor Augustus (27 BCE–14 CE), featuring as its prized symbol a temple dedicated to Jupiter Optimus Maximus located on the Campidoglio, with a new Catholic empire whose touchstone would be the new S. Pietro, begun by Julius in the role of "Maximus Caesar et Pontifex Maximus." Referring to the warrior-pope's most recent victories in the name of the Church, the conclusion of Giles's sermon rises to dizzying rhetorical heights on the wings of Vergilian epic poetry, singing of "arms and a man":

> Among the things you [Julius] have most nobly accomplished [is] the rule of the greatest prince. For you used peace, clemency, and war with equity and justice; you pacified the faithful, spared the contentious; and with war and arms, you subdued the proud....Thus have I made immortal your felicity, Julius, most august *pontifex*; thus immortalized your mind and the great things you have accomplished with hope and good counsel—so that you will know the memory of all the good things you have accomplished shall not perish from the earth, and so that you will be exalted in order that all these things be followed by those who come after you. For the sake of this, it is right and fitting that the name of Julius moves you—with all its connotations of mind, character, and power.... Consider, Julius, the gravity of your authority and great strength of Christians; consider both kinds of rewards—those which immortal god alone bestows upon those who die, and those which living mortals give. That which we, in our labors, sow is brief; whereas that which we, in our reaping, collect is eternal. And among all that over which you cast your gaze so frequently, carefully, and cleverly, fear not that what our princes have lost, through a span of a thousand years, shall be returned and given by your efforts unto your joyous flock as the golden fruits of your oak, just as through you a golden age shall be restored.
> (Latin text by O'Malley (1969); trans. courtesy of Gretchen Meyers)

Giles was not alone in seizing the moment. On the first day of January 1508, ten days after this "golden age" sermon, the Roman humanist Battista Casali (1473–1525), one of the finest rhetoricians of the day, delivered a rousing oration in the Cappella Sistina, also in the presence of Julius himself. This speech invoked the entire classical tradition as background for the Rome of Julius's reign, for Casali declared that the Rome of Julius not only had restored the grandeur of the ancient city, but also had created a new Jerusalem and new Athens. In his oration, delivered just a few months before Julius commissioned Raphael to paint his Stanze, Casali concludes by placing emphasis upon Julius's enterprise as the completion of a providential plan:

> [J]ust as Sixtus, your father... laid the foundations of learning, you set the cornice upon it. There is the pontifical library he erected, in which he has, as it were, brought over Athens herself; gathering what books he could from the shipwreck [of the Ottoman conquest] he established the very image of the Academy. You, now, Julius II, Supreme Pontiff, have founded a new Athens when you summon up that prostrated world of letters as if raising it from the dead, and command ... that Athens be restored. To be sure, your other projects are indeed magnificent and splendid, yet they would remain voiceless and mute without learning and rhetoric to celebrate them. This Athenaeum you have restored shall never grow silent. Every day it will sing your praises in a hundred tongues, and when those other projects are ruins, as these texts are read, they shall rise again day after day, and forever the memory of them shall be renewed. This is why you achieve what soldiers shall never conquer by arms, shackling your adversaries with bonds of learning.
>
> (Trans. by O'Malley (1968))

By invoking the name of Athens and its renowned philosophical schools, Casali first proposed the idea that the erudition of ancient Greece had been resurrected in the books of the Biblioteca Vaticana. Inspiring a hope in the books themselves as the weapons and armour of the Church against the armies of Islam and the Turk (both being major geopolitical concerns of the era), his sermon praised Julius as the founder of a new age, celebrating the Biblioteca Vaticana as the most magnificent monument in the legacy of Julian Rome—and an antidote to the ideological claims of rival regimes. Casali's oration and Giles's sermon together proclaimed the Rome of Julius to be the heir of Periclean Athens and Augustan Rome.

The Legacy of Pope Julius II

However praiseworthy, such words about the impact of Julius on both the institution of the papacy and the city of Rome still do not do justice to the full magnitude of his vision and accomplishments. Much of what we take for granted about High Renaissance Rome, including what has been described as Rome's "Renaissance quarter" along the Via Giulia, was either his own commission or an epilogue to the powerful new spirit of civic humanism and cultural renewal that he had set in motion. Speaking only of the Via Giulia, the hundred years that followed Julius would see a building spree in the neighbourhood created by the pope that included such magnificent structures as Palazzo Spada, Palazzo Falconieri, and Palazzo Farnese. The same can be said for so many other places where Rome's premier patron turned his attention. As the great patron of Bramante, Raphael, and Michelangelo, among others, Julius created mighty opportunities for his generation's brightest talents, empowering them to produce some of their greatest and most iconic masterpieces. They owed a debt of gratitude to Julius and the vision of greatness, and renewal, that he embraced, although this debt is rarely grasped by the millions of visitors each year who travel to Rome and the Vatican City to pay homage to its art and architecture. While the legacy of Julius as pope and patron has been obscured, for those who know where to look, the city is full of visual evidence for his substantial contribution to the arts and visual rhetoric of High Renaissance. For the coat-of-arms and symbol of Julius's papacy, the Della Rovere oak tree and acorns, can be seen gracing several of the most unforgettable works of High Renaissance art and architecture by Bramante, Raphael, and Michelangelo. A few determined visitors will also discover the ironic honour paid to Pope Julius II by the humble circumstances of his final resting place. After being moved from another location in the seventeeth century, Julius's relics are currently buried together with his uncle Pope Sixtus IV (r. 1471–84) within the marble pavement of a side chapel of S. Pietro. The grave marker says nothing at all about his accomplishments and enterprises as pope, and yet it rests beneath the immense dome of the Basilica di S. Pietro that he himself was instrumental in creating.

Essential Reading

Hall, Marcia, ed. *Raphael's School of Athens*. Cambridge and New York: Cambridge University Press, 1997.

Holmes, George, ed. *Art and Politics in Renaissance Italy*. Oxford and New York: Oxford University Press, 1993.

O'Malley, John W. "Fulfillment of the Christian Golden Age under Pope Julius II: Text of a Discourse of Giles of Viterbo, 1507." *Traditio: Studies in Ancient and Medieval History, Thought and Religion* 25 (1969): 265–338.

——, *A History of the Popes: From Peter to the Present*. Lanham: Rowman and Littlefield, 2011.

——, *Giles of Viterbo on Church and Reform: A Study in Renaissance Thought*. Leiden, Brill: 1968.

Ott, Michael. "Pope Julius II." In *The Catholic Encyclopedia*, vol. 8, edited by Charles George Herbermann, et. al., 562–64. New York: Robert Appleton Co., 1910.

Rowland, Ingrid. *Culture of the High Renaissance: Ancients and Moderns in Sixteenth-Century Rome*. Cambridge and New York: Cambridge University Press, 1998.

Shaw, Christine. *Julius II: The Warrior Pope*. Oxford: Wiley-Blackwell, 1997.

Stinger, Charles. *The Renaissance in Rome*. Bloomington, IN: Indiana University Press, 1985.

The Vatican Collections: The Papacy and Art. New York: The Metropolitan Museum of Art, 1982.

Other Places to Encounter Pope Julius II in Rome

- Cappella Sistina (Musei Vaticani): frescoes commissioned by Julius, painted by Michelangelo.
- Cortile del Belvedere: Julius commissioned Bramante to establish a sculpture gallery here.
- Castle of Julius II (Ostia Antica, west of Rome): commissioned by Julius.

ROME

S. Maria del Popolo
9

Piazza
del Popolo

Via Crescenzio

Città del
Vaticano **Musei Vaticani**

S. Pietro
3

Castel
Sant' Angelo

Piazza
Cavour

13 Piazza
San Pietro Via Della Conciliazione

Via del Corso

Tevere

Palazzo
Montecitorio

S. Maria della Pace
10

6 **S. Agostino**

Corso Vittorio Emanuele II

Piazza
Navona

Pantheon 5
11
S. Maria sopra Minerva

Via Giulia

Campo
de' Fiori

Largo
Argentina

Villa Farnesina
15

Ponte Sisto

Via Arenula

Isola Tiberina

Trastevere

Giard
de
Aran

Aventino

S. Paolo fuori le mura 12

MAP OF ROME FOR CHAPTERS 17–19

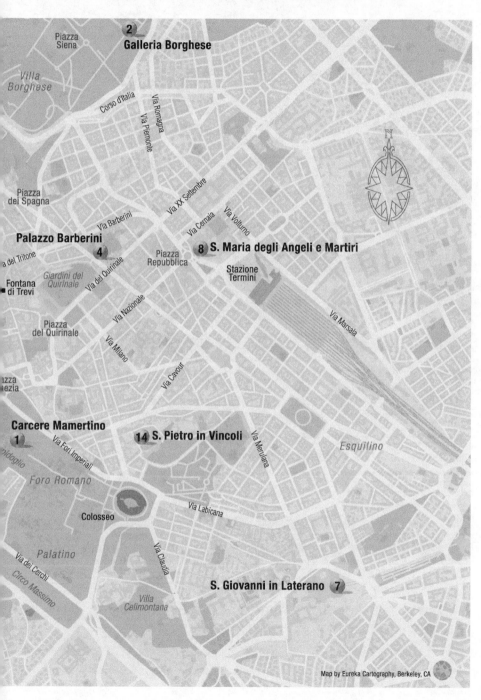

Piazza
Siena

2

Galleria Borghese

Villa
Borghese

Corso d'Italia

Via Romagna

Via Piemonte

Piazza
dei Spagna

Via Barberini

Via XX Settembre

Via Cernaia

Via Volturno

Palazzo Barberini

a del Tritone

4

Via del Quirinale

Piazza
Repubblica

8 **S. Maria degli Angeli e Martiri**

Giardini del
Quirinale

Stazione
Termini

Fontana
di Trevi

Via Nazionale

Piazza
del Quirinale

Via Milano

Via Marsala

Via Cavour

zza
ezia

Carcere Mamertino

1

Via Fori Imperiali

14 **S. Pietro in Vincoli**

Via Merulana

Esquilino

doglio

Foro Romano

Colosseo

Via Labicana

Via dei Cerchi

Palatino

Via Claudia

Circo Massimo

S. Giovanni in Laterano **7**

Villa
Celimontana

Map by Eureka Cartography, Berkeley, CA

Fig. 46: View of Piazza San Pietro, the Via della Conciliazione,
and Castel Sant'Angelo, Rome. Photo courtesy of Ann Molash.

Chapter Seventeen

ST. PETER (ca. 10–64 CE) AND ST. PAUL (5–67 CE) AT THE BASILICA DI SAN PIETRO, THE BASILICA DI SAN PAOLO FUORI LE MURA, AND THE ABBAZIA DELLE TRE FONTANE

FR. THOMAS ESPOSITO, O. CIST.

I Due Santi: Rome's Most Prominent Saints

One would perhaps expect to find the name *Petrus* (Peter) emblazoned on the façade of the Basilica di S. Pietro, the edifice built to honour the sacred relics of the first pope and the appointed "rock" of the Church (Matt. 16:18). However, the prominent inscription running across the front of S. Pietro features *Paulus* (Paul) in a central position instead. It was the proud Borghese pope, Paul V (r. 1605–21), who elected to honour his famous namesake in this special way upon his completion of S. Pietro in 1612, and doubtless this decision to use the apostle Paul's name to promote his own papal name ruffled some ecclesiastical feathers. Peter, after all, was a companion of Jesus and universally regarded as the "prince of the apostles," whereas Paul was not among the first disciples, and violently persecuted the first Christians. Both history and tradition thus weighed against the pope's decision. Yet Paul V boldly put his own name on the façade of S. Pietro anyway, counting on his great power and influence to win over skeptics. History was not positioned entirely against this pope's plans either. Indeed, the presence of *Paulus* on *Petrus*'s territory nicely symbolized the connection between the two greatest apostles of the early Church. In later centuries, the bond between Peter and Paul came to be further emphasized at the corners of the steps leading up to S. Pietro. Holding vigil over the Piazza San Pietro and guarding the entrance to the basilica are two grand statues, placed there in 1847. To the right is Paul, looking out toward the piazza and bearing a sword, a scroll, and a scowl; to the left stands Peter, clutching the keys representing the temporal and spiritual power of the bishop of Rome.

The origins of the Christian Church in Rome are bound up with the lives and glorious martyrdoms of these two men. In recognition of that fact, visitors have come to Rome for centuries to commemorate them and walk in their footsteps, and in doing so they have encountered many traces of their memory. Regarding Paul, for example, there is the main church at the Abbazia delle Tre Fontane—the site of his martyrdom—and the Basilica di San Paolo fuori le mura, where he is buried. Regarding Peter, multiple sites preserve one memory or another of his years in Rome, including most prominently the early Constantinian church and Petrine shrine that lie under Paul V's seventeenth-century church, both of which are today accessible to the public.

The Lives of Peter and Paul According to the New Testament

The four Gospels testify to Peter's unique relationship to Jesus. Peter, along with his brother Andrew, is among the first disciples called by Jesus (Matt. 4:18–22; Mark 1:16–20; John 1:35–42). Furthermore, his name always appears first in the list of the twelve disciples chosen by Jesus (Matt. 10:2–4; Mark 3:14–19; Luke 6:13–16). In Luke's presentation of the Last Supper, Jesus foretells Peter's denial of him, but also bestows on him a stunning commission: "Behold, Satan has demanded to sift all of you like wheat, but I have prayed that your own faith may not fail; and once you have turned back, you must strengthen your brethren" (Luke 22:31–32). The conclusion of John features the risen Jesus reversing Peter's threefold denial, charging him with the task of feeding and shepherding his flock (John 21:15–17).

The most famous Gospel scene involving Peter supplies the classic iconographical detail of the keys. Peter confesses that Jesus is "the Messiah, the Son of the living God," prompting Jesus to confer upon him a new name and a great authority: "And so I say to you, you are Peter (in Greek, *Petros* or Πέτρος; in Aramaic *Cephas*), and upon this rock (*Petra/Cepha*) I will build my Church, and the gates of the netherworld shall not prevail against it. I will give you the keys to the kingdom of heaven. Whatever you bind on earth shall be bound in heaven, and whatever you loose on earth shall be loosed in heaven" (Matt. 16:18–19).

The only first-century document detailing the events spanning the initial decades of the Christian Church is the Acts of the Apostles, written by Luke, who also composed the Gospel bearing his name. The first half of Acts presents Peter as the unquestioned leader of the disciples in Jerusalem. In the opening chapters, Peter organizes the election of a disciple to replace Judas Iscariot (Acts 1:15–26), and is the first to preach after the descent of the Holy Spirit at Pentecost (Acts 2:14–41). Though Paul is regarded as the "apostle to the gentiles," it is Peter who converts the first gentile, a Roman centurion named Cornelius (Acts 10:1–11:18).

It is through the book of Acts that we learn both about Paul's introduction to Christianity and the intersection between his and Peter's lives and ministry. In Acts 7, the deacon Stephen is stoned to death on account of his bold proclamation of the Gospel, and the Jews throwing the rocks lay their cloaks at the feet of a young man named Saul. This zealous persecutor of the novel Christian movement goes to Damascus to arrest Christians, but he is blinded on the way by a mysterious light. He then hears a voice crying, "Saul, Saul, why are you persecuting me?" (Acts 9:4). After regaining his sight, Saul is embraced by Barnabas, who vouches for his genuine conversion and introduces him to the apostles in Jerusalem (Acts 9:27). In Galatians 1:13–16, Paul gives a theological summary of his turn to Christ, and in Galatians 1:18 speaks of his meetings with Peter in Jerusalem,

In Galatians 2, Paul recounts a meeting in Jerusalem with the apostles Peter, James, and John, the "pillars" of the Church. These leaders confer with Paul about his teaching, and give him the approving "handclasp of fellowship" to signify their approval of his Gospel presentation. He zealously preaches the Gospel he once sought to eliminate in Antioch, where believers in Jesus are first called "Christians" (Acts 11:26). Perhaps in honour of a patron named Sergius Paulus whom he meets in Cyprus, Saul begins to be called Paul (Acts 13).

Peter and Paul assemble in Jerusalem, together with other leaders of the Church, to decide the proper course of action regarding gentile converts and the demands of the Jewish law. This "council" of Jerusalem, narrated in Acts 15, concludes with the agreement that non-Jewish converts do not need to follow the regulations of the Torah, including circumcision and dietary restrictions. After this decisive meeting, Peter disappears entirely from the narrative, and accounts of Paul's missionary journeys comprise the remaining chapters of Acts. Paul, with the help of disciples such as Silas and Timothy, journeys to Asia Minor and Greece. During the course of his travels, he writes letters to communities he had founded (such as the Philippians, Thessalonians, and Corinthians in Greece), exhorting them to maintain the true bonds of faith and community which he established among them, and to ignore those preaching a contrary and divisive message.

Paul is eventually arrested by Jewish authorities in Jerusalem, and asserts, after a series of appeals, that his Roman citizenship guarantees him a hearing before Caesar. The Acts narrative thus moves from the Temple in Jerusalem to the heart of the empire, with the final chapters (21–28) detailing Paul's voyage to Rome. Paul's journey is a pivotal moment in the life of the apostolic Church. As described in Acts 23:11, it was an event willed by God, who tells Paul, "Take courage; just as you testified about me in Jerusalem, so you must bear witness also in Rome."

After a shipwreck on the island of Malta, the boat bearing Paul arrives at Puteoli (modern day Pozzuoli, near Naples). As Paul and his guards move toward Rome, "brothers" from Rome meet him at the Forum of Appius and Three Taverns (Acts 28:15), both located on the Via Appia south of Rome. Acts concludes with Paul under house-arrest yet free to preach to those who visit him (28:16–31).

Prior to his arrival in Rome (perhaps several years beforehand), Paul wrote a letter to the Christians dwelling there, telling them that he hoped one day to greet them in person (Rom. 1:11–13; 15:23–24). These verses acknowledge that he was not the founder of the Christian community in Rome. He had befriended a Roman couple named Priscilla and Aquila while in Corinth (Acts 18). They had been exiled from Rome, probably in 49, as part of Claudius's decree banishing Jews from the city. This historical detail is confirmed by the historian Suetonius, who writes that a conflict regarding a certain "Chrestus" was disturbing the peace (*Divus Claudius* 25). This intriguing statement is usually interpreted as a misspelling of "Christus," referring to Jesus, and could suggest that Jews were upset that their fellows were converting to the Christian faith. In his letter, Paul greets Prisca and Aquila, who had returned to Rome after the death of Claudius in 54, "and those who gather in their house-church" (Rom. 16:4–5); the Chiesa di Santa Prisca on the Aventino stands atop what is traditionally regarded as the foundations of that house-church.

The Martyrdom of Paul at Tre Fontane

Acts ends with the arrival of Paul in Rome without mentioning anything about his death. Several of the letters attributed to Paul mention his readiness for death (2 Cor. 1:23–28;

Fig. 47: Chiesa di San Paolo, traditional site of the martyr's beheading,
Abbazia delle Tre Fontane, Rome. Photo courtesy of Fr. John Bayer.

Phil. 20:25; 2 Tim. 4:6–8), and Paul delivers a formal farewell discourse to the elders of Miletus (Acts 20:17–38). For information regarding his martyrdom, we must however look outside the New Testament. Pope Clement's (r. 88–99 or 101) letter to the Corinthians, one of the communities established by Paul, acknowledges his martyrdom (1 Clem. 5:2). An apocryphal document from the second century, the *Acts of Paul*, asserts that Paul was beheaded by order of Nero, though we cannot be certain of the details given in this text (such as Paul's preaching to the emperor). A later witness, *The Acts of Peter and Paul* by Pseudo-Marcellus (ca. fifth century), provides a plausible location for his martyrdom, *ad Aquas Salvias*, and notes that the beheading took place near pine trees.

Aquae Salviae is a swampy area several miles south of Rome. Christians venerated the site as the place of Paul's martyrdom almost immediately after his death. A tradition developed that his decapitated head bounced three times after meeting the executioner's sword, each bounce generating a gushing stream of water (see fig. 47). This tradition gave rise to the name of the place as it is still known today: *Tre Fontane* (Three Fountains). The site is a testimony to the strength of layered tradition in Church history. The oldest monument is the church built to shelter the springs of water. Rebuilt by Giacomo della Porta (1536–1602) in 1599, it is located at the back of the property, and may be reached by a short path lined with pine trees. The second church to be built on this property, standing about two hundred metres in front of the church commemorating Paul's martyrdom, is S. Maria Scala Coeli. It was purportedly built to house the relics of St. Zeno and some ten thousand soldiers in Diocletian's army who were martyred around 300. The largest church in the complex houses the relics of Saints Vincent of

Saragossa (ob. ca. 304) and Anastasius of Persia (ob. ca. 628). It was given by a sixth-century pope to the Benedictines, who established a monastery there.

Around 1140, Pope Innocent II removed Cluniac Benedictines from the monastery and entrusted the grounds to the great Cistercian Bernard of Clairvaux (1090–1153). The current church dates from this time period. Cistercians lived at Tre Fontane until 1812, when the Napoleonic invasion of Italy sent them packing. A group of Cistercians from the French abbey of La Trappe resumed monastic life there in 1868, and the Trappists remain the proprietors to this day. The monastic setting of Tre Fontane, with its rustic assortment of trees and little city noise, offers welcome relief from the urban hub-bub of Rome.

Paul's Tomb at the Basilica di S. Paolo fuori le mura

St. Paul may have been buried in a small cemetery next to the present-day S. Maria Scala Coeli, but this was not his final resting place. Christian sources from the second through the fifth centuries relate that the body of the Apostle was moved to a burial plot about two miles from the Aurelian wall along the Via Ostiense. A monument, or *cella memoriae*, was then erected over his grave. This site, like all Christian catacombs, was located outside the city walls; the superstitious Romans did not want the spirits of the dead roaming in the city itself, and the Christians, members of an illegal religion until 313, could gather safely at the tombs of their forerunners in faith. After legalizing Christianity, Constantine ordered the construction of a basilica above the tomb of Paul. Subsequent emperors and popes modified and adorned the basilica. From the tenth century onward, its care was entrusted to the Benedictines, who still live in an adjoining monastery.

In 1823, a fire ravaged the basilica, though the fifth century mosaics on the triumphal arch were spared. The basilica was quickly rebuilt according to the previous structure but several new features were added. Among the highlights of the new additions are the spacious portico and courtyard featuring quadrants of grass and palm trees which greet visitors. An imposing statue in the centre depicts Paul, "Apostle to the Gentiles," glaring fiercely. The sword he bears, its tip pointing skyward, is a standard iconographical feature; it represents "the sword of the Spirit, which is the word of God" (Eph. 6:17), as well as the instrument of his martyrdom.

Beneath the high altar is a *confessio*, a place for prayer which pilgrims can access by a staircase. A chain reputedly used during Paul's imprisonment is displayed in a case above a glass wall, which offers a view of the side of the white marble sarcophagus in which the apostle's bones reside. Excavations of this area were carried out from 2002–6. A marble slab on top of the sarcophagus bears the phrase "Paul Apostle Martyr" in Latin, and carbon dating of the bones within yielded an origin between the first and second centuries. Samplings of incense, purple linen with gold sequins, and blue linen were also collected from the tomb. Little controversy greeted Pope Benedict XVI's (r. 2005–13) announcement in 2008 that the sarcophagus almost certainly contains the mortal remains of the apostle.

As if to underscore the intrinsic connection between Peter and Paul, the interior of the basilica features a famous series of medallions running down the nave and aisles depicting every bishop of Rome from Peter to the current pontiff. This feature of the church probably owes its origins to the intervention of Pope Leo I (ca. 440–61). On the feast of the conversion of Saint Paul, January 25, popes visit the basilica to inaugurate the annual week of prayer for Christian unity.

The Martyrdom of Peter on the Vatican Hill

No New Testament writing chronicles Peter's movements after the council in Jerusalem, though some indirect evidence may be gleaned. Paul writes of a memorable confrontation with Peter in Antioch in which Paul publicly scolded him for refusing to eat with Gentiles, as the apostles had agreed to do in Jerusalem after a group of Jewish converts pressured him to eat separately from the non-circumcised (Gal. 2:11–15). The Gospel of John alludes to Peter's death. The risen Jesus appears to his disciples at the Sea of Galilee, and prophesies Peter's martyrdom in the following terms: "'Amen, amen, I say to you, when you were younger, you used to dress yourself and go where you wanted; but when you grow old, you will stretch out your hands, and someone else will dress you and lead you where you do not want to go.' He said this signifying by what kind of death he would glorify God" (John 21:18–19). The phrase "to stretch out your hands" may reasonably be interpreted as a reference to Peter's crucifixion. This concluding chapter could be a later addendum to John's Gospel, composed after the deaths of both Peter and "the beloved disciple."

A patristic tradition holds that Peter was the first bishop of Antioch, succeeded by Ignatius (ca. 35–107), the most famous early Christian martyr after the apostles. In 1 Cor. 1:12, Paul mentions a party of Christians in Corinth who claim to belong to Cephas, suggesting that Peter might have preached there as well (this tradition is confirmed by a second-century bishop of Corinth named Dionysius). The date of Peter's arrival in Rome, as well as the extent of his activity there, are unknown. Irenaeus of Lyon (ca. 120–202) reports that Peter, a simple fisherman from Galilee, was accompanied by Mark, his interpreter and translator. It was Mark who eventually compiled Peter's preaching and composed the book known today as the Gospel according to Mark (*Adversus Haereses* III.1.1). One other New Testament text, First Peter, implies that Peter was in Rome. This letter contains a verse which speaks of "the chosen one at Babylon" who sends greetings to the anonymous recipient of the letter, "as does Mark, my son" (1 Peter 5:13). Though the authorship and date of this letter are uncertain, it likely originated with Peter. Since Babylon is an early Christian code word for Rome, the verse could infer that Peter ministered in the capital city.

The occasion for Peter's martyrdom is probably the great fire in the year 64. The historian Tacitus writes of Nero's scapegoating of the Christians, accusing them of setting the city ablaze. He savagely persecuted them, using their bodies as torches for the night-time illumination of his parties (*Annales* XV.44). The circus where some of Nero's murderous reprisals took place was located on the Vatican Hill west of the Tiber. The obelisk currently in Piazza S. Pietro once stood in the centre of this circus; a plaque marking its original location is visible today as one walks pass the Swiss Guards to the *Scavi* office adjoining the basilica on the south side.

The apocryphal Acts of Peter narrates a beloved story about Peter's final days. According to this second- or third-century document, Peter flees the city to avoid Nero's bloodthirsty rage. On the Appia, barely a mile outside the city walls, Peter encounters Jesus walking in the opposite direction and asks him, "Where are you going, Lord?" Jesus responds, "I am going to Rome to be crucified." Peter then realizes that he himself must die, and returns to the city. The famous question, *Quo vadis, Domine?*, actually comes from John 13:36. A church commemorating this encounter is located near the first mile marker of the Appia, not far from the Catacombe di San Callisto.

Though details are sparse, Peter's death in Rome is confirmed in 1 Clement 5:3–4, usually dated to the last years of the first century. Tradition asserts that Peter requested to be crucified upside down, not wishing to die in the same manner as his Lord. After his crucifixion, Christians took charge of his body. Since the custom of the early Christians was to bury their martyrs close to the site of their death, they placed Peter's corpse in a nearby pagan necropolis along the Via Cornelia, on the southern slope of the Vatican Hill.

The history prior to the legalization of Christianity is murky regarding the bones of the apostles. Graffiti found at the catacombs of San Sebastiano on the Appia suggest that the remains of both Peter and Paul may have been moved there for a time, perhaps due to fear of vandalism during the persecution of Valerian (r. 258–60). Nevertheless, the two present-day basilicas housing their tombs can claim legitimate authority as the resting places of the principle apostles. Eusebius (II:25) preserves the statement of a presbyter named Gaius, who boasts near the end of the second century that he can point out the "trophies" of the two apostles "who founded the Church" in Rome: that of Paul along the Via Ostiense, and that of Peter at the Vatican.

The Search for Peter's Bones

The story of Peter's bones and their discovery is a fascinating one that spans the entire history of the Roman Church. Pope Pius XI (r. 1922–39) wanted to be buried as close to the bones of Peter as possible. Since it was generally supposed that the prince of the apostles was buried beneath the high altar, Pius XI's successor, Pius XII (r. 1939–58), ordered the excavation of that subterranean area. The work took place from 1940–49, and was not interrupted by the Nazi occupation of Rome in 1943–44. These excavations (or *scavi*) uncovered an ancient necropolis composed of funerary houses and monuments, many of them pagan, which were originally located above ground. A tomb carved from bare earth, around which other tombs had been arranged, was also discovered.

An above-ground trophy marking Peter's grave, named later for the presbyter Gaius, was an *aedicula* without any apparent Christian symbols. It featured a red plaster wall, which archaeologists dated to the reign of Marcus Aurelius (161–80) thanks to the imprint on the bricks used to build the wall. Touching this red plaster wall at a right angle was another wall built sometime later to support it; labelled the "graffiti wall," it bore the scratchings of various Christian symbols and names, among them Jesus, Mary, and Peter.

The veneration of Peter's relics at the Vatican necropolis, evidenced by the graffiti wall, prompted Constantine to erect a basilica over the saint's bones around 325. The location of the grave on the southern slope of the Vatican Hill required Constantine to level part of the hill; the monuments and chambers of the necropolis, still active at the time Christianity was legalized, were filled with dirt, fortuitously preserving them and the original trophy. Constantine wished to construct the altar of his basilica directly above the trophy identifying Peter's grave. Subsequent popes built or refurbished altars on top of the bones. Their exact location, however, became lost with the passage of time, and no search was made for them during the construction of the new basilica in the sixteenth and seventeenth centuries.

A most intriguing Vatican mystery took place in the middle of the twentieth century. Inside the graffiti wall adjoining the red plaster wall, a small repository lined with marble had been created. A collection of bones was removed from this repository in 1941 but the men who removed them did not inform the main archaeologists about their removal. As a result, the bones were placed in a wooden box and stored in a Vatican cupboard, forgotten for over a decade!

An epigraphist, Margherita Guarducci, had deciphered the graffiti wall, figuring out the symbols revealing Peter's name in abbreviated word puzzles and letters attached to other letters. She learned that a piece of red plaster had been found in the marble repository of the graffiti wall bearing the phrase "Peter is here" in Greek. After questioning the archaeologists who worked on the graffiti wall, she turned her attention to the forgotten bones in the wooden box. An analysis revealed them to be the remains of an elderly man with encrusted dirt attached to them. In addition, strands of purple wool and gold thread had been detected. Guarducci came to the tantalizing conclusion that the bones of the Galilean fisherman had at some point been removed from his grave and then transferred to the marble repository of the graffiti wall. Though many questions remain unanswered to this day (why were the bones stashed in a wall of the tomb, rather than in a more honourable space? And when would that relocation have occurred?), Pope Paul VI declared in 1968 that the bones of St. Peter had been found. The necropolis underneath the basilica may be visited as part of the scavi (excavations) tour, during which a guide explains the history of the necropolis while leading a

Fig. 48: *Saint Peter Enthroned*, bronze statue attributed to Arnolfo di Cambio, c. 1300, Basilica di S. Pietro, Rome. Photo courtesy of Peter Hatlie.

group through its streets, houses, and memorials of Peter's tomb. The tour ends at a viewing platform from which one can see the bones of Peter, which were returned to their repository in the graffiti wall after Guarducci's investigations.

The ancient tradition that the basilica's high altar stands over the bones of the fisherman explains the architectural space inside and outside the basilica. The construction of the new S. Pietro, which required the demolition of the decrepit Constantinian basilica, included the immense dome of Michelangelo and, directly beneath it, the majestic *Baldacchino* of Gian Lorenzo Bernini (1598–1680). Before and beneath the *Baldacchino*, Bernini fashioned the confessio, accessible by two flights of stairs and illuminated by candles. This space contains a gold box which holds the *pallia*, the wool stoles given to new archbishops by the pope, as a symbol of their connection to Peter, the chief shepherd of the Church. The term "confessio" is appropriate for this area, which stands almost level with the bones of Peter, for it is here that Catholic pilgrims from all over the world renew their baptismal profession of faith.

The dominant image linking Peter to his successors, the bishops of Rome, is the set of keys, recalling Matthew 16:18–19. A beloved twelfth-century statue of St. Peter sitting solemnly on a throne, his left hand clutching two keys and his right extended in blessing, stands in front of a huge column near the confessio in the main nave. The saint's right foot is completely worn away due to centuries of rubbing by devoted pilgrims. The biblical passages asserting Peter's presidency over the apostles (and, by extension, the pope's authority over his brother bishops) are also prominently displayed inside the basilica. The words of three passages mentioned above, Matthew 16:16–19, Luke 22:31–32, and John 21:15–19, form continuous gold banners running above the central nave and wrap along the back sanctuary. The texts are written in Latin, though Jesus's words from John 21 about shepherding his sheep are written in Greek above the *cathedra* (chair), another symbol of Peter's universal authority.

The Petrine keys are also easy to spot outside the basilica. Hovering over the two clocks on either side of the façade are interlocking keys underneath papal tiaras. The piazza itself, reconfigured by Bernini, takes the shape of a keyhole, though the two semicircle colonnades, dotted with statues of saints, are commonly understood to be arms embracing all visitors.

Conclusion: Blood of the Martyrs, Seed of the Church

Jesus never set foot in Rome. His ministry took place exclusively in the Roman province of Palestine, and he was crucified in Jerusalem. His disciples used Jerusalem as their headquarters in the initial years after his death and resurrection and their evangelical efforts took them "to the ends of the earth" (Acts 1:8). The capital of that world was Rome, but this does not suffice to explain why Rome quickly acquired its primacy among all Christian churches. The most suitable explanation, from both historical and theological points of view, is that the apostles Peter and Paul shed their blood in this city.

Several patristic sources claim that Peter and Paul were martyred at the same time, but no conclusive evidence to support this is available. A majority of scholars hold that Peter died in the year 64 and that Paul died either in 64 or 67. The implications of their final testaments of faith were immediately recognized by the first Christian writers. It is possible that the author of the Revelation of St. John has Peter and Paul in mind when he presents the image of the two olive trees and two witnesses, both of whom are murdered and desecrated in the streets (Revelation 11). The manifest references in Revelation to Rome under the guise of "Babylon," and even to Emperor Nero, suggest that the two apostles martyred in Rome are symbolized in John's vision.

St. Ignatius of Antioch, writing just before his own martyrdom around the year 110, tells the Romans that he does not give them orders like Peter and Paul did (Rom. 4:3). Both Ignatius and Irenaeus speak of the primacy of the Roman Church "in love." Irenaeus, writing near the end of the second century, bases his argument for Rome's primacy on the fact that Peter and Paul "founded and built up the Church" and that every other Church must be in harmony with this one, since its "most excellent origin" as the place where the two great leaders shed their blood has faithfully preserved its apostolic heritage (*Adversus Haereses* III.3.2). Tertullian offers a beautiful interpretation of the apostles' martyrdoms when he writes around the year 200, "how fortunate is this Church into which the apostles poured forth all their teaching along with their blood" (*Prescription of Heretics* 3). The blood of the martyrs, for Tertullian, is the seed from which the Church sprouts (*Apologeticus* 50:13). The fact that these apostles deposited the seed of their teaching and their blood in Roman soil makes the eternal city not only an essential place of pilgrimage but also the focal point of the universal Church's confession of faith.

Today, the visit made by all bishops to the bishop of Rome is known as the pilgrimage *ad limina apostolorum* (to the threshold of the apostles), not simply to the threshold of Peter. It may be said that while the bishop of Rome possesses the primacy of governing and strengthening the faith given to Peter by Jesus (Matt. 16:16–18; Luke 22:32), he is also heir to the teaching authority of Paul, who wrote of his daily concern "for all the Churches" (2 Cor. 11:28).

Essential Reading

Confraternity of Christian Doctrine. *The New American Bible.* Rev. edition. Oxford and New York: Oxford University Press, 2011.

Eusebius. *The History of the Church.* Revised edition. Translated by G. A. Williamson. New York: Penguin Classics, 1989.

Farmer, William and Roch Kereszty. *Peter and Paul in the Church of Rome: The Ecumenical Potential of a Forgotten Perspective.* Mahwah, NJ: Paulist Press, 1990.

Pope Benedict XVI. *Saint Paul.* San Francisco: Ignatius Press, 2010.

Walsh, John E. *The Bones of Saint Peter.* Manchester, NH: Sophia Institute Press, 2011.

Other Places to Encounter Saints Peter and Paul in Rome

– Basilica di S. Giovanni in Laterano: besides the imposing statues of apostles (including Paul) lining the nave, tradition has it that the head of Peter is housed in the church's *Baldacchino*.

– Carcere Mamertino: just off the Foro Romano, this small dungeon was reportedly the place where Peter was held before his martyrdom.

– S. Maria del Popolo: its Cappella Cerasi features two paintings by Caravaggio: *The Crucifixion of St. Peter* and *The Conversion of St. Paul*.

– San Pietro in Vincoli: a chain which, according to tradition, was bound to Peter during his imprisonment, is displayed in this church.

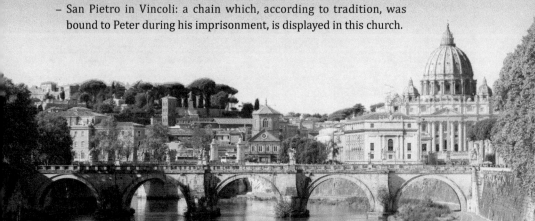

Fig. 49: *Portrait of Tommaso "Fedra" Inghirami*, by Raphael, 1515–16, Palazzo Pitti, Florence. Photo Credit: Erich Lessing / Art Resource, NY.

Chapter Eighteen

RAPHAEL SANZIO (1483–1520 CE), TOMMASO "FEDRA" INGHIRAMI (1470–1516 CE), AND POPE JULIUS II (1443–1513, r. 1503–13 CE) AT THE STANZA DELLA SEGNATURA (1508–11 CE)

CLARE P. FRANK AND WILLIAM A. FRANK

A Room with Many Conversations

The Stanza della Segnatura is an elegant, modest-sized room on the second floor of the Vatican palace (now the Musei Vaticani) designed to house Pope Julius II's personal library. The room was decorated by Raphael in the early years of the sixteenth century. Like many great works of art, Raphael's *Stanza* asks the visitor to stay awhile, to dwell with it, a proposal particularly apt for a library. Art historian Timothy Verdon distinguishes the Renaissance visitor from today's typical learned viewer: "Renaissance visitors to the Stanza della Segnatura 'registered' the frescoes with their eyes and 'read' them with mind and heart—poetic processes that differed substantially ... from those with which modern art historians read them" (Verdon 116–17). As we shall see, the walls of the *Stanza* portray many conversations, inviting the viewer to be part of them.

The paintings of this room tell two stories. One is the story of the characters depicted, for the most part "heroes" who played important roles in the tradition of ancient classical learning. This learning was in the process of recovery by Renaissance scholars, builders, poets, and artists. The second story is that of the three men most responsible for the room's program and embellishments: the program's inventor, Tommaso "Fedra" Inghirami (1470–1516); its painter, Raphael Sanzio (1483–1520); and its patron, Pope Julius II (1443–1513, r. 1503–13). What is expressed on the room's frescoed walls and ceiling is informed by the humanism that developed in papal Rome during the fourteenth and fifteenth centuries. Every least detail of Raphael's painting fits into a unified program that portrays the intellectual, cultural, and spiritual aspirations of Rome's renewal after a long period of decline. Part of the wonder and delight of visiting the Stanza is understanding what it all signifies.

In this regard, scholars in the last half of the twentieth century have greatly advanced our understanding of the Renaissance humanism specific to Rome, including questions of the influence of humanism on artistic programs such as that of the Stanza. John F. D'Amico and John W. O'Malley are just two among these scholars. Their scholarship helps us appreciate how the humanists in the Roman academies and in the papal curia employed scholarly, poetic, and oratorical gifts in fashioning an effective ideology that wed Rome's cultural achievements to its political and ecclesiastical aspirations. Building on this body of historical scholarship, in her book *Raphael's "Stanza della Segnatura": Meaning and Invention*, art historian Christiane L. Joost-Gaugier demonstrates the influence exercised by Roman humanists in fashioning the room's program. Although there is as yet no decisive agreement on the mind behind the program, she has persuasively argued that it was Tommaso Inghirami, famed orator and head of the Biblioteca Vaticana, who invented the program that Raphael executed with such extraordinary creative brilliance (Joost-Gaugier 57).

Raphael and Inghirami

The last twelve years of Raphael's brief life, passed in Rome, were his most productive and masterful. After growing up and learning his craft in his native Urbino, he perfected his painting in various cities across Italy as a young adult, working either under or with some of the masters of his day, including Perugino (1448–1523). By his mid-twenties, he had already gained considerable fame and influence, notably through such works as the revolutionary *Marriage of the Virgin* (1504, now in the Pinacoteca di Brera, Milan) and the massive *Madonna of the Baldacchino* (1506–8, now in the Galleria Palatina, Florence). The unexpected call to Rome by Julius came just as the artist was completing the latter work and initiated an intensive and remarkably productive concluding phase of his brief career. Nearly fifty separate works commissioned by a wide range of patrons date to Raphael's Roman years, 1509–20, including a lively picture of Inghirami (see fig. 49). Arguably the most celebrated of these, however, was that commissioned by Julius and guided by the same Inghirami to give further momentum to the great era of renewal and humanistic fervour that had been stirring in Rome in recent decades and reached its high point under Julius. Raphael's Stanza della Segnatura represented a triumph in the cultural history of this age. For this project brought one of the age's most gifted painters together with one of the age's premier humanist intellectuals, both of whom received encouragement and support from one of the age's most powerful and far-seeing popes in Julius.

Setbacks and Renewal in Renaissance Rome

For a hundred years or so prior to the age of Inghirami, Raphael, and Julius, the city of Rome and its popes had suffered two major blows to their prestige and power. Between 1309 and 1376 the popes resided not in Rome but rather in Avignon, France, in a historical period that is sometimes called the second Babylonian Captivity. It was Pope Gregory XI (r. 1370–78) who in 1376 left Avignon and returned the papal court to Rome. But on his death two years later, the papal election deteriorated into two uncompromising factions, each declaring its own pope and thus provoking a bitter struggle among anti-popes between 1378 and 1417. Both this struggle and the earlier Avignon interlude dealt a near fatal blow to both papal prestige and the economy and infrastructure of the city of Rome, over which popes had presided for most of the previous one thousand years. To make matters worse still, the papacy's return to relatively normal operations by the second quarter of the fifteenth century was met with hostility by their Italian neighbours and certain powerful European nations. Even if the papal states were not the single or even central focus of these hostilities, as a sovereign state located within a complex and tense geopolitical predicament, it was evident that Rome would get dragged into war. More than one war followed, in fact, over the course of the fifteenth and sixteenth centuries. These so-called Italian Wars or Great Italian Wars pitted the relatively weak Italian states of Rome, Milan, Naples, Florence, Genoa, and Venice against one another in differing combinations of alliance and antagonism. Carried on for over sixty years (1494–1559), the Italian Wars produced few winners and plenty of losers, Rome among them. To add to the eternal city's troubles, the fall of Constantinople to the Ottoman Turks in 1453 and the latter's subsequent push westward toward Catholic Europe was troubling, and in Europe itself the Reformation movement was at also at hand. It came not just from Martin Luther's Germany, Henry VIII's England, or Erasmus's Netherlands. Calls for reform came from within the Vatican curia as well.

Despite these multiple challenges at home and abroad, some progress at renaissance and reform did come to Rome over the course of the fifteenth and sixteenth centuries. Culturally speaking, Roman humanism advanced on several political, cultural, and religious fronts. Religiously, the period begins with the Council of Constance (1414–18), which brought to an end the Avignon Papacy, and ended with the ambitious reforming Council of Trent (1545–63). Finally, the city of Rome enjoyed a quiet rebirth during the period. It was Pope Martin V (r. 1417–31) who began the massive task of urban and artistic renewal for a city which had lapsed into political chaos and financial bankruptcy over the course of the previous century. With this historic move toward the eventual restoration of civic order and public services in Rome, energies turned toward the rebuilding of the Basilica di S. Pietro and the adjoining Vatican Palace.

Three popes played especially significant roles in advancing in these last efforts. Nicholas V (r. 1447–55) believed that the popes, "as custodians of the keys given by Christ to Peter, should exercise that authority from the sacred precincts of the apostle's tomb" (Johnson 120). It was he who added to the Vatican Palace the wing that contains the Raphael rooms, while also founding the Biblioteca Vaticana. Then, three pontificates later, Pope Sixtus IV (r. 1471–84), "with stunning vigor and intelligence transformed Rome into an incomparable center of art and learning" (Johnson 125). Himself a learned humanist, Sixtus IV took great interest in augmenting the library begun by Nicholas. Finally, and most importantly, Pope Julius II (r. 1503–13) consolidated the independent political governance of Rome and the Papal States against its many enemies and furthermore made himself "immortal for his patronage of Bramante, Raphael, and Michelangelo" (Johnson 129). With these and other commissions, Julius's goal was nothing less than restoring Rome to its ancient prestige and power: not merely the exalted power of Rome under earlier popes of the Middle Ages but rather the insuperable Rome of ancient times. Indeed, Julius was inspired by the ancient Rome of Julius Caesar, Augustus, and Constantine. Equally important was the model of Cicero's Rome, the latter a man who understood that Rome's greatness was sustained by more than its *arma virumque*, its men and wars: it needed the wisdom and beauty of Athens's philosophy and art. Although Julius was happy to think of himself as the warrior-pope, whose hand was more comfortable with a sword than a book, he was nevertheless keenly concerned that, in accord with the humanist vision of ancient Greece and classical Rome, Christian Rome be a centre of law, poetry and art, philosophy and theology. Julius II was a patron with wealth, judgment, vision and purpose.

Celebrating Rome through Its Key Renaissance Popes

A couple of historical references give us a good sense of the renewed spirit and intellectual aspirations of the age. At the entrance of the Biblioteca Apostolica Vaticana, founded by Nicholas V and substantially reorganized by Sixtus IV with the assistance of his nephew, Guiliano della Rovere (the future Pope Julius II), there is a caption that extols the civic works of Sixtus with regards to the new construction of Rome's churches, its streets, parks, city walls, bridges, and aqueducts. It praises the reopening of Rome's age-old shipping port and the building a new wall around the Vatican. The caption then ends with the lines: "Still, Rome owes you [Sixtus] more than this: where a library languished in squalor / Now it is visible in a setting befitting its fame" (trans. Rowland 135–36). The caption celebrates, as a crowning achievement, the renewal of the Vatican's library.

In a comparable spirit, Battista Casali, papal orator, delivered a speech in the Cappella Sistina before Pope Julius on January 1, 1508. He clearly projects the role cast for Julius's Rome as the new Athens. Casali set before the pope the vision of classical Athens as the well-spring of religion, learning, and law that spread "to every land." The ancient city is depicted as a place of schools where "the princes of learning" are tutored in the moral virtues of fortitude, temperance, and justice. But ancient Athens, the birthplace of moral and civic virtue, had long since been destroyed in the whirlwind of the "Mohammedan war machine" (trans. Rowland 139). Casali is well aware that Greek learning has been given a new birth in Rome. He commends Julius and his uncle Sixtus for their rich contributions to its renaissance. With his patronage of the Biblioteca Vaticana and the revitalization of the world of the arts and letters, Julius has "founded a new Athens." Casali concludes this line of thought with an image calculated to appeal to the warrior in Julius's character:

> This is why, Blessed Father, you achieve what your soldiers shall never conquer by arms: shackling your adversaries with bonds of learning, learning with which, as with a sponge, you will erase all the errors of the world and circumcise the ancient roots of evil at the base with a sickle of adamant. (trans. Rowland 140)

Against this sketch of the historical context of Julius II's papacy, we turn to the Stanza della Segnatura. Our purpose will be to appreciate how the Roman renaissance advanced by Julius was understood and interpreted by Tommaso Inghirami and Raphael Sanzio in the program of the Stanza.

Setting for the Stanza della Segnatura (1508–11)

Walking into the Stanza della Segnatura, one immediately encounters remarkable paintings on its ceiling and four walls. The high ceiling is a complex symbolic puzzle integrating personifications of philosophy, poetry, law, and theology together with incidents from classical mythology and holy scripture. Altogether no less than 164 persons (human, mythical, angelic, divine) are collected into various groups, each is engaged in active conversation. Many of these figures are almost life-size and most represent real historical individuals: philosophers, mathematicians, natural philosophers, painters, architects, legislators, evangelists, theologians, popes, poets, saints and apostles, as well as Jesus Christ, God the Father, and the Holy Spirit. It was common in Renaissance art to

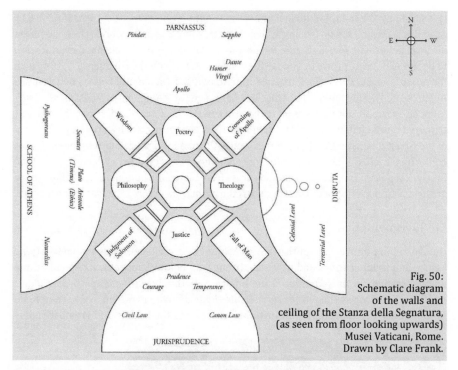

Fig. 50:
Schematic diagram
of the walls and
ceiling of the Stanza della Segnatura,
(as seen from floor looking upwards)
Musei Vaticani, Rome.
Drawn by Clare Frank.

show great characters in conversation, but Raphael's Stanza develops the motif with a creativity and scale that is altogether unprecedented. In addition to the people depicted therein, one soon realizes that one is surrounded by words. There are the silent words spoken in the many conversations, and there are the many more words of the fifty-four books, scrolls, and manuscripts depicted in the room's paintings. Some lines of conversation span more than two thousand years. It's what today we might call a communion (*communio*) of the holy and the learned.

This room, we remember, was originally intended as Julius II's personal library. In accordance with the custom of the day, the books of the collection were classified into four groups: poetry, philosophy, law, and theology. Correspondingly, each of the four walls is dedicated to one of the four arts. It is the genius of Inghirami and Raphael that brings the books and scrolls alive through conversations on the walls. There also seem to be conversations between the arts: philosophy with civil law, theology with canon law, poetry with both theology and philosophy, and philosophy with theology. Let's now look at particular images on the ceiling and walls.

On Parnassus

On the ceiling above the north wall is the personification of Poetry. She holds a book and a lyre, while *putti* (little angels) at her sides hold up the words *"numine afflatur"* (Breath of Divinity). These words likely come from Virgil's *Aeneid*, specifically the scene where Aeneas, founder of Rome, stands with the Sybil at the opening to the underworld as she is inspired by the breath of divine authority: *adflata est numine ... dei* (*Aeneid* 6.50–51). As she is seized by the divine spirit, Aeneas passes into the underworld. There he meets his dead father who reveals to him the destiny of Rome: "Roman, remember, your arts are to be these: to bring peace, to impose the rule of law, to spare the conquered, battle down the proud" (*Aeneid* 6.847–53, Fitzgerald trans. modified). On the wall below Poetry we see Apollo, seated beside the source of the Castalian Spring at the summit of Mt. Parnassus, surrounded by the Muses. He gazes off to the heavens, perhaps transfixed, as he plays his lyre. Gathered on the left and right flanks, in four different conversations, are the great poets of the Greek and Latin traditions. For instance, Dante and Virgil gather with blind Homer on the upper left. On the bottom left we see Sappho, who is credited with being one of the first lyrical poets in ancient Greece, and across from her on the bottom right sits Pindar, the greatest of Greek lyric poets. Directly across the room from Poetry is Law or Jurisprudence.

On Jurisprudence

On the ceiling above the south wall, opposite Poetry, we see a figure personifying Justice and holding scales and a sword. On the wall below, Raphael has depicted three distinct scenes. On the left side, on the Justice wall, the Byzantine emperor Justinian I (r. 482–565) receives the *Corpus Juris Civilis* (*Body of Civil Law*). This book, completed in 534 under the sponsorship of Justinian, represents the largest and greatest collec-

Fig. 51:
School of Athens (detail): scientists discussing a problem, fresco by Raphael, Stanza della Segnatura, Stanze di Raffaello, Musei Vaticani, Rome. Photo Credit: Erich Lessing / Art Resource, NY.

tion of Roman law ever produced. Justinian believed that law flows from reason. Since it is not based on force, "the minister of justice must be a follower of "true philosophy" (d'Entrèves 27). The emperor wrote that "of all subjects none is more worthy of study than the authority of Laws, which happily disposes all things divine and human, and puts an end to iniquity" (*Digest* 1.1). The attraction of seeing law this way would be irresistible to a Renaissance mind attentive to moral and cosmic harmony. The Stanza's elevated understanding of law is taken up into Julius's vision of himself as the new Caesar.

On the right side of the same (south) wall, Pope Gregory IX (r. 1227–41) receives the *Decretals* from St. Raymond of Pennafort. An important development in canon law, the *Decretals* was conceived of as the mother of all canon law collections, and to this extent it was similar to Justinian's *Corpus*, which aimed to do the same for civil law. It pairs well with Justinian's *Corpus* in another way as well, and that is in its claim to be authoritative not merely within the Church, but universally. Both the selection of the *Decretals* motif itself and its placement in conversation with Justinian's *Corpus* emphasize papal dignity and supreme papal authority.

In the lunette overarching both scenes are three female figures representing three of the cardinal virtues: courage, prudence, and temperance. Courage, on the left, wears a helmet, holds a lion at her side, and wears the warrior's protective foot gear. In the middle, Prudence wears her two faces: one, that of a young woman gazing into a mirror and the other face, that of an older bearded man looking backwards. Temperance, holding reins in her hand, is seated at the right.

On the School of Athens

On the ceiling above the east wall, with Poetry to the right and Justice to the left, we find the personification of Philosophy. She is flanked by putti holding up the words "*causarum cognitio*" (knowledge of the causes). On the wall below is the *School of Athens*, which has almost become a visual cliché. For the contemporary tourist, it is *the* attraction to the Stanza della Segnatura. In large part this preference has been prompted by art critics and historians who have restricted their attention to just the ancient philosophers. To do so, however, is to miss the significance of how all four walls and the ceiling work together to celebrate the classical learning in the new Rome.

The *School of Athens* represents a congregation of Greek philosophers from Pythagoras to Porphyry. Its composition expresses the Renaissance philosopher Pico di Mirandola's *pax philosophica*. Pico held that there is concord among the variety of philosophical schools. In line with this sentiment, Plato and Aristotle stand shoulder to shoulder at the centre of the east wall, under the arched structure open to the sky. Plato holds in his hand his *Timaeus* and Aristotle his *Ethics*.

On the right side, the Aristotelian philosophers gather in distinct groups. Most prominent are the students huddled around Euclid as he demonstrates one of his geometrical theories (see fig. 51). Just above them and with his back to us, Ptolemy, wearing his golden crown, holds the globe of the earth with the continents marked off. Facing him is Strabo, the famed geographer, holding up a globe of the starry universe. Immediately to the left of Plato himself is a small group of men thought to include Parmenides and Zeno.

Further left stands Socrates actively engaged with Xenophon, Phaedo, and Crito. Toward the lowermost section there's a group gathered around Pythagoras. Immediately to his left is Empedocles and standing off to his right insistently gesturing to the book in his hand is Anaximander. Taken as a whole, Raphael has depicted a seven hundred year tradition of classical Greek pagan philosophy.

Brian Copenhaver has observed the influence of Pico di Mirandola who, in his *Oration on the Dignity of Man* (1486), sets out a course of studies in which "the student starts with moral philosophy and then moves through dialectic and natural philosophy toward theology" (Copenhaver). The move into philosophy and beyond into theology is essential to understanding the meaning of the *School of Athens*. The viewer is meant to see these philosophers of classical antiquity, with Plato and Aristotle at the centre, oriented forward, across the floor, towards the scene of the *Disputa* on the opposite wall.

On the *Disputa*

On the ceiling of the west wall the personification of Theology presides over what has come to be called the *Dispute of the Most Holy Sacrament* (in Italian: the *Disputa*) (see fig. 52). The wall expresses the life of Christian theology: holy conversation probing the mysteries of creation and redemption under the guidance of sacred revelation. The picture shows a great dynamism and diversity of characters, saintly, papal, learned and artistic. For the most part the characters focus directly toward the central line, following the presence of God upward. In viewing the scene, one's eye travels in two directions. Starting from lower middle with the Holy Eucharist on the altar, one's eye is drawn up a vertical line to the Holy Spirit directly above, then further up to the resurrected Christ in glory, and finally to God the Father in the golden Empyrean, surrounded by angels, holding the world in his left hand and blessing Creation with his right hand. At the top of the arch the eye then follows the rays of divine light downward embracing the scenes below even to the farther ends, left and right, of the terrestrial level. From these extremities the eye is drawn back towards the altar at the centre.

Raphael has divided the scene into a hierarchy of three levels: terrestrial, heavenly, and the supra-celestial Empyrean. Many of the personalities are readily identified by their iconography or by the titles of the books that accompany them. A few even have their names inscribed inside the circumference of their halos. On the terrestrial level, immediately flanking the Holy Eucharist, are the four Fathers of the Latin Church: Gregory the Great and Jerome on the left, Ambrose and Augustine on the right. Farther to the right are Aquinas with Pope Innocent III and Bonaventure. Yet a little more to the right and behind are Sixtus IV and Dante. On the higher celestial level Christ presides at the centre seated on a throne of clouds, with the Virgin Mary on the left and John the Baptist on the right. Seated on clouds arching inward toward Christ are twelve figures from the Old and New Testaments: patriarchs Adam, Abraham, Moses, and David; martyrs and apostles, Stephen, James, John, and possibly Lawrence; holy warriors, likely Joshua and Judas Maccabees; and bookended by the two martyr-founders of the Christian Church in Rome, Peter on the foremost left and Paul on the foremost right. God the Father stands forth at the summit from within the golden light of the Empyrean. The sense of a fullness of ordered energy, of intellectual interest and expectation impresses itself on the viewer.

Fig. 52: *La Disputa*, fresco by Raphael, Stanza della Segnatura, Stanze di Raffaello, Musei Vaticani, Rome. Photo Credit: Erich Lessing / Art Resource, NY.

On the Ceiling

The ceiling of the Stanza della Segnatura is an intricate puzzle of imagery and symbol. Julius's papal emblem is suspended at the centre in a celestial blue octagon. Surrounding the centre are four circles representing the personifications of the arts which we've already described, along with four rectangles representing founding moments of those four arts. As we make our way around the ceiling it is interesting to observe the conversations between these scenes and the personification at their sides.

- In the northwest corner of the ceiling we find the *Crowning of Apollo* (fig. 53, top-right). The seated Apollo holds his lyre as he raises his right hand and faces the unfortunate Marsyas, who has just lost a musical competition with the god. Apollo is now recognized as the undisputed god of music and of poetry. To the right of this image sits the personification of *Poetry* (fig. 53, top-centre). Reigning above *Parnassus* on the north wall, winged *Poetry* wears a laurel crown, a white gown, and a royal blue cloak about her middle. She is looking off toward the crowning of Apollo and the wall of *Theology*. The clouds beneath her are pink, and the putti flanking her hold up the words *numine afflatur*, "the breath of divinity." Directly below her, seated on Mt. Parnassus, Apollo is also crowned in laurel as he plays a lute, gazing into the heavens.

- Next to *Poetry*, in the northeast corner, is the striking image of a woman leaning over, her right hand on a globe and her left arm raised in a signal of attention, the

Fig. 53: Ceiling of the Stanza della Segnatura, fresco by Raphael, Stanza della Segnatura, Stanze di Raffaello, Musei Vaticani, Rome. Photo Credit: Scala / Art Resource, NY.

ends of her sash swept into the breeze beside and behind her. The globe is a celestial blue, marked with the constellations and studded with gold stars. At the centre is the green and blue globe of the earth. The imagery evokes the iconography of the Prime Mover; but this is clearly a woman who represents Sophia, or *Wisdom* (fig. 53, top-left), said to exist before the Creation: "By wisdom the Lord laid the earth's foundations, by understanding he set the heavens in place (Prov. 3.19). *Wisdom* lies at the origin of the knowledge of causes sought by philosophers. Visually, this celestial globe is paired with the globes below held by Ptolemy and Strabo in the *School of Athens* (see fig. 51) and by God the Father in the *Disputa* (see fig. 52).

– Next to *Wisdom* we find the personified *Philosophy* (fig. 53, centre-left) enthroned on the ceiling above the *School of Athens*. Her gown and cloak represent the four elements of air, fire, water, and earth. With her face towards *Wisdom* and with Justice on the left, she rests the book "Naturalis" on her left thigh and above it she props the book "Moralis," facing it towards *Judgment of Solomon* and Justice.

– In the southeast corner of the Stanza's ceiling stands the *Judgment of Solomon* (fig. 53, bottom-left), depicting the first manifestation of Solomon's shrewd wisdom. Raphael shows Solomon on his throne, pronouncing the verdict, while a courtier with drawn sword holds the babe by his feet, ready to cleave him in two, as the true mother lunges forward to stop him. The scene represents a founding moment of Jurisprudence. Its placement between Philosophy and Justice seems most fitting.

– Situated over *Jurisprudence* on the south wall, *Justice* (fig. 53, bottom-centre) with her right arm raising a sword and her left hand supporting a balance, presides over the great law-givers below. Winged putti carry tablets with the words *ius suum unicuique*, "to each what is due to him."

– Next to *Justice*, in the southwest corner, Adam and Eve are depicted in the Garden of Eden in conversation with the serpent, the moment just before Adam's fall. Situated between Justice on the left and Theology on the right, the *Fall of Man* (fig. 53, bottom-right) depicts the moment of humankind's fall from grace and entrance into iniquity. Original justice is lost; its restoration will require divine action in human history. It is the beginning of salvation history. The image is fittingly set between Justice and Theology.

– Next to the *Fall of Man*, *Theology* (fig. 53, centre-right) is enthroned on grey clouds. She wears a crown and a transparent white veil across her head. The two ends of the veil are swept away towards the right, billowing as if in a strong wind. With a book propped on her left thigh, she points downward with her right hand, into the *Disputa* while gazing towards the *Crowning of Apollo* and *Poetry*'s "breath of divinity." Putti flank *Theology* holding up plaques with the words *divinarum rerum notitia*, "knowledge of divine things."

Julius's Library and Renaissance Humanism

In making our tour of the ceiling we enter the poetic process of observing the imagery and references, which reveal Inghirami's unified understanding of the four arts of Poetry, Philosophy, Justice, and Theology. We've seen how each personification of the arts opens to conversation with the scenes at either side of it. Most notable are the ways in which the life of each personification is acted out in human history on the wall just below it. Our study of the ceiling has shown how its complex of images extends and unifies the conversations taking place below it. One more element remains. At the centre of the ceiling, uniting all these images and scenes, is the octagonal medallion of celestial blue with the Julius II's heraldic shield at the centre. Julius's emblem serves as the single point that unites the whole of the room and the spheres of knowledge it symbolizes. Its unity is not only *one* by design, but also, it is implied, *one* by authority.

This, then, is the Stanza della Segnatura, devised by Tommaso Inghirami and painted by Raphael Sanzio. It represents the arts and learning of Renaissance humanism, inherited from the ancient Greeks and classical Romans. The genius of this great room tells the story of the richly integrated theological vision and the artistic and political aspirations of Julius II and Renaissance Rome.

Essential Reading

Beck, James. *Raphael: The Stanza della Segnatura*. New York: George Braziller, 1993.

Copenhaver, Brian. "Giovanni Pico della Mirandola." *The Stanford Encyclopedia of Philosophy*. Edited by Edward N. Zalta. http://plato.stanford.edu/archives/sum2012/entries/pico-della-mirandola.

D'Amico, John F. *Renaissance Humanism in Papal Rome: Humanists and Churchmen on the Eve of the Reformation*. Baltimore and London: Johns Hopkins University Press, 1983.

Hersey, George L. *High Renaissance Art in St. Peter's and the Vatican: An Interpretive Guide*, Chicago and London: University of Chicago Press, 1993.

Johnson, Paul. *The Papacy*. Edited by Michael Walsh. New York: Barnes & Noble, 1997.

Joost-Gaugier, Christiane L. "Raphael's Disputa: Medieval Theology Seen through the Eyes of Pico della Mirandola, and the Possible Inventor of the Program, Tommaso Inghirami." *Gazetta des Beaux-Arte* 129 (1997): 65–84.

——, *Raphael's Stanza della Segnatura: Meaning and Invention*. Cambridge and New York: Cambridge University Press, 2002.

O'Malley, John W. *Giles of Viterbo on the Church and Reform: A Study in Renaissance Thought*. Leiden: Brill, 1968.

——, "Fulfillment of the Christian Golden Age under Julius II: Text of a Discourse of Giles of Viterbo, 1507." *Traditio* 35 (1969): 265–333.

——, "The Vatican Library and the Schools of Athens: A Text of Battista Casali, 1508," *Journal of Medieval and Renaissance Studies* 7.2 (1977): 271–89.

——, "An Ash Wednesday Sermon on the Dignity of Man for Pope Julius II, 1513." In *Essays Presented to Myron P. Gilmore*, Volume 1, edited by S. Bertelli and G. Ramakus, 193–209. Florence: La Nuova Italiana, 1978.

Rowland, Ingrid D. "The Intellectual Background of the *School of Athens*: Tracking Divine Wisdom in the Rome of Julius II." In *Raphael's "School of Athens"*, edited by Marcia Hall, 131–61. Cambridge: Cambridge University Press, 1997.

Verdon, Timothy. "Pagans in the Church: The *School of Athens* in Religious Context." In *Raphael's "School of Athens"*, edited by Marcia Hall, 114–30. Cambridge: Cambridge University Press, 1997.

Other Places to Encounter Inghirami and Raphael* in Rome

Raphael

- Pantheon: burial place of Raphael.
- Musei Vaticani, Pinacoteca: Ten tapestries based on Raphael cartoons, together with mutiple paintings, including *The Transfiguration*, *The Coronation of the Virgin, Annunciation, Adoration of the Magi, Presentation at the Temple, Madonna of Foligno;*
- Musei Vaticani, Raphael Stanze: Multiple frescoes decorating the walls and ceiling of the Stanza di Eliodoro e Stanza della Segnatura.
- Basilica di Sant'Agostino: *The Prophet Isaiah*, fresco.
- Chiesa di S. Maria della Pace: *Sibyls*, (also called *Sibyls Receiving Angelic Instruction*), fresco.
- Basilica di S. Maria del Popolo: architecture of the Chigi Chapel.
- Villa Farnesina: *Galatea* (also called *The Triumph of Galatea*), fresco.
- Galleria Nazionale d'Arte Antica, Palazzo Barberini: *La Fornarina*, painting.
- Borghese Gallery: two paintings, *Portrait of a Man* and *The Deposition* (also called the *Pala Baglione* or the *Borghese Entombment*).

Inghirami

- Musei Vaticani: one figure within Raphael's *School of Athens*, that of Epicurus, is said by some scholars to resemble Fedra Inghirami.

* For Julius, see chapter 16 in this volume.

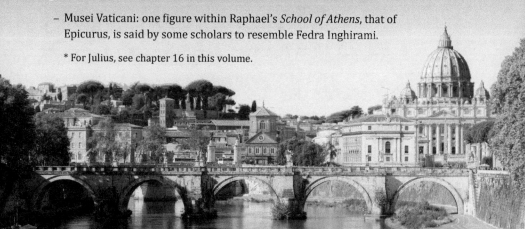

Fig. 54: *School of Athens* (detail): portrait of a man identified as Michelangelo, fresco by Raphael, Stanza della Segnatura, Stanza di Raffaello, Musei Vaticani, Rome. Photo Credit: Scala / Art Resource, NY.

Chapter Nineteen

MICHELANGELO BUONARROTI (1475–1564 CE) AT THE CAPPELLA SISTINA

SCOTT F. CRIDER

> [Beauty] creates, without itself satisfying, the aspiration for certitude.
> Elaine Scarry, *On Beauty and Being Just*

What All of Rome Saw

On October 31, 1512, Michelangelo's finally completed Cappella Sistina ceiling was unveiled, and Giorgio Vasari tells us in *The Lives of the Artists* that all of Rome came to see it. For Vasari, imitating Michelangelo is like imitating nature because Michelangelo has imitated nature so well that he is almost a second Creator: He is a "blessed artist" who has "removed the blinders of the eyes from your minds" (449–50), "something divine rather than mortal" (414). Vasari comes close to proclaiming that the artist is a second Incarnation, at least a new prophet—"a man sent by God into the World" (482)—as an example of moral, intellectual and artistic perfection. What did all of Rome see that day? What sight so aroused Vasari's latent paganism that he could conceive of Michelangelo as an artistic god? All Rome saw what one still sees when straining to see the ceiling of the Cappella Sistina with one's head bent upward, disoriented by the physical effort of contortion: an artistic complexity so bright and varied that it is overwhelming. Only by patient attention can one begin to discern the patterns in the ceiling, the patterns which establish the work's complex harmony. Harmony is not identical to unity, though. The ceiling is harmonic, but as one sees how Michelangelo reads the Bible, how story becomes image, one begins to see creative tensions in the harmony.

Those tensions arise from Michelangelo's deliberate decision to juxtapose a precisely-conceived theological program on the ceiling of the Cappella Sistina with a boldly articulated artistic one. The theological program must be understood in terms of a much-used interpretative approach of the artist's day called typology, which attempted to fuse the Hebrew Bible and the New Testament into a unified account of Christian salvation by reading the New Testament back into the Hebrew Bible, now called the Old Testament and thought to be a promise fulfilled. But with Michelangelo, that theological program is in tension with a bold artistic program whose interest in classical beauty challenges Christian doctrine. In other words, the beauty of Michelangelo's perfect bodies is not easily reconcilable with the Christian metanarrative of the Fall. If, as Matthew Arnold would have it, the culture of the West is defined by the relationship between the Hebraic and the Hellenic—Jerusalem and Athens—then Michelangelo's early modern Cappella Sistina ceiling enacts that relationship. Or to put more simply, Michelangelo is an unapologetic Christian humanist, and his humanist fascination with the body is in a dialectical relationship with the Christian theology of the body in both the Cappella

Sistina and many of his other works. In Rome alone, his *Pietà* in the Basilica di S. Pietro, *Moses* in the Basilica di S. Pietro in Vincoli, and *Christ Carrying the Cross* in the Basilica di S. M. sopra Minerva embrace this same spirit.

Michelangelo and Rome

Most of Michelangelo's youth was passed in Florence at a time, in the late fifteenth and early sixteenth centuries, when the city enjoyed an unmatched reputation for excellence and innovation in learning and the arts. From a young age, he resisted attempts by parents and guardians to keep him in school. Painting and sculpting occupied most of his time in these childhood years until finally, at age thirteen, he was apprenticed to Domenico Ghirlandaio (1449–94), one of the finest Florentine painters of the day. Ghirlandaio quickly recognized Michelangelo's extraordinary talent and effectively launched his career by introducing him into the court circle of Lorenzo "The Magnificent" de' Medici (1449–92), Florentine's *de facto* duke and a major patron of arts and letters. With Lorenzo de' Medici as patron, Michelangelo went on to study under some of the most famous humanists of Renaissance Florence during the years 1490–92, gaining a reputation of his own as a sculptor. By 1496, while still only twenty-one years old, he was well enough known to receive two commissions in Rome, the most famous being his *Pietà* that was completed in 1499 and now stands in the Basilica di S. Pietro. Other important commissions followed, including his famous statue of *David* in 1504 and one of his few known stand-alone paintings, the *Doni Tondo*, now in the Uffizi Gallery in Florence. It was on the strength of these and other of his works in circulation that the powerful and ambitious Pope Julius II (r. 1503–13) invited Michelangelo back to Rome to undertake two massive projects. The first was a sculptural program for Julius's tomb that, while unfinished, still graces Rome's Basilica di S. Pietro in Vincoli with its impressive statue of *Moses* flanked by *Rachel* and *Leah*. Michelangelo's second Julian commission was the ambitious fresco program for the Cappella Sistina's ceiling, a work he completed in the years 1508–12 while in his early thirties. Widely regarded as a masterpiece in the history of art, Michelangelo's completed fresco cycle covered some five hundred square metres and included over three hundred separate figures taken from both the Hebraic and the Hellenic traditions.

The Harmony of the Cappella Sistina Ceiling

The ceiling is not actually as architectural as it appears. Although the lunettes, spandrels, and pendentives are actual features of the chapel's architecture, the rest of the apparent architecture is fictional. Michelangelo paints the ceiling to look as though the central panels are framed by stone, not fresco. This painting-within-a-painting technique allows him to paint figures whose substantiality has a grade. The scenes within the lunettes, spandrels, pendentives, and the panels themselves are painted as paintings: The caryatids are painted as sculpture; the prophets, sybils, and *ignudi* (decorative nudes) are

55 (opposite): Cappella Sistina Ceiling, fresco by Michelangelo, 1508–12,
sei Vaticani, Rome. Photo Credit: Scala / Art Resource, NY.

painted as live figures. Michelangelo's fictive architecture allows him to represent three orders of being: those of paint, stone, and flesh.

Within this fictive architecture, there are four acts of the Christian metanarrative of salvation from Creation to the birth of Christ. First, within the central panels, there is Michelangelo's reading of three episodes from Genesis—Creation, Adam and Eve, and Noah. We will look at those in detail in a moment, especially the Adam and Eve panels. Second, in the four corners (or pendentives), there are four episodes of liberation from tyranny with two male and two female liberators: David and Goliath, Judith and Holofernes, Moses and the brazen serpent, and the death of Haman. Typologically, Moses and David are types for Christ; Judith and Esther, for Mary and the Church. Third, along both the north and south sides of the ceiling's central panels are pagan sybils and Hebrew prophets, both of whom, in a typological reading, foresee the coming of the Christian Messiah. Zechariah sits across from Jonah; Joel, from the Delphic oracle; Isaiah, from the Erythraean Sybil; Ezekiel, from the Cumaean Sybil; Daniel, from the Persian Sybil; Jeremiah, from the Libyan Sybil. The juxtaposition of pagan sybil and Hebrew prophet extends the typological horizon of interpretation not only to the Hebrew stories of the Old Testament, but also to the literary texts of the classical tradition. Christ is foreseen not only by pre-Christian Judaism, but also by ancient paganism. Fourth and last, in the lunettes and spandrels, there are the ancestors of Christ, those Old Testament figures cited in Matthew's opening genealogy of Christ's line back to David (1:1–17), images which emphasize child-rearing.

The four acts of the Christian metanarrative from Creation to the birth of Christ provide, within a typological reading, a unified story of universal salvation. God the Father, according to this narrative, creates a world which, through the human failures of Adam and Eve, then Noah, falls, only to be redeemed by the Father's incarnation as the Son, an incarnation prefigured in Hebrew liberation and prophesied by Hebrew and Hellenic seers. This is an incarnation which brings to historical fulfillment the human genealogy from Adam to Christ, who is at the centre of *The Last Judgment*, Michelangelo's later fresco that completes his work on the chapel and resides behind the alter in the chapel, right below the first image of Creation. End meets beginning and knows it for the first time.

Reading Michelangelo While He Is Reading Genesis

According to Michael Buxandall, a painter from early modern Italy was "a professional visualizer of the holy stories." He turned biblical story into image. This artistic act is not mere illustration. To visualize is to interpret because, in deciding which episodes to visualize, in deciding which exact moment in the episodes to visualize, and in deciding how to visualize them, the artist re-reads and re-interprets the text. To make an obvious point, Michelangelo chooses not Abraham as his patriarch after Adam, but instead Noah. And each panel is the result of a highly focussed selection of one visual moment or point in a narrative continuum of line. Early modern painters are not mere recorders of holy narrative; they are, at least, emphasizers of it and perhaps even re-makers of it. Any number of observations about Michelangelo's interpretative interest and abilities could be discussed here. His interest in bodies, however, is perhaps most apparent. That is, in his selection of episodes from Genesis, in the exact moments he chooses to represent, and in his emphases, Michelangelo isolates and investigates three topics: first, the human body, especially the unashamed naked body; next, God as the artist of that natural body; and finally, the relationship between God as the fashioner of natural bodies and Michelangelo as fashioner of artistic ones. Michelangelo reads Genesis as an artist whose primary interest—indeed, the object of his obsession—is the human body. Reading him reading the Bible as we try to understand how he turned story into image, we will see that it matters that it is Michelangelo himself who is re-reading and reimagining the Bible. No reader comes from nowhere, and this particular reader from somewhere brings with him his own central concerns.

Nine panels are found at the highest point of the vaulted ceiling of the Cappella Sistina (see fig. 55), and these are framed by an elaborate selection of supporting scenes further down into the lunettes, spandrels, and pendentives. These panels recount the story of the physical Creation (panels one through three), human creation and the Fall (panels four through six), and the consequences of the Fall (panels seven through nine). Within this sequence of nine visual narratives it is probably true that the three panels depicting Adam and Eve are the most important: they take pride of place both because they are located at the centre of the ceiling, and because an enlarged figurative format is employed in two of the three panels (panels four and six) in contrast to the reduced format used by Michelangelo in his depictions of physical creation before the Adam and Eve sequence and the consequences of the Fall for Noah after that sequence. Within the Adam and Eve story at the centre of the ceiling, panel four gives us the creation of Adam, panel five that of Eve, and panel six their temptation, fall, and expulsion from Eden.

Michelangelo's scene of God's creation of Adam (panel four) depends on Genesis 2:7, the second of two accounts of human creation, one slightly different from the other, that are found there. Michelangelo knew the Bible in a recent Italian translation and (perhaps) in the Latin Vulgate, and had read Genesis. "[T]he LORD God formed man out of the clay of the ground and blew into his nostrils the breath of life, and so man became a living being." What does Michelangelo choose to represent, and how? God has apparently just made Adam from dust, but has either not yet or just breathed the breath of life into him—that infusion of breath here represented as touch—finger to finger. Reclining in a languorous pose, Michelangelo's Adam is a bodily form either without a living soul just yet, or just now ensouled. Is God reaching toward that touch or retreating from it? It is difficult to tell but, if Adam is only body but not yet soul, he is then a kind of statue. Michelangelo thought of himself first and foremost as a sculptor, not a painter, and there is almost always a sculptural quality to his painted figures. He may be thematizing here his own sculptural activity. Michelangelo's God is a sculptor of a human form just given, or yet to be given, animating soul. He is a kind of Michelangelo, who, after all, fashioned from stone material forms which *seem* to be animated by soul. The point in the story Michelangelo chooses is ambiguous, but it takes place as near as possible just before or after the singular point of the first ensouled human form.

Notice that this God discloses his own bodily form to view, a visual representation of the first account of Creation (Gen. 1:26): "Let us make man in our own image, after our likeness." This God has a body. He is not naked, but his clothing is tight, and his ancient musculature is visible, strained at the moment of creation. Michelangelo represents God; that is, he imitates He who made the nature to be imitated. He shares none of Dante's reticence in not representing God directly in the *Commedia*. In Michelangelo's Genesis, as he transforms biblical story into papal image, Adam's body—in the image of God's—is a perfect body, the body before the fall of the world. Yet Michelangelo himself paints both essentially perfect forms of God and of its Adamic likeness.

How, though, can a post-fallen human being imagine pre-fallen bodies in their shameless perfection? The next narrative ceiling (panel five), depicting the creation of Eve, assists us. Michelangelo's point of departure for this scene was Genesis 2:21–25:

> So the LORD God cast a deep sleep on the man, and while he was asleep, he took out one of his ribs and closed up its place with flesh. The LORD God then built up into a woman the rib that he had taken from the man. When he brought her to the man, the man said: "This one, at last, is bone of my bones and flesh of my flesh. This one shall be called 'woman,' for out of 'her man' this one has been taken." That is why a man leaves his father and mother and clings to his wife, and the two of them become one body. The man and his wife were both naked, yet they felt no shame.

Fig. 56: Cappella Sistina Ceiling (detail): Temptation, Fall, and Expulsion from Paradise with ignudi in the corners, fresco by Michelangelo, 1508–12, Musei Vaticani, Rome. Photo Credit: Scala / Art Resource, NY.

Pre-fallen bodies—perfect bodies—were not only free from age, disease and death, according to the Genesis account. They were free from the self-consciousness of shame: "[T]hey felt no shame."

It is in the next panel (panel six), treating the temptation, fall, and expulsion from paradise, where we begin to see that Michelangelo suggests that the fall did not make the body a form to be ashamed of, even if it can be ravaged by time. The painting's composition is very interesting since the Tree of Knowledge literally separates paradise from exile (see fig. 56, corners). Equally interesting is his careful, nuanced, and clearly selective reading of the Genesis 3:1–24 account upon which it is based. Michelangelo ignores some key sequences of the Genesis account while supplementing or altering it in other ways. Most remarkable of all, perhaps, is his decision to de-emphasize the shame of Adam and Eve's nakedness. There is no interview with God to accommodate Genesis 3:11's "Who told you that you were naked?" Nor do we see that "the Lord God made leather garments, with which He clothed them" (Gen. 3:21). And, of course, they begin their exile *without clothing*. Although Adam and Eve are clearly marked by time and sorrow already, they reveal no shame in their nakedness. They are not clothed, and neither one covers genitals or face, both visual signs of shame in early modern paintings. Compare Michelangelo's expulsion with Masaccio's in the Brancacci Chapel in Florence, a painting Michelangelo knew quite well, where Adam covers his face and Eve her breasts and genitals. Michelangelo's Adam and Eve leave in sorrow and fear, but they are not ashamed of their nakedness. In Michelangelo's Genesis, the fall brought death, not shame.

Perfect Bodies: The Ignudi

The nine central panels of Michelangelo's Genesis inaugurate a topic which Michelangelo explores throughout the ceiling: Is the naked body shameful? Is its beauty, a beauty made by the Creator Himself, undermined by sin, or is it somehow—in its freedom from shame—perfectly if only temporarily beautiful? Is beauty the incarnation of divine presence or the vanity of human idolatry? Does it lead to, or from, the divine?

We might be better able to answer that question by examining that part of the ceiling which is not at all part of its theological program: the ignudi, the twenty male nudes framing Michelangelo's Genesis. Such figures pop up in his earlier work, for example, in the *Holy Family*, dating to 1503–6—just a few years prior to his Cappella Sistina commission—and now located in the Uffizi Gallery in Florence. The scholar Howard Hibbard says that the ignudi are particularly expressive of Michelangelo's intent and character, insofar as they are "expressions of Michelangelo's unique artistic daemon" and "his most personal and revealing contribution to the ceiling, having no necessary function" (121)—no function, that is, within its theological program. Be that as it may, the complex harmonics of the ceiling reflect a serious, creative tension between that theological program and Michelangelo's own artistic program, notably his obsession with classical ideals of beauty.

In order to put Michelangelo's obsession with classical ideas of beauty in context, it is necessary to recall just how passionate he and his contemporaries were about the recently discovered classical statues of their day. Michelangelo himself was an eyewitness to the excavation of the famous *Laocoön* in Rome in 1506. As one witness, Francesco da Sangallo, put it in a letter recounting events surrounding the statue's discovery:

"Then they dug the hole wider so that they could pull the statue out. As soon as it was visible, everyone started to draw, all the while discoursing on ancient things." Michelangelo was there. The artist was not an eyewitness to the discovery of another famous work of his day, the *Belvedere Torso*, but he certainly knew it well. Having come to light in Rome by the late fifteenth century, the *Torso* found its way into the Vatican's existing collection of classical sculpture by the mid-sixteenth century and became a celebrated piece worldwide over the course of Michelangelo's lifetime.

The ignudi are Michelangelo's painted torsos, his imaginative reconstructions of that fragmentary piece into twenty whole, beautiful young men framing creation. Each of the smaller panels is surrounded by four ignudi who sit upon fictive blocks of stone (see fig. 56). What one notices is that they grow increasingly larger as Michelangelo progresses so that by the time one gets to the first scene of creation, they are at least as large as God; indeed, by then, it is arguable that they begin to crowd Him out. The framing ignudi obscure the central deity. The ignudi are beautiful, but their beauty is clearly Hellenic, not Hebraic. Or, to put it more precisely, their beauty is only Christian within the cultural frame of the early modern fascination with classical beauty. Michelangelo appropriates the pagan, homoerotic beauty of classical sculpture and uses it to frame images from Genesis, images themselves influenced by such classical beauty! (Although this is a topic beyond the scope of this essay, there is a Renaissance Christianity that is not that of the Reformation, and Michelangelo is one of its most important inventors.) Some art historians evade the character of the ignudi with safe discussions of angels, but, in fact, the ignudi may be a problem theologically. My supposal is not anachronistic, by the way. A contemporary of Michelangelo's, Pietro Aretino (1492–1556), devotes a portion of one of his dialogues to the following exchange over Michelangelo's ignudi. One character complains of them:

> "Who will be daring enough to affirm that it is proper, that in Rome, in the Church of St. Peter, the chief of the apostles; in Rome, where all the world assembles, in the chapel of that high priest, who ... is the representative of God on earth, figures should be seen, who immodestly discover what decency conceals? A thing, in truth, utterly unworthy of that most holy place."

To which his interlocutor replies,

> "Sound eyes, my friend, are incorrupt and unoffended by seeing natural objects."

My analysis begins with the ceiling's first reception. The Florentine Savonarola's bonfire of the vanities ought to be a reminder that not all early modern Christians applauded the introduction of classical humanism into their culture. Perhaps the dialogue's last speaker is right, though: the figures are beautiful, natural objects, nudes without shame, the enjoyment of which need arouse no anxiety.

Indeed, Michelangelo goes even further. In one of his sonnets (*Rime* 83), he explains his love for Tommaso Cavalieri (1509–87) in neo-platonic terms thus:

> I see in your beautiful face, my lord,
> what in this life words cannot well describe;
> with it my soul, still clothed in flesh,
> has already risen to God. (1–4)

Fig. 57: *Christ Carrying the Cross*, statue by Michelangelo, Basilica di S. Maria Sopra Minerva, Rome. Photo courtesy of Peter Hatlie

The last two lines of this sonnet in Italian—[L]*'anima, della carne ancor vestita, / con esso è già più volte ascesa a Dio*—affirm the body's potentially ideal beauty, even in its classical form, as a simulacrum of the perfection of the resurrected body. Beauty, for Michelangelo, is thus incarnation.

Perhaps, then, the ignudi are commensurate with the theological program of the ceiling's biblical stories, provided we see Hebrew narrative, Christian typology and neo-platonic beauty all participating in his early modern vision. Beauty may be divine. Perhaps, however, they are not commensurate. The male nude is Michelangelo's favourite object of artistic interest, even love: As he confesses in Sonnet 41, "[L]ove takes me, and beauty binds me [*l'amor me prende, e la beltà me lega*]" (9). The body's actual beauty is a perfection of an earthly body, after all. Beauty may be only human.

Conclusion: A Perfectly Beautiful Body

Does Michelangelo believe that beauty is divine and therefore eternal, or does he believe that it is human and therefore finite? Perhaps what dissolves the tension within the harmony of the Cappella Sistina ceiling is incarnation itself. Christ's body is both human and divine and is (one presumes) the perfect male body—as Mary's is the perfect female one. Yet, as we see in the *Pietà*, Michelangelo is not very interested in Mary's body. He is interested in Christ's figure at the moment he has given his perfect body to death in order to free humankind from death. One can see, as well, in his *Christ Carrying the Cross* (see fig. 57) in S. Maria Sopra Minerva near the Pantheon that he imagines Christ as one of the ignudi. The disfiguring "fig-leaf" of cloth added later is an act of vandalism that misunderstands Michelangelo's central concerns. Christ's body is, for Michelangelo, the perfect nude.

In conclusion, I would like to turn to a later piece of sculpture, one of Michelangelo's purposely unfinished sculptures, the *Atlas Slave*, now found in the Galleria dell'Accademia museum in Florence among a group of his *Prigioni* ("Prisoner") statues in the same hall as the *David*. Why did Michelangelo not finish some of his later pieces? One hears that it was because the stone was flawed, or that he was called away to other commissions, and both of these reasons may very well be true. Are there other reasons, perhaps? Does he become ashamed of the body in his old age? One can surely see that in *The Last Judgment* the bodies have lost their delicacy and become torpid. Does he grow frustrated that even perfectly sculpted or painted bodies decay? After all, many of the statues being recovered in Rome were fragments, their beauty becoming dust. Or does he hope to represent that very process of the birth of form from dust and the death of form into dust—from dust to dust, whether body or image? Allow me to suggest the last option. One cannot tell in these late pieces if the form is emerging from or declining into matter. *From* or *to* dust? Are these bodies being born, or are they dying?

One old man, the finest artist of the male body in the world, decides in his own decline to represent the very mystery of the Christian faith: the death of the perfect body raises imperfect bodies into perfection. Throughout his career, Michelangelo, as a reader of the stories of Bible and a maker of images from them—that is, as a re-writer of the Bible—becomes the perfectly beautiful body of our mysterious world.[1]

---

1   I have presented this interpretation of the ceiling to several gatherings of University of Dallas students, both in Rome, Italy and in Irving, Texas. Their questions and comments have been crucial to helping me understand Michelangelo's project. Special thanks to Peter Hatlie, who helped me a great deal in a revision of an earlier draft. This chapter is dedicated to John Norris in gratitude for his teaching, collegiality, and friendship.

Essential Reading

Arnold, Matthew. *Culture and Anarchy.* Edited by J. Dover Wilson. Cambridge: Cambridge University Press, 1932.

Barkin, Leonard. *Unearthing the Past: Archaeology and Aesthetics in the Making of Renaissance Culture.* New Haven and London: Yale University Press, 1999.

Buxandall, Michael. *Painting and Experience in Fifteenth-Century Italy: A Primer in the Social History of Pictorial Style.* 2nd ed. Oxford: Oxford University Press, 1988.

Graham-Dixon, Andrew. *Michelangelo and the Sistine Chapel.* New York: Skyhorse Publishing, 2009.

Hibbard, Howard. *Michelangelo.* 2nd ed. New York: Harper & Row, 1974.

King, Ross. *Michelangelo and the Pope's Ceiling.* New York: Walker & Company, 2003.

Seymour Jr., Charles. *Michelangelo: The Sistine Chapel Ceiling.* New York: Norton, 1972.

Unger, Miles J. *Michelangelo: A Life in Six Masterpieces.* New York: Simon & Schuster, 2014.

Vasari, Giorgio. The Lives of the Artists. Translated by Julia Conaway Bondanella and Peter Bondanella. Oxford: Oxford University Press, 1991.

Wallace, William E. *Michelangelo: The Artist, the Man and his Times.* Cambridge: Cambridge University Press, 2011.

Other Places to Encounter Michelangelo in Rome

- Campidoglio: the architecture of the piazza and buildings designed by Michelangelo (see chapter ten in this volume).

- S. M. degli Angeli: design for the transformation of Diocletian baths into a church is Michelangelo's.

- Dome of the Basilica di S. Pietro: central contribution of Michelangelo to architecture of this building.

- Basilica di S. Pietro in Vincoli: parts of the tomb of Pope Julius II are preserved here under the high altar.

CONCORDANCE OF PLACE NAMES
ITALIAN AND ENGLISH

Place names marked with an asterisk are either unknown or beyond walking distance of Rome's city centre. Therefore, they have not been included on the maps within this volume.

Place Name in Italian	Place Name in English
Abbazia delle Tre Fontane*	Abbey of Tre Fontane*
Appia Antica	Appian Way
Ara Pacis	Ara Pacis
Arco di Costantino	Arch of Constantine
Arco di Giano	Arch of Janus
Arco di Settimio Severo (Foro Romano)	Arch of Septimius Severus (Roman Forum)
Arco di Tito (Foro Romano)	Arch of Titus (Roman Forum)
Aventino	Aventine Hill
Basilica dei Santi Giovanni e Paolo	Basilica of Sts. John and Paul
Basilica dei Santi Quattro Coronati	Basilica of the Santi Quattro Coronati
Basilica dei Santi XII Apostoli	Basilica of the Twelve Holy Apostles
Basilica di Massenzio	Basilica of Maxentius (alt. Basilica Nova)
Basilica di Nettuno (Via della Palombella)	Basilica of Neptune (Via della Palombella)
Basilica di S. Giovanni in Laterano	Basilica of St. John Lateran
Basilica di S. Lorenzo fuori le mura	Basilica of St. Lawrence Outside the Walls
Basilica di S. Marco al Campidoglio	Basilica of St. Mark's at the Capitoline
Basilica di S. Paolo fuori le mura	Basilica of St. Paul Outside the Walls
Basilica di S. Sisto Il Vecchio	Basilica of St. Sixtus the Elder
Basilica di San Clemente al Laterano	Basilica of Saint Clement
Basilica di San Giovanni dei Fiorentini	Basilica of San Giovanni dei Fiorentini
Basilica di San Pietro	Basilica of St. Peter (alt. St. Peter's Basilica)
Basilica di San Pietro in Vincoli	Basilica of St. Peter in Chains
Basilica di San Sebastiano fuori le mura	Basilica of St. Sebastian Outside the Walls
Basilica di Santa Cecilia in Trastevere	Basilica of Santa Cecilia
Basilica di Santa Croce in Gerusalemme	Basilica of the Holy Cross in Jerusalem
Basilica di Santa Maria degli Angeli e dei Martiri	Basilica of St. Mary of the Angels and Martyrs
Basilica di Santa Maria del Popolo	Basilica of Santa Maria del Popolo
Basilica di Santa Maria in Aracoeli	Basilica of St. Mary on the Altar of Heaven
Basilica di Santa Maria in Cosmedin	Basilica of Santa Maria in Cosmedin
Basilica di Santa Maria Maggiore	Basilica of St. Mary Major

Place Name in Italian	Place Name in English
Basilica di Santa Maria Sopra Minerva	Basilica of Santa Maria Sopra Minerva
Basilica di Santa Sabina	Basilica of Santa Sabina
Basilica di Sant'Andrea delle Fratte	Basilica of Sant'Andrea delle Fratte
Basilica Emilia (alt. Fulvia; alt. Paulii) (Foro Romano)	Basilica Aemilia (alt. Fulvia; alt. Pauli) (Roman Forum)
Basilica Giulia (Foro Romano)	Basilica Julia (Roman Forum)
Battistero lateranense	Lateran Bapistery (alt. Baptistry of St. John Lateran)
Biblioteca Apostolica Vaticana	Vatican Library
Campidoglio	Capitoline Hill
Campo de' Fiori	Campo de' Fiori
Campo Marzio	Campus Martius
Cappella Sistina (incorporated within the Musei Vaticani)	Sistine Chapel (incorporated within the Vatican Museums)
Carcere Mamertino	Mamertine Prison
Casa di Augusto (Palatino)	House of Augustus (Palatine Hill)
Casa di Livia (Palatino)	House of Livia (Palatine Hill)
Castel Sant'Angelo	Castel Sant'Angelo
Castelgandolfo*	Castelgandolfo*
Catacombe di Domitilla	Catacombs of Domitilla
Catacombe di San Callisto	Catacomb of St. Callixtus
Catacombe di San Sebastiano	Catacombs of St. Sebastian
Chiesa di Domine Quo Vadis*	Church of Domine Quo Vadis*
Chiesa di S. Maria del Rosario a Monte Mario*	Church of S. Mary of the Holy Rosary*
Chiesa di S. Maria in Tempulo	Church of St. Mary in Tempulo
Chiesa di S. Stefano il Protomartyre*	Church of St. Stephen Protomartyr*
Chiesa di San Giorgio in Velabro	Church of San Giorgio in Velabro
Chiesa di San Girolamo della Carità	Church of San Girolamo della Carità
Chiesa di San Giuseppe dei Falegnami	Church of St. Joseph the Carpenters
Chiesa di San Lorenzo in Miranda	Church of San Lorenzo in Miranda
Chiesa di Santa Bibiana	Church of St. Bibiana
Chiesa di Santa Maria in Vallicella (ovvero Chiesa Nuova)	Church of Santa Maria in Vallicella (alt. Chiesa Nuova)
Chiesa di Santa Maria Liberatrice	Church of Santa Maria Liberatrice
Chiesa di Santa Prisca	Church of Santa Prisca
Chiesa di Santi Cosma e Damiano	Church of Santi Cosma e Damiano
Chiesa di Santi Luca e Martina	Church of Santi Luca e Martina
Cimitero Acattolico	Protestant Cemetery
Circo Massimo	Circus Maximus

Place Name in Italian	Place Name in English
Città del Vaticano	Vatican City
Collegio Inglese (alt. Venerabile Collegio Inglese)	English College (alt. Venerable English College)
Collegio Romano	Roman College
Colosseo	Colosseum
Cortile del Belevedere (incorporated within Musei Vaticani)	Belvedere Courtyard (incorporated within the Vatican Museums)
Curia (Foro Romano)	Curia (Roman Forum)
Domus Aurea	Nero's Golden House
Fontana del Tritone	Triton Fountation
Fontana della Barcaccia	Fontana della Barcaccia
Foro di Augusto	Forum of Augustus
Fori Imperiali	Imperial Fora
Foro di Giulio Cesare	Forum of Julius Caesar
Foro Romano	Roman Forum
Galleria Borghese	Borghese Gallery
Galleria Nazionale d'Arte Antica	National Gallery of Ancient Art
Giardini degli Aranci	Garden of the Oranges
Horti Sallustiani	Gardens of Sallust
Keats-Shelley House	Keats-Shelley House
Mausoleo di Adriano	Mausoleum of Hadrian
Mausoleo di Augusto	Mausoleum of Augustus
Musei Capitolini (=Palazzo Conservatori, Palazzo Senatorio, Palazzo Nuovo e resti del Tempio di Giove Ottimo Massimo)	Capitoline Museums (=Palazzo Conservatori, Palazzo Senatorio. Palazzo Nuovo and remains of the Temple of Jupiter Optimus Maximus)
Musei Vaticani	Vatican Museums
Obelisco lateranense	Lateran Obelisk
Ospedale di Santo Spirito in Sassia	Hospital of the Holy Spirit
Palatino	Palatine Hill
Palazzo Barberini	Palazzo Barberini
Palazzo Barberini ai Giubbonari	Palazzo Barberini ai Giubbonari
Palazzo Cenci	Palazzo Cenci
Palazzo Conservatori (see Musei Capitolini)	Palazzo Conservatori (see Musei Capitolini)
Palazzo dei Tribunali	Palazzo dei Tribunali
Palazzo di Propaganda Fide	Palace of the Propagation of the Faith
Palazzo Falconieri	Palazzo Falconieri
Palazzo Farnese	Palazzo Farnese
Palazzo Massimo alle Terme	Palazzo Massimo
Palazzo Masssimo alle Colonne	Palazzo Massimo alle Colonne
Palazzo Muti (alt. Palazzo Balestra)	Palazzo Muti (alt. Palazzo Balestra)

Place Name in Italian	Place Name in English
Palazzo Senatorio (see Musei Capitolini)	Palazzo Senatorio (see Musei Capitolini)
Palazzo Spada	Palazzo Spada
Palazzo Verospi	Palazzo Verospi
Pantheon	Pantheon
Piazza Barberini	Piazza Barberini
Piazza di Sant'Eustachio	Piazza di Sant'Eustachio
Piazza di Spagna	Spanish Steps
Piazza San Pietro	St. Peter's Square
Piazza Santi Apostoli	Piazza Santi Apostoli
Piazza Venezia	Piazza Venezia
Ponte Sant'Angelo	Ponte Sant'Angelo
Ponte Sisto	Ponte Sisto
Pontificia Università S. Tommaso D'Aquino Angelicum	Pontifical University of St. Thomas Aquinas "Angelicum"
Pyramide di Caio Cestio	Pyramid of Cestius
Rostri (Foro Romano)	Rostra (Roman Forum)
Teatro di Pompeo	Theater of Pompey
Tempio del Divo Giulio	Temple of Divine Caesar
Tempio della Magna Mater (Palatino)	Temple of the Great Mother (Palatine Hill)
Tempio della Vittoria (Palatino)*	Temple of Victory (Palatine Hill)*
Tempio di Antonino e Faustina (Foro Romano)	Temple of Antoninus and Faustina (Roman Forum)
Tempio di Adriano	Temple of Hadrian
Tempio di Apollo Palatino	Temple of Apollo Palatinus
Tempio di Augusto (alt. di Divo Augusto)	Temple of Augustus (alt. of Divine Augustus)
Tempio di Ercole Vincitore	Temple of Hercules Victor
Tempio di Giove Ottimo Massimo (see Musei Capitolini)*	Temple of Jupiter Optimus Maximus (see Capitoline Museums)*
Tempio di Marte Ultore (Foro di Augusto)	Temple of Mars Ultor (Forum of Augustus)
Tempio di Saturno (Foro Romano)	Temple of Saturn (Roman Forum)
Tempio di Venere Genetrice (Foro di Giulio Cesare)	Temple of Venus Genetrix (Julius Caesar's Forum)
Tempio di Venere e Roma	Temple of Venus and Rome
Terme di Agrippa	Baths of Agrippa
Terme di Caracalla	Baths of Caracalla
Via Giulia	Via Giulia
Via Sacra (Foro Romano)	Via Sacra (Roman Forum)
Villa Adriana*	Hadrian's Villa*
Villa di Livia ad Gallinas Albas*	Villa of Livia ad Gallinas Albas*

APPENDIX B

TIMELINE OF THE PEOPLE AND PLACES MENTIONED IN THIS VOLUME

FOR THE DATING of monuments, works of art and texts, the year or approximate year of the work's completion is given. The "+" symbol signifies a very approximate date and/or significant uncertainties about the dating. Where the advisable original construction of a monument and its later reconstruction are indicated by *(original)* and *(reconstructed)*, respectively.

ca. 750 BCE	Circo Massimo
ca. 750 BCE	Curia (Foro Romano)
ca. 750 BCE	Foro Romano
7th c. BCE+	Carcere Mamertino
500 BCE+	Rostri (Foro Romano)
497 BCE	Tempio di Saturno (Foro Romano)
294 BCE	Tempio della Vittoria (Palatino)
191 BCE	Tempio della Magna Mater (Palatino)
179 BCE	Basilica Emilia (Foro Romano)
ca. 120 BCE	Tempio di Ercole Vincitore
100 BCE	**Birth of Julius Caesar**
55 BCE	Teatro di Pompeo
ca. 50 BCE	Caesar's *Commentarii de Bello Gallico*
46 BCE	Basilica Giulia (Foro Romano)
46 BCE	Foro di Giulio Cesare
44 BCE	**Death of Julius Caesar**
63 BCE	**Birth of Emperor Augustus**
58 BCE	**Birth of Empress Livia**
ca. 29 BCE	Beginning of Augustus's reign
29 BCE	Tempio del Divo Giulio (Foro Romano)
28 BCE	Mausoleo di Augusto
28 BCE	Tempio di Apollo Palatino
25 BCE	Terme di Agrippa
ca. 20 BCE	Casa di Augusto (Palatino)
17 BCE	Horace's *Carmen Saeculare* in honour of Augustus
ca. 12 BCE	Pyramide di Caio Cestio

9 BCE	Ara Pacis
2 BCE	Foro di Augusto
2 CE	Tempio di Marte Ultore (Foro di Augusto)
1st c. CE+	Casa di Livia (Palatino)
1st c. CE	Villa di Livia ad Gallinas Albas
1st c. CE+	Catacombe di Domitilla
ca. 10 CE	Horti Sallustiani
ca. 10 CE	**Birth of St. Peter**
ca. 14 CE	Augustus's *Res Gestae Divi Augusti*
ca. 40 CE	Peter's apostolic mission begins
ca. 30 CE	Peter meets and follows Jesus
14 CE	**Death of Emperor Augustus**
29 CE	**Death Empress Livia**
ca. 35 CE	**Birth of Pope Clement I**
37 CE	Tempio di Augusto
64 CE	**Death of St. Peter**
68 CE	Domus Aurea
80 CE	Colosseo
76 CE	**Birth of Emperor Hadrian**
ca. 80 CE	Clement's *First Epistle*
82 CE	Arco di Tito (Foro Romano)
88 CE	Beginning of Clement I's papacy
ca. 101 CE	**Death of Pope Clement I**
117 CE	Beginning of Hadrian's reign
123–39 CE	Castel Sant'Angelo (ex-Mausoleo di Adriano)
ca. 125 CE	Villa Adriana
126 CE	Pantheon
ca. 138 CE	Hadrian's poem *To My Soul*
138 CE	**Death of Emperor Hadrian**
141 CE	Tempio di Antonino e Faustina (Foro Romano)
141 CE	Tempio di Venere e Roma
203 CE	Arco di Settimio Severo (Foro Romano)
212–17 CE	Terme di Caracalla
ca. 277 CE	**Birth of Emperor Constantine**
3rd c. CE+	Catacombe di San Callisto

3rd c. CE+	Catacombe di San Sebastiano
ca. 300 CE	Basilica di San Sebastiano fuori le mura
312 CE	Beginning of Constantine's reign
312 CE	Basilica di Massenzio
315 CE	Arco di Costantino
324 CE	Basilica di S. Giovanni in Laterano (original)
ca. 324 CE	Basilica di S. Paolo fuori le mura (original)
ca. 325 CE	Basilica of the Holy Cross in Jerusalem
336 CE	Basilica di S. Marco al Campidoglio
337 CE	**Death of Emperor Constantine**
ca. 350 CE	Basilica di S. Lorenzo fuori le mura
ca. 350 CE	Basilica di San Pietro (original)
382 CE	S. Girolamo della Carità (original)
ca. 392 CE	Basilica di San Clemente al Laterano (original)
4th c. CE+	Santa Bibiana (original)
4th c. CE+	SS. Quattro Coronati (original)
4th c. CE+	Santa Prisca
ca. 400 CE	**Birth of Pope Leo I "the Great"**
ca. 400 CE	Basilica di Santa Cecilia in Trastevere
ca. 400 CE	S. Sisto Il Vecchio
5th c. CE+	S. Maria in Tempulo
ca. 430 CE	Basilica di S. Maria Maggiore
432 CE	Basilica di Santa Sabina
439 CE	Basilica di S. Pietro in Vincoli
440 CE	Battistero lateranense
440 CE	Beginning of Leo I's papacy
449 CE	Leo's christological *Tome*
452 CE	Leo's defence of Rome against Attila the Hun
461 CE	**Death of Pope Leo I the Great**
ca. 500 CE	Basilica di Santo Stefano Protomartire a Via Latina
ca. 500 CE	SS. Giovanni e Paolo
527 CE	SS. Cosma e Damiano
ca. 550 CE	Basilica dei Santi XII Apostoli (original)
7th c. CE	Abbazia delle Tre Fontane (original)
7th c. CE	S. Giorgio in Velabro

7th c. CE	SS. Luca e Martina (original)
7th c. CE	S. Maria in Cosmedin
7th–8th c. CE	Ospedale di Santo Spirito in Sassia (original)
7th c. CE+	San Lorenzo in Miranda
9th c. CE	Chiesa del Domine Quo Vadis (original)
early 12th c. CE	SS. Quattro Coronati (reconstructed)
12th c. CE	Abbazia delle Tre Fontane (reconstructed)
12th c. CE	Basilica di S. Maria in Aracoeli
ca. 1123 CE	Basilica di San Clemente al Laterano (reconstructed)
1170 CE	**Birth of Dominic de Guzmán**
1216 CE	Foundation of Dominican Order
1221 CE	**Death of Dominic de Guzmán**
ca. 1224 CE	**Birth of Thomas Aquinas**
1265 CE	Aquinas's *Contra Gentiles*
1273 CE	Aquinas's *Summa Theologica*
1274 CE	**Death of Thomas Aquinas**
ca. 1370 CE	Basilica di S. Maria Sopra Minerva
1475 CE	Ospedale di Santo Spirito in Sassia (reconstructed)
1443 CE	**Birth of Pope Julius II**
1468 CE	**Birth of Pope Paul III**
1470 CE	**Birth of Tommaso "Fedra" Inghirami**
1475 CE	Biblioteca Apostolica Vaticana
1475 CE	**Birth of Michelangelo Buonarroti**
1477 CE	Basilica di S. Maria del Popolo
1483 CE	**Birth of Raphael Sanzio**
1499 CE	Michelangelo's *Pietà*
16th c. CE	Palazzo dei Tribunali
1503 CE	Beginning of Julius II papacy
1504 CE	Michelangelo's *David*
1510 CE	Raphael's *La disputa* (Stanza della Segnatura)
1510 CE	Raphael's *School of Athens* (Stanza della Segnatura)
1514 CE	Raphael's *Expulsion of Heliodorus* (Stanza di Eliodoro)
1512 CE	Michelangelo's *Cappella Sistina Ceiling*
1513 CE	Machiavelli's *The Prince*
1513 CE	Raphael's *Triumph of Galatea*

1513 CE	**Death of Pope Julius II**
1514 CE	Raphael's *Meeting of Leo and Attila* (Stanza di Eliodoro)
1514 CE	Raphael's *Deliverance of St. Peter* (Stanza di Eliodoro)
1514 CE	Raphael's *Mass at Bolsena* (Stanza di Eliodoro)
1515 CE	Michelangelo's *Moses*
1515 CE	**Birth of Philip Neri**
1516 CE	**Death of Tommaso "Fedra" Inghirami**
1520 CE	Michelangelo's *Christ Carrying the Cross*
ca. 1520 CE	Raphael's *Transfiguration*
1520 CE	**Death of Raphael Sanzio**
ca. 1530 CE	Palazzo Farnese
ca. 1532 CE	Palazzo Masssimo alle Colonne
1534 CE	Beginning of Paul III's papacy
1536 CE	Michelangelo begins work on Piazza del Campidoglio
1538 CE	Equestrian statue moved from Lateran to Campidoglio
1541 CE	Michelangelo's *Last Judgment*
1545–63 CE	Council of Trent meets
1545 CE	Michelangelo ceases work on the *Tomb of Julius II*
1549 CE	**Death of Pope Paul III**
1556 CE	Foundation of Neri's Oratory
ca. 1560 CE	Palazzo Verospi
1561 CE	Basilica di S. Maria degli Angeli e dei Martiri
1561 CE	S. Maria in Vallicella (Chiesa Nuova)
1564 CE	**Death of Michelangelo Buonarroti**
1568 CE	**Birth of Pope Urban VIII**
1579 CE	Venerabile Collegio Inglese
1584 CE	Collegio Romano
1585 CE	Palazzo Cenci
1595 CE	**Death of Philip Neri**
17th c. CE	Basilica di San Giovanni dei Fiorentini
1600 CE	Palazzo Barberini ai Giubbonari
1622 CE	Congregation of Propaganda Fide founded
1623 CE	Beginning of Urban VIII papacy
1624 CE	Bernini's *David*
1625 CE	Bernini's *Apollo and Daphne*

1626 CE	Bernini's *Santa Bibiana*
1626 CE	Basilica di San Pietro (reconstructed)
1627 CE	Bernini's *Fontana della Barcaccia*
1632 CE	Bernini's *Bust of Urban VIII*
ca. 1632 CE	Bernini's *Portrait of Urban VIII*
1633 CE	Palazzo Barberini
1634 CE	Bernini's *Baldacchino* in S. Pietro
1637 CE	Chiesa del Domine Quo Vadis (reconstructed)
1640 CE	Bernini's *Memorial Statue of Urban VIII*
1643 CE	Fontana del Tritone
1644 CE	**Death of Pope Urban VIII**
1647 CE	Bernini's *Tomb of Urban VIII*
1649 CE	Palazzo Falconieri
1654 CE	S. Girolamo della Carità (reconstructed)
1660 CE	Palazzo Muti
1663 CE	S. Giuseppe dei Falegnami
1664 CE	SS. Luca e Martina (reconstructed)
1667 CE	Palazzo di Propaganda Fide
1667 CE	Bernini's *Elephant and Obelisk*
1693 CE	Battle of Vienna
1702 CE	**Birth of Maria Clementina Sobieska**
1714 CE	Basilica dei Santi XII Apostoli (reconstructed)
1716 CE+	Protestant Cemetery
1717 CE	Pope Clement XI grants Palazzo Muti to Stuarts
1719 CE	Marriage of James the Old Pretender to Maria Clementina Sobieska
1720 CE	Birth of Charles Edward Stuart (1720–88) in Rome
1722 CE	First Wogan biography of Sobieska
1725 CE	Birth of Henry Benedict Stuart (1725–1807) in Rome
1745 CE	Second Wogan biography of Sobieska
1726 CE	S. Maria del Rosario a Monte Mario
1735 CE	Basilica di S. Giovanni in Laterano (reconstructed)
1735 CE	**Death of Maria Clementina Sobieska**
1766 CE	Death of James the Old Pretender in Rome
1792 CE	**Birth of Percy B. Shelley**
1795 CE	**Birth of John Keats**

1801 CE	**Birth of John Henry Newman**
1811 CE	Shelley's *The Necessity of Atheism*
1818 CE	Keats's *Endymion*
1818 CE	Shelley's "Ozymandias"
1819 CE	Keats's six great odes, including "To Autumn"
1819 CE	Shelley's *The Cenci*
1820 CE	Keats's *Lamia, Isabella, The Eve of St. Agnes and Other Poems*
1820 CE	Shelley's *Prometheus Unbound*
1821 CE	**Death of John Keats**
1821 CE	Shelley's *Adonaïs*
1826 CE	Basilica di Sant'Andrea delle Fratte
1833–41 CE	Newman's *Tracts for the Times*
ca. 1840 CE	Basilica di S. Paolo fuori le mura (reconstructed)
1852 CE	First edition of Newman's *The Idea of a University*
1855 CE	Newman's *Callista*
1858 CE	Second edition of Newman's *The Idea of a University*
1864–65 CE	Newman's *Apologia Pro Vita Sua*
1865 CE	Newman's *The Dream of Gerontius*
1890 CE	**Death of John Henry Newman**
1906 CE	Pontificia Università S. Tommaso D'Aquino Angelicum
1906 CE	S. Maria Liberatrice (in Testaccio)
1932 CE	Giardino degli Aranci

INDEX